Scaling Generative AI

Scaling Generative AI

An Operational Readiness Framework for Enterprises

Amit Prabhu

BEP
BUSINESS EXPERT PRESS
Leader in applied, concise business books

Scaling Generative AI: An Operational Readiness Framework for Enterprises

First published in 2025 by
Business Expert Press, LLC
222 East 46th Street, New York, NY 10017
www.businessexpertpress.com

ISBN-13: 978-1-63742-798-9 (paperback)
ISBN-13: 978-1-63742-799-6 (e-book)

Business Expert Press Big Data, Business Analytics, and Smart Technology Collection

First edition: 2025

10 9 8 7 6 5 4 3 2 1

EU SAFETY REPRESENTATIVE
Mare Nostrum Group B.V.
Mauritskade 21D
1091 GC Amsterdam
The Netherlands
gpsr@mare-nostrum.co.uk

To all the AI evangelists striving to better humanity

Description

Different enterprises have reacted differently to the generative AI hype. The real value of generative AI lies in the scaled adoption. Only 10 percent of enterprises have been able to scale. A staggering 90 percent of them are lagging. This has caused a *huge gap* between the scaling and lagging firms. Closing this huge gap is a daunting task.

To bridge this gap, enterprises must achieve operational readiness in the following four areas:

- Customer
- Technology
- Data
- People

This book contains the operational readiness framework, providing step-by-step guidance for enterprises to prepare themselves for the scaled adoption of generative AI.

Although the framework is primarily for executives, leaders, managers, consultants, strategists, and transformation drivers at the lagging firms, the scaling firms can use it to assess their current operational readiness levels and mitigate the prevailing gaps. It can also provide useful insights for entrepreneurs in the generative AI value chain to develop unique solutions. Additionally, it can help technology and management students align themselves better to embrace new challenges of the corporate world they will soon enter.

The success of this book lies in how effectively the readers apply the framework at their workplace. This book is not just about information … it's all about *transformation*!

Contents

Praise for Scaling Generative AI

"Amit has masterfully distilled his extensive experience across multiple engagements into clear, bite-sized steps that provoke proactive thinking among readers. His insights resonate deeply, aligning closely with our own enterprise experience through our 3W framework (ways of thinking, working, and doing). The book effectively highlights that adopting generative AI is not just about technology but a broader cultural transformation that reshapes how businesses operate. Amit's structured approach provides a roadmap for organizations to navigate this shift with confidence and clarity."—**Pankaj Rai, Group Chief Data and Analytics Officer, Aditya Birla Group**

"As more and more companies enter the foray of AI, the demand and expectations will surge at an unprecedented pace. AI is already transforming the way businesses, governments, and individuals operate, and this evolution will only accelerate, reshaping societies worldwide. This change is unavoidable, and those who fail to implement and leverage AI will quickly wither away. Businesses must act swiftly to harness the power of AI, enhancing productivity and efficiency. Amit Prabhu's timely book explores the profound impact of AI, offering a practical guide to navigating this transformation. It provides valuable insights and support for businesses looking to implement AI effectively. This book is essential reading for organizations seeking to adapt and thrive in this new era."—**Robin Joffe, Managing Director-Middle East, South Asia and North Africa, Frost & Sullivan**

"Amit Prabhu has written an incredibly timely and essential guide for any organization looking to move beyond the hype (and the pilot stage) to effectively implement generative AI at scale. I truly appreciate his constructive and pragmatic approach to the roadblocks and issues. The book provides a reasonable step-by-step framework filled with common sense practices that can enhance the corporate culture. Prabhu does a great job not adding to the

AI hype. He instead offers a balanced perspective on genAI, acknowledging both its potential and its challenges along with fantastic tools and solutions to break through the noise and get you from point A to Z in a way that makes sense for your unique organizational capacity and capabilities. If you're in the bottom 90%, you must read this book."—**Dr. Cari Miller, Founder, AI Procurement Lab and Center for Inclusive Change.**

"Amit Prabhu presents a practical guide for businesses looking to effectively integrate and scale AI. He highlights the gap between companies that have successfully scaled AI and those that are still facing challenges, while show- casing lessons from recent large-scale successes. His Operational Readiness Framework, which focuses on Customer, Technology, Data, and People, offers actionable insights for achieving this readiness. Prabhu's work serves as a valuable resource for business leaders and AI practitioners alike, offering best practices for overcoming the hurdles of AI adoption. As someone deeply involved in the genAI field, I love how his framework simplifies the com- plex task of scaling AI into clear, manageable components. By focusing on the readiness areas and pairing them with practical concepts like "convertible pilots", he turns the huge challenge into steps we can realistically approach." — **Ofir Zan, Vice President, AI Solutions & Enterprise Lead at VAST Data, Ex-AI21 Labs**

"Amit Prabhu's Scaling Generative AI *is a comprehensive guide that explores the key factors for successful enterprise-wide adoption of generative AI. Draw- ing from my experience in AI transformations, I've often seen organizations struggle with identifying the right problem AI should solve and scaling beyond small pilots—both of which this book effectively addresses through a struc- tured framework. Beyond these insights, the book offers practical, field-tested strategies, making it an essential resource for anyone looking to drive large scale AI value."*—**Johan Harvard, Global AI Advisory Lead, Tony Blair Institute for Global Change.**

Introduction

2023 was the year of *discovery*, 2024 was the year of *piloting*, and 2025 and beyond will be the years of *adoption* for generative AI or simply genAI. As shown in Figure I.1, we can estimate the starting points of these phases based on when enterprises adopted them first. The discovery phase started on November 30, 2022, the launch date of ChatGPT; the piloting phase began in the second quarter of 2023; and the adoption phase began in the fourth quarter of 2023.

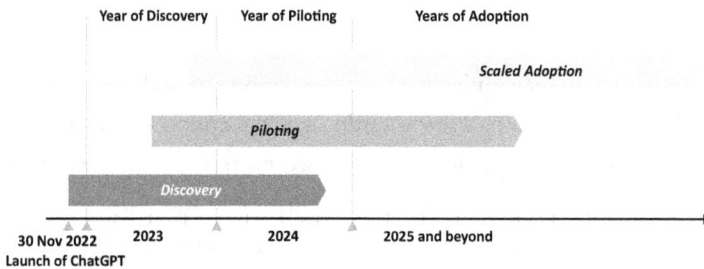

Figure I.1 GenAI timeline

In the year of discovery, though different enterprises reacted differently to the genAI hype, almost all of them explored how this technology would impact them. GenAI became a hot topic at customer meetings, team lunches, coffee breaks, internal project meetings, town halls, conferences, seminars, events, and C-suites. A Gartner survey in the year 2023 with 285 board of directors revealed that AI/genAI is being discussed in the boardroom 3.4 times more frequently than cloud and 2.5 times more frequently than digital transformation.[1] The enterprises began learning about genAI through courses, YouTube videos, articles, blogs, posts, seminars, demos, analyst reports, industry experts, and hands-on experimentation with text generation tools such as ChatGPT and image generation tools such as Midjourney and DALL-E. *Prompt engineering* emerged as a focal point of discussion where people shared ideas about how to make prompts better to generate output with fewer inaccuracies. During this phase, the ethical considerations of genAI took center stage, where people often raised concerns about bias, privacy, and misuse. Enterprises either started developing new policies or revising the existing ones around *responsible AI* (RAI). There were new regulations from regulatory bodies across the globe about the fair use of AI and genAI.

GenAI was everywhere.

In November 2023, I met a recruiter from one of the top consulting firms at a digital transformation event in Olympia, London. She jokingly said, "All of a sudden everyone seems to be working on genAI. I hardly see a CV without it. I wonder how and where people get this experience from."

Although there were no significant investments seen in the discovery phase, the transition from discovery to piloting was very rapid. Alex Singla, senior partner and global leader of QuantumBlack, AI by McKinsey, said:

> It's amazing how quickly the conversation around generative AI has evolved. Just a few months ago, the conversation in the C-suite was pretty rudimentary, focused on trying to understand what it was and seeing what hype versus reality was. Now in just about six months, business leaders are having much more sophisticated conversations. Almost a third of companies are using generative AI in at least one business function. This underscores the degree to which companies understand and accept that generative AI is viable in business.[2]

GenAI is a digital transformation technology that has the potential to transform businesses. It can impact all three areas of a business: customer engagement, internal operations, and corporate culture.

As per a report by Boston Consulting Group (BCG), by the end of 2023, 10 percent of companies were leading the way in scaling genAI technology across their entire organization. As a result, they were not just experimenting with genAI but using it to unlock efficiency gains, improve the customer experience, and boost revenue. However, a major 90 percent of companies were lagging in their use of genAI, causing a *huge gap* between the scaling and lagging firms. Among these 90 percent, 40 percent of companies had taken no action or were still in the

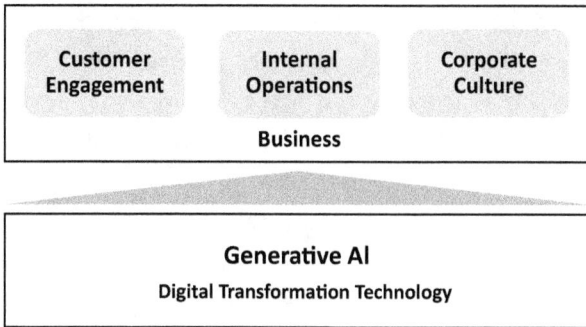

Customer Engagement	Internal Operations	Corporate Culture

Business

Generative AI
Digital Transformation Technology

Figure I.2 Business impact of GenAI

discovery phase. They had developed an understanding of the genAI very rapidly. But when it was time to act, these companies didn't know how to get started.[3]

A business consultant from a Nordic consulting firm said:

I had been interacting with several customers including the C-level, almost every week. Not a single meeting went by where generative AI was not discussed. It somehow used to get dragged into the discussions even when it was not on the agenda. The customers were eager to seek as much information as possible on the latest developments in genAI. They wanted to be the first ones to go to the market with genAI products. They wanted to improve their operations and achieve cost efficiencies. We presented them with the demos of our genAI chatbot. But when we asked if they would like to go for a paid assessment or pilot, they showed resistance.

A solution architect at a business incumbent firm in Nordics said:

Our team has seen several demos from various vendors on the genAI chatbots—Lucy, Macy, Alice, Andy—that can generate some clever text content and emulate the voices and styles of famous celebrities. We were blown apart by their potential to outperform humans. I feel it can add a significant value to our business. We put a proposal to our senior management to develop a pilot. And the response is, "Let us wait until next week, for one more demo from this vendor, and then we shall decide." We have met so many vendors but still haven't received a decision from our management. I am tired of this endless cycle of demos and presentations. So far, they have been only successful in entertaining us. I see no substantial business value in them.

These are the "all talks, no actions" type of enterprises that discussed genAI only at a strategic and conceptual level. They did not go deeper and address it at an operational level.

The remaining 50 percent of 90 percent of the lagging firms have begun piloting, as per the BCG report. There are more pilots in customer-facing functions such as customer support, marketing, and sales than administrative functions such as HR, legal, or finance.[4] The most popular use case is of an AI-powered chatbot developed using a technique known as *retrieval augmented generation*, popularly known as RAG. We can put these firms into the second category "few talks, more actions."

A study named Project Excalibur was conducted by Digiculum, a Stockholm-based AI reskilling, ecosystem orchestration management, and consulting firm. They asked the enterprises, primarily in Europe, if they had any scaled adoption plans in place when they kicked off the pilots, to which an astounding 95 percent of them said, "No." These enterprises were in such a rush to jump on the genAI bandwagon that they just wanted to get started with pilots, with no long-term strategy in place.

Randomly selecting pilots and deploying them without a scaled adoption plan is not a good practice. Enterprises should address the underlying challenges and develop the scaled adoption plan simultaneously. The pilots should lay the foundation; and the organizations, after leveraging the lessons learned from them, should scale incrementally. People from different areas of business should be involved in selecting the use cases for pilots. However, piloting is done in silos in most organizations, either by a team or a function, lacking a unified goal and vision toward scaled adoption. The chief digital officer of a British incumbent bank said, "There is a strategic disconnect between the genAI pilots run by the enterprises at present and their scaled adoption that the enterprises may be likely to embrace in the future." Moreover, Peter Bendor-Samuel, the CEO of Everest Group, said, "We expect that 90 percent of the pilots started in 2023 will not make it to production in 2024. However, the 10 percent which do make it will still drive a significant amount of business."[5]

The scaled adoption can fail due to the following two reasons:

1. Lack of convertible pilots
2. Lack of scaled adoption plan

Convertible pilots are those that have higher probabilities of being successfully moved to the scaled adoption phase. And a part of the scaled adoption plan includes *operational readiness*. Note that convertible pilots are a part of piloting, though dependent but different from operational readiness as shown in Figure I.3.

Note that operational readiness:

- Does not necessarily guarantee scaled adoption of genAI, but it certainly improves its success probability.
- Implies taking critical actions.

The operational readiness of genAI should ideally happen in parallel with the discovery and piloting phases. However, most enterprises are running a higher percentage of nonconvertible pilots and do not have operational readiness. And those who are considering it lack a comprehensive, structured, and well-defined framework that can provide them with step-by-step guidance.

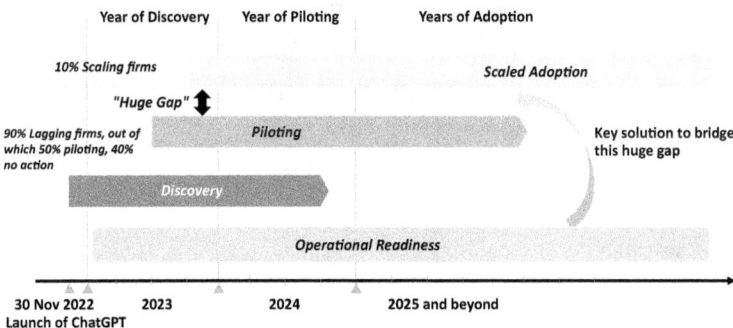

Figure I.3 Operational readiness

I am a pragmatic believer in genAI, neither too excited by its hype and promises nor too concerned about its potential threats. Through RAI frameworks (see Chapter 15) and responsible actions from humans, the threats can be mitigated. Over the past three years, I have developed a good understanding of needs, challenges, and concerns of enterprises regarding genAI through various interviews with key stakeholders, cultivation of knowledge, and personal observation. I consider the following four main reasons for the huge gap between scaling and lagging firms:

1. Suboptimal mindset
2. Low AI maturity
3. Low VITA score
4. Either no pilots, nonconvertible pilots, or convertible pilots, without operational readiness

Authoring two books, *Digital Strategy Framework* and *Digital Leadership Framework*, and publishing them in 2024, I had no intention of writing a third one so soon. But looking at the genAI hype sweeping the enterprises away, the challenges faced by them during piloting, the large number of nonconvertible pilots, and the huge gap between the scaling and lagging firms, I thought it was urgent and time-critical to write this book now. I discussed this idea with Scott Isenberg, the executive editor at Business Expert Press, the publisher of my two previous books. He strongly advocated it and encouraged me to write my third book on the operational readiness framework for generative AI. We both agree that it can have a strong impact on the business community consisting of various enterprises that have embarked on the genAI transformation journey in their respective capacities.

There are many unresolved problems in various areas of an organization that need to be fixed first in order to harness the full potential of genAI. I broadly classify them into four areas:

1. Customer
2. Technology
3. Data
4. People

These are the four main readiness areas of the operational readiness framework proposed in this book. The framework comprises genAI maturity assessment, scaled adoption strategy, four readiness areas, three boosters, and one launchpad. It is also known as the *readiness rocket* (see Chapter 2).

The objective of the lagging firms should be to reach the scaled adoption phase, close the huge gap, and catch up with the scaling firms as soon as possible, through the implementation of the readiness rocket detailed in this book.

The four readiness areas are interconnected through processes and workflows. While I briefly mentioned them in the readiness area Data—since data is central to any process—I intentionally kept the discussion concise to prevent the book from becoming too lengthy. For more details, you can book a consultation at www.scalinggenai.com.

This book contains seven parts spread over 18 chapters. Part 1 covers the fundamentals, where details on the scaled adoption using the readiness rocket are discussed. Part 2 reveals the three boosters that facilitate the enterprises to scale. The VITA mystery will be unraveled in this part as well. From Parts 3 to 6, each of the readiness areas—customer, technology, data, and people—is discussed in detail. The details about the launchpad will be revealed in Part 6. Part 7 contains the practical implementation of scaled adoption of genAI through a fictitious case study. I suggest that you read Parts 1 to 6 first, before you start with Part 7. Whenever I mention AI in the book, I mean traditional AI and not genAI. I would explicitly say generative AI or genAI to avoid confusion. For those who are not familiar with genAI, please enroll in the course Generative AI Fundamentals from www.digiculum.com/reskilling.

Like my previous two books, the success of this book lies in how effectively the readers apply the operational readiness framework at their workplace. This book is not just about information ... It's all about *transformation*!

PART 1

Fundamentals

CHAPTER 1

The Scaled Adoption

Imagine there are three enterprises: alpha, beta, and gamma. Alpha is a mid-sized U.S.-based media company. Beta is a large-sized European-based retail company. Gamma is a large-sized Asian-based utilities company. Impacted by the genAI hype, all of them began with the discovery phase very early in December 2022. Within six months, they became well-equipped with genAI knowledge and could foresee its strong potential in transforming their enterprises. In the second quarter of 2023, the executives of these three enterprises attended an online webinar by one of the leading global consulting companies, where they came across a startling statistic—the global market size of genAI is estimated to reach U.S. $62.72 billion in 2025 and U.S. $356.05 billion by 2030 at a compounded annual growth rate (CAGR) of 41.52 percent.[1] This reinforced their belief in the potential of genAI and fueled their ambitions to capitalize on this multi-billion dollar opportunity. After heavy brainstorming with their respective leadership teams, they targeted to scale genAI by the end of 2025.

It is the first quarter of 2024. Figure 1.1 shows their current statuses. Alpha took the "all talks, no actions" approach and did not do any pilots.

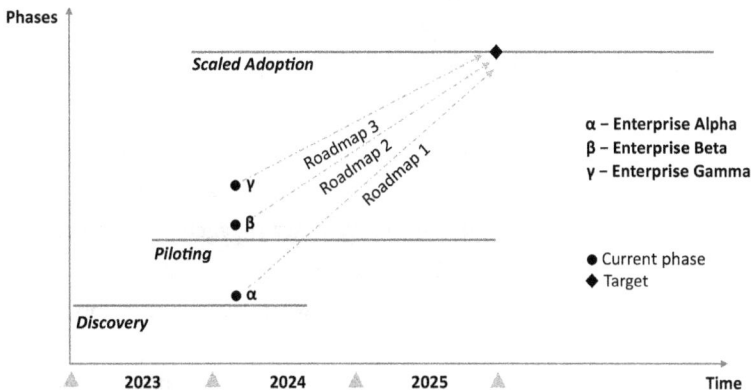

Figure 1.1 Alpha, Beta, and Gamma

It is still in the discovery phase, figuring out Roadmap 1 on how to reach the target. Beta took the "few talks, more actions" approach and is currently running three nonconvertible pilots. It is in the piloting phase, working on Roadmap 2. Gamma also took the "few talks, more actions" approach and is currently running three convertible pilots. It is in the piloting phase, working on Roadmap 3.

Which of them do you think is more likely to meet the target?

Adoption Phase

The adoption phase of genAI can be further divided into scaled adoption, large-scale adoption, and enterprisewide adoption. The scaled adoption phase can be characterized by:

- Minimum one convertible pilot scaled or minimum one new genAI solution (different from the pilots) deployed across at least one of the following three business areas: customer engagement, internal operations, and corporate culture, impacting at least 40 percent of the processes and workflows in either one or more areas combined.
- Minimum cumulative investments of U.S. $2 million up to $10 million.
- Minimum overall productivity gain of 5 percent.
- Perceived value by the users or stakeholders ≥ 7 (on a scale of 1 to 10, 1: lowest and 10: highest).

The large-scale adoption phase can be characterized by:

- Minimum one convertible pilot scaled or minimum one new genAI solution deployed across at least one of the following three business areas: customer engagement, internal operations, and corporate culture, impacting at least 75 percent of the processes and workflows in either one or more areas combined.
- Minimum cumulative investments of U.S. $10 million up to $25 million.

- Minimum overall productivity gain of 10 percent.
- Perceived value by the users or stakeholders ≥ 7.

The enterprisewide adoption phase can be characterized by:

- Multiple convertible pilots scaled or multiple new genAI solutions deployed across all three business areas: customer engagement, internal operations, and corporate culture, impacting more than 90 percent of the processes and workflows across all areas combined.
- Minimum cumulative investments of U.S. $25 million.
- Minimum overall productivity gain of 10 percent.
- Perceived value by the users or stakeholders ≥ 8.

A cumulative investment is the total sum of all the investments from the current and previous phases to date. Refer Chapter 8 to know more about productivity gains.

The Hype

The genAI hype can be explained based on the Gartner hype cycle that includes the following key stages:

1. Innovation trigger: At the start of the cycle, there is typically a pivotal moment that ignites curiosity surrounding a new technology or the discovery of new applications for existing technologies. The pivotal moment was the launch of ChatGPT on November 30, 2022.
2. Peak of inflated expectations: Following the trigger, there is a period of rapid publicity and hype. Excitement about the technology reaches its peak. Often, unrealistic expectations are set, and the technology is seen as a solution to a wide range of problems. The rise in expectations of genAI can be dated from December 2022 to 2023, which can be marked as the peak point of inflated expectations. The slow decline in excitement can range from the first quarter till the end of the year 2024.

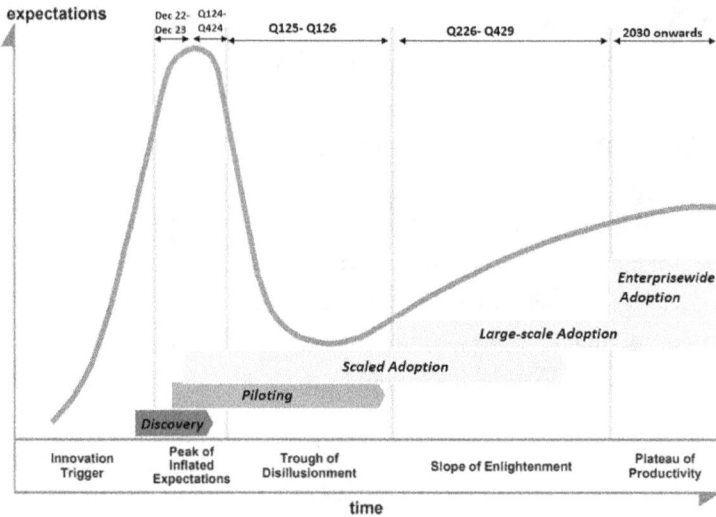

Figure 1.2 Mapping genAI adoption timeline to Gartner hype cycle

3. Trough of disillusionment: As the initial hype fades, people begin to realize the challenges and limitations of the technology. Some technologies may fail to meet expectations, leading to disappointment. This period can be marked from the first quarter of 2025 until the first quarter of 2026, where there will be scaled adoption of genAI. The estimated range of companies that will enter this phase is 10 to 25 percent.

4. Slope of enlightenment: During this phase, a more realistic understanding of the technology's potential emerges. Organizations learn from their initial experiences and improvements are made. This is the period that can be expected from the second quarter of 2026 until the end of 2029, where there would be scaled and large-scale adoptions.

5. Plateau of productivity: The technology reaches a level of maturity and stability. It becomes widely adopted and integrates into everyday practices. If everything goes right, then this stage can be marked from 2030 onwards, where there would be enterprisewide adoption.

The Probability of Scaled Adoption

Many employees around the globe might be confronted with the question—should we really invest our time in learning new genAI skills? What if it doesn't scale? Many enterprises around the globe might be confronted with the question—should we really put in efforts in building the genAI competence in our respective organizations? What if it doesn't scale? And many investors around the globe might be confronted with the question—should we really buy stocks of genAI companies? What if it doesn't scale?

It is very hard to predict whether any new digital transformation technology will scale or not after the stage of its initial hype. However, the probability of its successful adoption in the future can be somewhat estimated by the following factors observed during its hype:

1. Business case
2. Emergence of successful ecosystems
3. User acceptance

Let us consider three digital transformation technologies: cloud, 3D TV, and genAI. The cloud hype began around 2008/2009, when hyperscalers such as Amazon Web Services (AWS), Microsoft, and Google emerged and began expanding their offerings. The 3D TV hype began in 2010 and was heavily marketed as the next big thing in home entertainment, offering an immersive viewing experience. And the genAI hype began after the launch of ChatGPT by OpenAI in November 2022.

During the cloud hype, enterprises perceived it as a game-changer in the realm of IT infrastructure and service delivery. Cloud computing promised greater flexibility, scalability, and cost-effectiveness compared to traditional on-premises solutions. It was seen to reduce the burden of managing physical hardware and infrastructure, allowing enterprises to focus more on innovation and core activities. They were also wary of security risks, vendor lock-in, and reliability concerns. But as cloud matured, these concerns were addressed, and the enterprises became more comfortable adopting cloud solutions. To summarize, enterprises perceived the benefits and were able to develop a good business case for cloud.

During the 3D TV hype, enterprises considered the promise of a more immersive and engaging viewing experience a key selling point. However, a 3D TV was significantly more expensive than a traditional TV, making it a less attractive option for many consumers. Viewing 3D content required wearing special glasses, which some users found inconvenient. Early 3D technology had limitations in terms of picture quality and viewing angles, leading to a less-than-ideal viewing experience for them. To summarize, enterprises neither perceived the benefits nor could develop a good business case for 3D TV.

During the cloud hype, a strong ecosystem emerged comprising cloud providers such as AWS, Google, Microsoft, IBM, and Salesforce, who raced to establish themselves as leaders in the burgeoning cloud market. There were independent software vendors (ISV) who created new applications and services specifically designed to run on the cloud, which expanded the functionality and appeal of cloud computing for enterprises. There were system integrators such as Tata Consultancy Services, Accenture, and Infosys, who provided consulting and implementation services to help enterprises migrate to the cloud and integrate cloud services with their existing IT infrastructure. There were hardware manufacturers like server and storage companies, who adapted their products to better integrate with cloud services, ensuring compatibility and optimized performance for cloud deployments. There were open-source communities whose tools and libraries facilitated cloud development and innovation, allowing developers to build on existing solutions and contribute to the overall ecosystem growth and success.

During the 3D TV hype, the ecosystem comprised TV manufacturers, such as Samsung, LG, Sony, Panasonic, and Sharp, offering a wide range of 3D TV models with different features and price points; 3D glasses providers, such as Xpand; and content creators, such as Hollywood studios and production companies that experimented with 3D filmmaking. However, the lack of readily available 3D content was a major hurdle. While some 3D movies existed, there wasn't a vast library of content readily available for purchase or streaming in 3D formats. This limited the appeal of owning a 3D TV. There was no uniform standard for 3D technology, leading to compatibility issues between 3D TV manufacturers, 3D content providers, and 3D glasses providers from different brands. This caused the failure of 3D TV ecosystem, creating confusion and frustration for consumers.

The user acceptance of cloud grew steadily over time, rather than experiencing a single high peak and then falling. While there was initial excitement during the hype phase, user acceptance ultimately remained low for 3D TV, as the users did not understand how it was better than the traditional TV.

Cloud was successful at scaling due to a strong business case, the emergence of successful ecosystems, and gradual user acceptance, during its hype. 3D TV failed to scale due to a lack of these factors during its hype. From these two examples, we can deduce that:

The probability of successful scaled adoption of a new digital transformation technology is higher if there is a strong business case, emergence of successful ecosystems, and gradual increase in user acceptance during its hype.

In the current genAI hype, enterprises can see the clear benefits of genAI as a content differentiator. However, most of them, especially the lagging companies, have not been able to produce a compelling business case for scaled adoption (see Chapter 8). A strong ecosystem comprising different types of players have emerged during the genAI hype phase offering various products, services, and solutions (see Chapter 7). The user acceptance of genAI has been exceptionally high, with a high level of interest and enthusiasm to explore and adopt this technology.

So, if we make a comparative analysis of these three technologies during their hype phases, the cloud ranks highest with a strong business case presence, followed by genAI, and then 3D TV. GenAI ranks higher than cloud and 3D TV on the emergence of ecosystem and user acceptance.

As shown in Figure 1.3, genAI ranks number one in two of the three observed factors during the hype. So, as per the theory of deduction, the

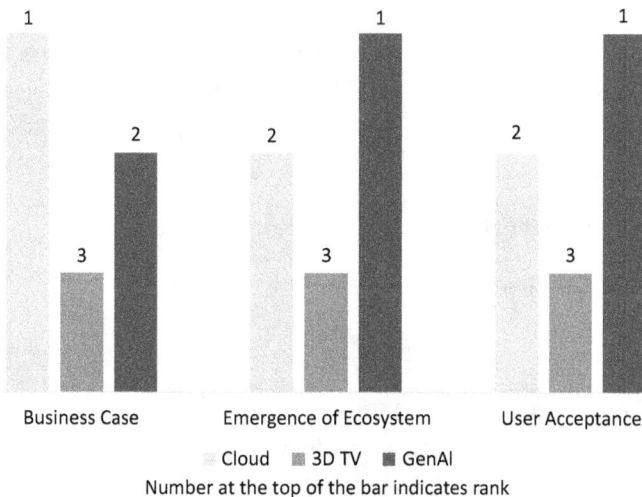

Cloud   3D TV   GenAI
Number at the top of the bar indicates rank

Figure 1.3 Comparison between cloud, 3D TV, and genAI during their hype

probability of genAI's scaled adoption can be estimated in the range of 55 to 65 percent.

It is most likely to scale.

However, it may or may not happen as per the estimated timelines shown in Figure I.1. Note that this is not an investment advice. It is my personal perspective on genAI's scalability.

Investing in GenAI Scaled Adoption

Whether to invest in the scaled adoption of genAI or not is an important decision for enterprises to make. The following are the four main criteria to consider investing:

1. If it generates new revenue streams or increases the value of my products or services
2. If it reduces my operational costs
3. If it enhances experience for my customers
4. If it enhances experience for my employees

If your business case meets at least one of the above four criteria, then you may consider investing in genAI. However, the final investment decision should be made after careful due diligence of various critical factors such as costs, resources, value, lead times, organizational strategy, and consultation with the legal team. If due diligence fails, then it is better to continue digital transformation with AI or other digital technologies and hold on investing in genAI for the moment.

Convertible and Nonconvertible Pilots

Whenever you pilot, there are three possible outcomes:

1. Pilot fails
2. Pilot succeeds but fails to scale
3. Pilot succeeds and scales successfully

First and second are the possible outcomes of a nonconvertible pilot. It can fail or succeed but cannot scale. All three above are the possible outcomes of a convertible pilot. It may not be always successful. It can fail too. However, its chances of successful scaling are higher.

One notable example of a failed AI pilot is Microsoft's chatbot experiment called Tay, launched in 2016. It quickly turned controversial as it began posting offensive tweets after being manipulated by internet users. Within hours, Tay's Twitter account was inundated with racist, sexist, and inflammatory messages, leading to its shutdown and an apology from Microsoft. The incident underscored the challenges of deploying AI systems in uncontrolled environments and highlighted the need for robust safeguards against misuse and abuse, revealing the potential risks of AI technology in real-world applications.

A financial services company in the Nordics developed an AI pilot to offer personalized investment recommendations and financial planning guidance through a chatbot interface. During initial testing, the chatbot effectively analyzed user input to generate tailored advice, receiving positive feedback for its intuitive interface and real-time accessibility. However, as the pilot scaled up to a wider user base, the chatbot struggled to handle increased inquiries, resulting in delays and declining accuracy in advice. Issues arose due to lack of scalability in the chatbot's architecture, infrastructure limitations such as low database capacity and processing power, and concurrency challenges in handling multiple user sessions. Ultimately, the company discontinued the scaled chatbot deployment. This is a good example of "pilot succeeds but fails to scale."

Deloitte's Omnia is an example of "pilot succeeds and scales successfully." Developed by Deloitte's audit and assurance practice, Omnia automates audit transactions, prioritizes human auditor reviews, and provides clients with insights into their businesses. With continuously evolving capabilities, sourced both internally and externally, Omnia has significantly advanced AI's role in external audits conducted by Deloitte & Touche LLP. The platform's architecture allows seamless integration of internal and external tools, tailored to meet data privacy and auditing standards across global markets. Additional tools like Signal and Reveal analyze financial data to identify risk factors and areas for audit scrutiny, while a trustworthy AI module ensures fairness and accuracy by evaluating AI models for bias. Deloitte continues to enhance Omnia's capabilities, exploring possibilities such as climate-related initiatives, visual displays of journal entries, and integration of genAI capabilities, cementing its position as a leading AI solution in the audit and assurance industry. The key reason behind Omnia's successful scaling is that, though first piloted with a U.S. client, it was built with a global deployment mindset.[2]

A systematic selection procedure based on best practices and guidelines is the major difference between convertible and nonconvertible pilots. A convertible genAI pilot includes clear purpose, strategic alignment, well-defined scope, impact analysis, leadership support, relevant data, metrics, right teams, technology collaboration, continuous evaluation and governance, communication plan, and final assessment.

Clear Purpose

The convertible genAI pilots are deployed with a clear long-term purpose of scaling them up in the future. The key questions to be addressed are:

- What business problem are we trying to solve?
- What value will it bring to the business?
- Is it a genAI or an AI pilot? Or both?

Strategic Alignment

All enterprises must create a genAI strategy, and the pilot must align with the strategic priorities. For example, if one of the genAI strategic priorities is to improve sales, it is important that the pilot development team works closely with the sales team. The key questions to be addressed are:

- How do we ensure alignment?
- Are there any prerequisites such as training, knowledge sharing, or awareness building?
- How soon can the value be realized?

Well-defined Scope

It outlines what the pilot aims to achieve, the key activities involved, and the resources required. The scope should also include how to scale the pilot. There are two approaches to scaling:

1. Incremental
2. Integrated

In incremental scaling, the focus is on gradually improving performance and expanding the project's scope. Take the example of a chatbot pilot. It involves continuous training on customer interactions, updating the bot regularly, and addressing underperformance in specific areas. Continuous efforts are made to broaden the chatbot's user base by introducing it to new customer segments over time.

In integrated scaling, you apply the lessons from one or more pilot projects to new projects that are larger in scope. For example, you can develop a pilot on customer sentiment analysis and integrate it into the bigger chatbot project.

The key questions to be addressed are:

- Are there any risks involved in scaling?
- How much time will it take?
- Do we have sufficient competence?

Impact Analysis

It involves understanding the key stakeholders impacted by the pilot. They could be either customers, internal employees, or both. It is important to communicate the change to them, explain its benefits, and make them understand the current and future scope of work. For example, if a team is currently using MS Excel and MS PowerPoint for the daily reports, it is important to communicate to them that in the future they should be using MS copilots. The key questions to be addressed are:

- How do we communicate effectively?
- Would this impact them positively or negatively?
- How to ensure stakeholder motivation?

Leadership Support

A strong support from leadership is needed in launching pilots. Leaders should play an important role of securing funding and approving budgets for pilots and making them an integral part of organization's digital transformation or AI/genAI strategy.

The key questions to be addressed are:

- What exactly should we expect from our leaders?
- How do we escalate the issues to them?
- How to manage their expectations?

Relevant Data

Though a pilot might need only a limited amount of data, the data strategy should be comprehensive, keeping in mind the scaled adoption. The key questions to be addressed are:

- Is the data available?
- Is it accessible?
- What new datasets would be required for scaled adoption?

Metrics

The development of a pilot project can be subdivided into different phases, each potentially accompanied by its own set of metrics to monitor and measure progress. Examples of core metrics are lead times, cost savings, and productivity gains. The key questions to be addressed are:

- Are the metrics realistic?
- Do they quantify the business value?
- Can they help my pilot scale?

Right Teams

A cross-functional team is essential in selecting the pilots. It is preferred that the same people involved in the pilot development are involved in the scaled adoption. If they are unable to stay, they should do a proper handover and set the right expectations for the new joiners. The key questions to be addressed are:

- How do we involve the right stakeholders?
- How do we align their different viewpoints?
- How do we keep them motivated?

Technology Collaboration

A pilot might be developed in isolation but scaled adoption would require genAI to be deployed collaboratively with other technologies such as data, AI, cloud, and automation. It is important to consider their implications while piloting. The key questions to be addressed are:

- How to understand the role and measure the impact of other technologies?
- How to integrate them with genAI?
- Do we have sufficient technology competence?

Continuous Evaluation and Governance

The pilot should undergo iterations and evaluations through continuous feedback from its users or early adopters. If something fails, it should fail fast, so that quick lessons can be learned from it. There should be regular governance meetings attended by different stakeholders. The key questions to be addressed are:

- How should the governance structure be laid out?
- What roles and responsibilities should be assigned to the different stakeholders?
- How to design an escalation matrix with quick access to the leaders?

Communication Plan

The benefits of piloting and its scaled adoption should be clearly communicated to a wide user base to generate interest and motivation. The key questions to be addressed are:

- Should the message be generic or customized?
- Who should communicate?
- How to ensure motivation?

Final Assessment

It involves a review with all key stakeholders and leaders at the conclusion of a pilot. It can have the following outcomes:

- Pilot is abandoned.
- Pilot is sent for rework.
- Pilot is ready for scaled adoption.

If it is ready for scaled adoption, one should assess the operational readiness. The key questions to be addressed are:

- What are the criteria for abandoning and reworking?
- What are the criteria for scaled adoption?
- What should we do if our business is not yet operationally ready?

The Case of Enterprises: Alpha, Beta, Gamma

So, coming back to the question—which of the three enterprises can meet the target?

Answer: All three of them.
How?
Answer: Through operational readiness.
Alpha can reach the scaled adoption phase through operational readiness and:

a. A new convertible pilot or
b. A new genAI solution

Beta can reach the scaled adoption phase through operational readiness and:

a. Learnings from three failed nonconvertible pilots and a new convertible pilot or
b. Learnings from three failed nonconvertible pilots and a new genAI solution

Gamma can reach the scaled adoption phase through operational readiness and:

a. Scaling at least one of the three convertible pilots or
b. Learnings from the three convertible pilots and a new genAI solution

Operational Readiness is a common requirement in all three above cases. Refer Chapter 2 for details.

Note that the new genAI solution is different from the convertible pilots. The following table illustrates the differences:

Nonconvertible Pilot	Convertible Pilot	GenAI Solution
Includes piloting phase	Includes piloting phase	Skips piloting phase
Focus on developing a proof of concept	Focus on developing a proof of concept with an intent to scale	Focus on developing a minimum viable product (MVP) with an intent to scale
Deployed without scaled adoption plan	Part of scaled adoption plan	Part of scaled adoption plan
No product-market fit evaluation	Optional product-market fit evaluation	Mandatory product-market fit evaluation
Focus only on genAI	Focus on adjacent technologies such as data, AI, cloud, automation, and so on, besides genAI.	Focus on adjacent technologies such as data, AI, cloud, automation, and so on, besides genAI.
No involvement of cross-functional teams	Involves cross-functional teams	Involves cross-functional teams
It can fail or succeed	It can fail or succeed	It can fail or succeed
It fails to scale	It has higher probabilities of successful scaling, either via incremental or integrated approach	It has higher probabilities of successful scaling through different phases of MVP: MVP 1, MVP 2...MVP n
Lowest cost, least planning	Medium cost, moderate planning	Highest cost, maximum planning

Can Skipping Pilots Help?

Yes, it can be beneficial in certain scenarios. According to a survey conducted by Accenture, involving 1,500 C-suite executives across 16 industries in 12 countries, it was revealed that while 84 percent recognized the importance of scaling AI to achieve strategic growth objectives, only 16 percent had progressed beyond the experimental phase. Interestingly, the successful 16 percent shared a common trait—they all had abandoned pilots. Pilot projects or proofs of concept carry a higher risk of failure.

For example, Nordea, the largest banking group in the Nordics, bypassed the proof of concept and directly pursued scalability. By ensuring data accuracy, building a minimum viable product, and incorporating customer feedback, Nordea successfully launched its chatbot in June 2017. It resulted in a 20 percent reduction in email and telephone traffic and a 30 percent increase in chatbot usage.[3]

So, a firm may choose to skip pilots if it has a genAI solution and operational readiness. Otherwise, it will be very difficult to reach scaled adoption.

Dependencies between Convertible Pilot, GenAI Solution, and Operational Readiness

At the final assessment, if a business decides to scale the convertible pilot, it should do so gradually in phases. There should be a budget allocated, teams mobilized, timelines created, and deliverables defined at every phase. Additionally, each phase should commence with a planning session, during which teams should review achieved targets, address any encountered issues or escalations, outline goals for the upcoming phase, and ensure control over costs and budget.

GenAI solution comprises genAI deployed with the adjacent technologies such as cloud, AI, and data. One business leader said:

Cloud is the enabler, data is the driver, AI is the enhancer, and GenAI is the differentiator.

Cloud serves as an enabler by offering infrastructure for hosting diverse AI platforms and applications while also serving as a storage solution for data. *Data* serve as the fundamental driver for AI and genAI applications, being essential for generating the desired outputs, without which these applications cannot function effectively. *AI* serves as an enhancer by boosting revenues, optimizing costs, and improving overall efficiency and system performance. *GenAI* serves as the differentiator through its unique content in the form of text, audio, image, or video, tailored to specific customer needs. The best practices of product development and product lifecycle management should be used in developing the genAI solution, which focuses on developing a minimum viable product first, and then gradually developing additional features and functionalities in phases.

Operational readiness is optional for deploying a convertible pilot but mandatory for deploying a genAI solution. Its combination with a genAI solution or convertible pilot is mandatory for scaled adoption.

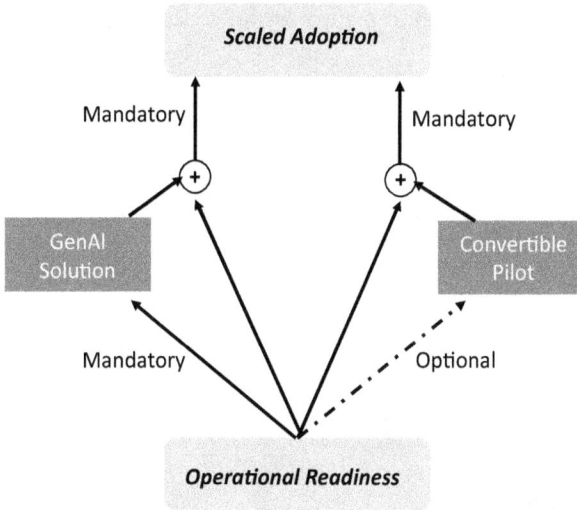

Figure 1.4 *Dependency on operational readiness*

Summary

- The adoption phase of genAI can be further divided into scaled adoption, large-scale adoption, and enterprisewide adoption.
- The probability of successful scaled adoption of a new digital transformation technology is higher if there is a strong business case, the emergence of successful ecosystems, and a gradual increase in user acceptance during its hype.
- Whenever you pilot, there are three possible outcomes:
  1. Pilot fails.
  2. Pilot succeeds but fails to scale.
  3. Pilot succeeds and scales successfully.
- A convertible genAI pilot includes clear purpose, strategic alignment, well-defined scope, impact analysis, leadership

support, relevant data, metrics, right teams, technology collaboration, continuous evaluation and governance, communication plan, and final assessment.

- GenAI solution comprises genAI deployed with adjacent technologies such as cloud, AI, and data.
- A combination of operational readiness with genAI solution or convertible pilot is mandatory for scaled adoption.

CHAPTER 2

Operational Readiness Framework

In February 2024, I was invited as a guest speaker at the Indian Institute of Technology, Bombay's (IIT-B) entrepreneurship cell summit. Upon reaching IIT-B's campus situated near Powai Lake, I was greeted by an event volunteer, a first-year mechanical engineering IIT-B student. He took me to the speaker's lounge, where I was seated among the executives of some of the top Indian corporations. We quickly started discussing genAI, the hot topic of the industry. Most of them lacked clarity on how to adopt genAI—should they pilot or wait for the hype to subside and the technology to mature?

I asked them, "Have you tried to seek your customer's perspectives on genAI? How do they feel about it? What new products or services are they expecting you to provide?"

One of the executives replied, "Yes, we had some conversations with our customers but at a very high level. Not in detail."

"Our customers are equally confused as we are," replied the other one.

I asked, "How is cloud adoption at your firms? Where would you rate your firm on cloud on a scale of 1 to 10, 1 being the lowest and 10 being the highest?"

The average of all the rating responses was 5. A few executives shared their stories, but from their responses, it was evident that they were not updated with details of cloud advancements in their firm.

Further, I asked, "Do you know your company's important data? Where is it located? How to access it?"

I saw blank faces and nervous expressions.

So, I changed the question, "Do you have any plans to reskill your employees on AI?"

One executive replied, "Yes, we have procured a few courses and learning modules from our partners."

Others replied, "Yes, we too."

"What is the enrollment rate?" I asked.

"Very less," said one.

"I don't know," replied the other.

Our conversation was interrupted as it was time for my talk. It was well received by the audience comprising some of India's brightest young talents. When I returned home, I reflected on the eventful day. I could not stop thinking about my conversation with the executives. It reinforced the need for an operational readiness framework. Thereafter, I interviewed a few more industry professionals. Based on their feedback, my knowledge of genAI, industry experience, and personal observation, I developed the first draft of the framework and then the final one, with feedback and validation from a few more experts.

Operational Readiness Framework

The operational readiness framework comprises the following components:

1. GenAI maturity assessment
2. Scaled adoption strategy
3. Readiness areas: customer, technology, data, people
4. Boosters
5. Launchpad

I call this framework *readiness rocket*, as it resembles a rocket. Just as rockets launch satellites into space, readiness rocket can launch enterprises into a new space of genAI.

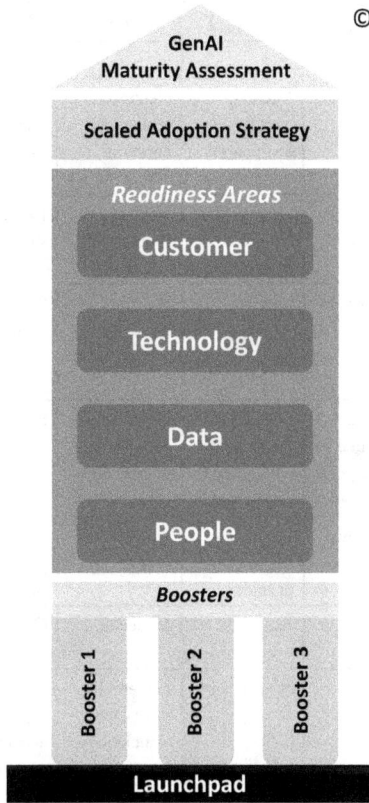

Figure 2.1 Readiness rocket framework

GenAI Maturity Assessment

It is an end-to-end analysis that shows the level of readiness of your firm to adopt genAI. There are five distinct and well-defined genAI maturity levels.

The following table shows the characteristics of different maturity levels:

Parameters	Level 1	Level 2	Level 3	Level 4	Level 5
Overall maturity	Very low	Low	Medium	High	Very high
Overall organizational mindset	Negative with lots of fears and doubts	Negative with few fears and doubts	Neutral with minor concerns	Positive with some belief in genAI	Very positive with a strong belief in genAI
GenAI strategy	No plans, no strategy	Some plans but no strategy	Unclear strategy	Developing strategy	Developed strategy
Understanding of customers' genAI requirements	Very poor	Poor	Some understanding	Good understanding	Very good understanding
Data	Siloed and fragmented, no willingness to clean	Siloed and fragmented, willingness to clean	Unorganized but cleaning in progress	Somewhat organized	Organized
Infrastructure	Insufficient, no plans to upgrade	Insufficient but plans to upgrade	Upgrade in progress	Good enough to support	Best in class
AI/genAI skills	Severe shortage	Shortage	Moderate	Good enough	Highly skilled
Reskilling programs	No plans	Some plans	Less enrollments, fewer completions	High enrollments, average completions	Full enrollments, full completions
GenAI usage in daily tasks	No usage	Very less usage	Average usage	High usage	Very high usage
Center of excellence	Not established	Plans to establish	Establishment in progress	Established, partially functional	Established, fully functional
Knowledge reuse and sharing	No	Low	Medium	High	Very high
GenAI investments	No	No	Low	Medium	High
Support from leadership	No support	Less support	Average support	Good support	Very good support
Go-to-market strategy	No	No	Unclear, under development	Yes	Yes
GenAI monetization	No	No	Low	Medium	High
Scaled adoption plans	No	No	Unclear	Yes	Yes

For scaled adoption of genAI, the minimum maturity required is *Level 4*.

Group Activity

1. Distribute the assessment to all the key stakeholders in your organization. It contains 33 statements in total.
2. To each statement in the assessment, assign a score between 1 and 6, depending on the extent to which you agree or disagree, 1: strongly disagree, 2: disagree, 3: somewhat disagree, 4: somewhat agree, 5: agree, and 6: strongly agree.
3. Calculate the average score of individual stakeholders.
4. The final score is the average of the average score of individual stakeholders.
5. Compare the final score (fs) with the following legend to determine the genAI maturity level:

Score	Level
$1 \leq fs < 1.5$	Level 1
$1.5 \leq fs < 2.5$	Level 2
$2.5 \leq fs < 4$	Level 3
$4 \leq fs < 5$	Level 4
$fs \geq 5$	Level 5

Assessment

#	Statements	Your score
1	We are not worried about the potential risks and harms of genAI.	
2	Responsible AI can help mitigate the risks.	
3	We believe that genAI can transform our industry.	
4	Our corporate strategy is the digital transformation strategy.	
5	We have a clear strategy and roadmap with genAI.	
6	We have a clear strategy and roadmap with data, AI, cloud, and automation.	
7	We provide thought leadership on genAI to our customers.	
8	We constantly innovate new ways of engaging with customers.	
9	We have a clear understanding of our customers' genAI requirements.	
10	Our data is structured and organized.	

(Continued)

(*Continued*)

#	Statements	Your score
11	Our data is accessible.	
12	We derive meaningful insights from our data.	
13	We have excelled in cloud migration and modernization.	
14	We have heavily implemented infrastructure as code (IaC).	
15	We manage and reduce our technical debt effectively.	
16	We have strong AI competence.	
17	We have strong data competence.	
18	We have strong cloud competence.	
19	The content quality of our learning programs is very high.	
20	Most of our employees have enrolled in and completed genAI courses.	
21	We apply new skills learned in the reskilling programs in our daily jobs.	
22	We use genAI tools in our daily jobs.	
23	We achieve high productivity with genAI tools.	
24	Our genAI tools produce accurate output.	
25	We have a fully functional AI/genAI center of excellence (CoE).	
26	CoE has clear AI/genAI objectives and drives lots of initiatives.	
27	CoE effectively streamlines and governs AI/genAI across our organization.	
28	We have a clear go-to-market genAI strategy.	
29	We monetize genAI.	
30	We have a clear scaled adoption plan.	
31	We have good support from our leadership on genAI.	
32	Our leaders have AI/genAI vision.	
33	Our leaders are champions of genAI.	
	Average score	

Scaled Adoption Strategy

Most of the leading firms (10 percent) have a clear strategy on how to scale genAI. The genAI strategy should be a part of overall AI strategy, which should be a part of the digital transformation strategy, which should be the corporate strategy. Normally in most of the big enterprises, there are two strategies, the corporate or the group strategy and the digital transformation strategy. There is not much of a sync between the two. The group strategy is owned and driven by the executives and the digital transformation strategy is owned and driven by a group of change enthu-siasts with an entrepreneurial mindset known as *intrapreneurs*.

Once I happened to be a delegate at the C-level summit in London. During a panel discussion on digital strategy, the panel members were challenged with one question from the audience—what do you exactly mean by one strategy? Do you mean that the existing corporate strategy should be discarded? The question was answered by two panel members. The first one replied that we keep the same corporate strategy. Its state-ment should not mention AI or any other technology. But we execute it with digital transformation technologies such as AI, cloud, and auto-mation. If we stress too much on technology in the strategy statements, it might cause concern among the employees with nontechnical back-grounds. I was very inspired by the reply from the second panelist, a leader at one of the top European insurance companies. He said:

> I disagree here. The corporate strategy statements should be rephrased to explicitly include keywords such as AI, cloud, data, or digital. And we should execute the strategy using these digital technologies. By doing so, we send a strong message and con-stantly remind our employees that we are not an insurance com-pany. We are a data and AI company that happens to be in the insurance industry.

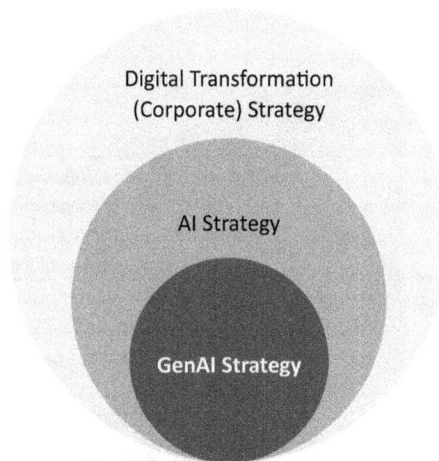

Figure 2.2 GenAI strategy as part of overall corporate strategy

The scaled adoption strategy comprises two components: wanted position and strategic priorities. *Wanted position* is a vision or objective where your firm wants to be with genAI adoption in a certain number of years. *Strategic priorities* are the steps that determine how you can attain your wanted position. You can refer to my book *Digital Strategy Framework* for details.

Group Activity

In this activity, we create a wanted position and strategic priorities.

Developing a wanted position:

1. Refer to the genAI maturity assessment results to determine your current genAI maturity level.
2. Discuss within your group the future genAI maturity level your firm aspires to achieve and the expected time frame for reaching it.
3. Write a wanted position statement: To be at a maturity level __ from level __ in __ months. Fill in the blanks with the appropriate details.

Developing strategic priorities:

1. Conduct the following genAI-related situation analysis by discussing the following sample open-ended questions in your group. You can add more questions to the list.

Situation analysis	Questions
Industry	1. What is the level of genAI hype in our industry? 2. What are the popular genAI use cases for our industry? 3. Are there any regulatory or compliance requirements specific to our industry that may impact the implementation of genAI solutions?
Customer	1. What are the main needs and pain points of our customers that could potentially be addressed by genAI? 2. What percentage of our customers are in the piloting phase? What is their feedback or experience? 3. What percentage of our customers are in the discovery phase? What is their feedback or experience?

Situation analysis	Questions
Process	1. What specific processes could be impacted by genAI? 2. Are there any potential risks? 3. By how much can the lead times be reduced?
Data	1. Are we aware of our critical data? 2. Where is it located? 3. Is it easily accessible?
People	1. What is the current AI, data, and cloud competence? 2. Are people eager to develop genAI competence? 3. Are there any reskilling programs in place?
IT tools and infra-structure	1. Do we have adequate IT infrastructure and tools to support genAI initiatives? 2. Are there any gaps in our existing IT capabilities that need to be addressed? 3. Are our IT systems scalable to support genAI?

2. List 3 preliminary strategic priorities corresponding to each of the analyses. Note them down in the sheet below.

Analysis	Preliminary strategic priorities	Final strategic priorities
Industry/Customer	1. 2. 3.	Best of 1,2,3
Process	4. 5. 6.	Best of 4,5,6
People	7. 8. 9.	Best of 7,8,9
Data	10. 11. 12.	Best of 10,11,12
IT tools and infrastruc-ture	13. 14. 15.	Best of 13,14,15

3. After discussing with your group, from the list of three preliminary strategic priorities corresponding to each analysis, pick the best one.
4. You can further narrow down the list to the top three final strategic priorities or have five strategic priorities, one for each of the analyses.

Readiness Areas

The success of a business depends on the following three factors: the value your business offers to the customers, the profits the customers bring into your business, and how you manage the relationships with your customers. With genAI, you can create differentiated content for your customers, which can add value to the offerings. These new revenue streams are most likely to increase profits. Through responsible AI, you can gain the trust and confidence of your customers and further strengthen business relationships. Without understanding your customer's perspectives regarding genAI, it would be very difficult to devise a roadmap for scaled adoption. Thus, *customer* becomes the first readiness area of the readiness rocket.

GenAI systems often require robust technological infrastructure to handle complex algorithms, large datasets, and varying workloads. The resources should be accessible and scalable as per the requirements. The genAI solutions also need to seamlessly integrate with existing IT systems and workflows within an organization. To derive maximum value from them, it is important that technical debt is managed efficiently. This makes *technology* the second readiness area of the readiness rocket.

High-quality, diverse data is essential for accurate genAI models. The data needs to be clean, complete, and easy to acquire from different tools and systems. There should be rules and controls for managing and safeguarding data. Users should be able to extract meaningful insights from it. This makes *data* the third readiness area of the readiness rocket.

Competent people are needed to develop, implement, and maintain genAI systems effectively. For its successful implementation, it is important that leaders should nurture a culture of continuous learning and collaboration among employees. This makes *people* the fourth readiness area of the readiness rocket.

The operational readiness areas map well with the digital transformation business areas as shown in Figure 2.3. Readiness area customer maps to customer engagement only, whereas technology, data, and people map to all three business areas.

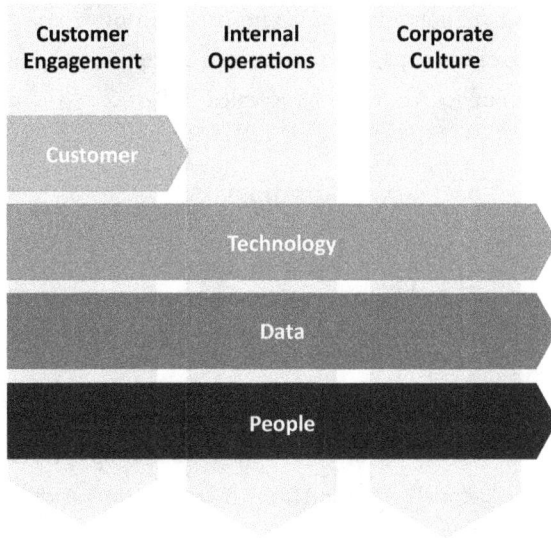

Figure 2.3 Mapping between operational readiness areas and digital transformation business areas

Boosters

Boosters play a crucial role in providing a significant amount of thrust to accelerate a rocket to escape velocity to overcome the earth's gravitational pull. Similarly, the three boosters of the readiness rocket can facilitate enterprises to escape the status quo and accelerate toward new realms of AI innovations. Without these boosters, the progress will be very slow. To ensure that the lagging firms catch up as soon as possible with the scaling firms, it is important to "fix the boosters." They will be revealed in Part 2.

Launchpad

The launchpad serves as the foundation for rocket launches, providing structural support and stability during ignition and liftoff. Its design includes various safety features to mitigate risks associated with the explosive force generated during launch, ensuring the safety of personnel and equipment. Additionally, it facilitates the controlled trajectory of the rocket as it ascends into space, guiding its path and minimizing deviations. Similarly, the launchpad of the readiness rocket provides a strong foundation and support, helps mitigate risks and overcome issues, and ensures deliverables are achieved at the end of respective phases for the scaled adoption of genAI. It will be revealed in Part 6.

Summary

- The readiness rocket comprises genAI maturity assessment, scaled adoption strategy, readiness areas, boosters, and launchpad.
- The genAI maturity assessment is an end-to-end analysis that shows the level of readiness of your firm to adopt genAI.
- For scaled adoption of genAI, the minimum maturity level required is Level 4.
- The scaled adoption strategy comprises two components: wanted position and strategic priorities.
- Wanted position is a vision or objective where your firm wants to be with genAI adoption in a certain number of years.
- Strategic priorities are the steps that determine how you can attain your wanted position.
- Readiness area customer maps to customer engagement only, whereas technology, data, and people map to all three business areas: customer engagement, internal operations, and corporate culture.

PART 2
Boosters

CHAPTER 3

Cultivating Right Mindset

Lisa Mitchell, deputy vice president of tech operations at Albright Cancer Centers (ACC), was eager to explore genAI's potential applications in customer support to revolutionize the calling experience for its patients and their families. She was backed by her manager, David Smithson, the vice president of customer service and business operations.

ACC, a private organization employing over 2,800 staff members and operating a network of healthcare facilities and outpatient centers in cities such as Chicago, Boston, and Denver, recognized the unique nature of each patient's health journey, including their distinct needs, challenges, preferences, and goals. The organization's philosophy, reflected in the Guardian Standard of Care, prioritized treating everyone with the same level of care and respect one would expect for their own family members—with kindness, honor, and compassion. Customer service played a crucial role at ACC, serving as the initial point of contact for patients and their families. However, Lisa faced significant challenges in this area.

Customer care representatives frequently struggled with technical issues, resulting in delays and frustration for callers. The cloud-based system, intended to enhance efficiency, often malfunctioned, providing inaccurate information and forcing representatives to navigate through misleading data. When calls needed to be escalated to higher authorities or specialized departments, callers had to repeat their stories from the beginning, causing additional stress for patients and their families. The emotional toll of recounting painful experiences, coupled with system-induced delays, was evident in the voices of callers. Determined to address these challenges, Lisa led an initiative to improve customer service. She was committed to ensuring that both staff and patients received the support and efficiency they deserved, exploring genAI as a potential solution.

Lisa introduced a new initiative called the "Guardian Level of Call," aimed not only at addressing current issues but also at enhancing the overall calling experience through the utilization of genAI capabilities. The initiative involved mapping out customer journeys for three distinct caller groups: new patients, existing patients, and family members advocating for them. Lisa believed that it was essential to use the genAI technology to understand it and thus, asked her team of customer service representatives to experiment hands-on with GPT-4, Google Gemini, and other AI tools.

The following table shows the findings and insights from her team members:

Name	Insights
Jane	GPT-4's ability to produce human-like responses can handle routine queries, allowing human reps to focus on more complex and emotionally charged calls.
Mark	Sentiment analysis can detect and categorize the emotions of the callers in real time.
Carlos	Predictive analytics can analyze past calls and data points to anticipate potential issues or concerns of the callers.
Sophia	Integrating natural language processing can better comprehend the nuances of the caller queries, ensuring more accurate and personalized experiences.
Layla	Integrating these technologies with the current CRM system can provide a holistic view of each patient's journey.

Lisa then informed David that the proposal would be ready in two weeks and scheduled a meeting to go through it. However, that afternoon, she received a phone call from him informing her that ACC's CEO Dr. Fernanda Rivera wanted to meet her to hear about her findings on genAI. Lisa asked if she could invite a few of her expert team members to the meeting. David declined. Lisa hung up the phone, feeling a mix of excitement and anxiety about the unexpected turn of events.

At the meeting with Dr. Rivera, Lisa presented the PowerPoint deck she had been working with till late into the evening before. But just 10 minutes into her presentation, Dr. Rivera interrupted:

Lisa, I appreciate that you did not have any customer service reps join us in this meeting, as I need to share something that they might not appreciate. Have you heard of Air.ai? They have developed a generative AI system that can potentially replace customer service reps. This could be a game-changer for us. Air.ai could be trained to take calls from our patients and their family members. It could significantly improve the quality and consistency of our customer service. Let us explore this avenue and what it would take to implement it at ACC.

Lisa was deeply unsettled by the sudden mention of Air.ai's AI system. She wondered if machines could understand people's feelings like humans do. People going through cancer treatment need more than just answers; they need comfort too. Lisa wasn't sure if AI could be as caring as humans. She thought it might be better to use AI to help human workers instead of replacing them completely. Her team had worked diligently from the beginning, carefully identifying problems in the current system and proposing solutions with great dedication. Also, it was important to fix the underlying foundational system before integrating it with genAI. Lisa believed in the promise of genAI but at the same time, she was concerned about its impact on her team.[1]

Like Lisa's, every business has a story about how it reacted to the genAI hype. Some enthusiasts think that ChatGPT is close to achieving artificial general intelligence and becoming as smart as or even smarter than humans. Some technology critics feel that generative AI will worsen the lives of workers, making their jobs more difficult and less fulfilling. And the most popular narrative which is often discussed and debated worldwide:

Will generative AI automate the current jobs and make them non-existent?

These negative viewpoints on genAI are quite unpleasing and likely to have a stronger impact on humans, causing fear and anxiety. They often outweigh the positive ones. In Nov 2023, in a breakout session at the SIME conference at Epicenter, Stockholm, I heard one of the participants say:

GenAI can generate a code, error free and incredibly faster than humans. It has the potential to make the software developer jobs obsolete.

There was some element of conviction in his narrative against the backdrop of many ongoing job cuts in the market. There were more than 200k employees laid off globally by different tech companies as per lay-offs.fyi. In 2024, the tech sector witnessed over 32,000 layoffs. AI and cost-cutting were reportedly the main reasons behind them.[2] Software developers comprise a massive 45 to 50 percent of the IT industry. If this narrative holds true, it can severely impact the industry workforce. The more the developments and advancements in genAI, the more will be the downsizing in the software developer jobs.

There were some solution architects in the same breakout session, who countered that software development is not just about writing lines of code; it involves understanding complex requirements, designing robust architectures, debugging, testing, and collaborating with multidisciplinary teams, which cannot be replaced by AI alone. It is an iterative process that requires constant adaptation and innovation tasks that are inherently human. In fact, as AI continues to evolve, the demand for software developers who can effectively leverage AI tools and integrate them into their workflow will only increase, making software developer jobs more indispensable than ever. The moderator at the breakout session went around asking everyone to present their views. She also asked for my perspective. Being a pragmatic believer of genAI, I said that I don't feel software jobs would be completely obsolete. However, as the technology advances, the job description will change. Jobs with AI will replace the ones without. People must remain relevant and competitive through AI/genAI reskilling.

When genAI was at the peak of inflated expectations stage, different enterprises reacted differently to it based on their organizational mindsets. Their mindsets can be grouped into the following categories:

- Optimistic
- Skeptic
- Pragmatic

Optimistic firms are enthusiastic early adopters of genAI, believing in its potential to revolutionize various industries, transform their businesses, and create significant value for their customers. They wholeheartedly embrace the hype surrounding genAI, viewing it as a harbinger of groundbreaking innovations to develop new products, services, and solutions. They are excited about the new job prospects and opportunities opened by genAI. They are willing to take risks with the expectation that the technology will yield significant benefits in terms of innovation, efficiency, and competitive advantage. They weigh profits more than ethics.

Skeptic firms approach genAI with caution and a degree of doubt, adopting a "wait-and-see" attitude, monitoring the technology's progress, and demanding concrete evidence of its value before considering its adoption. They are highly concerned about the ethical implications and the potential job losses caused by its large-scale adoption. They are hesitant to rush into adopting it without careful evaluation and risk mitigation. They weigh ethics more than profits.

Pragmatic firms fall somewhere between optimistic and skeptic firms. They are neither too excited about the promises of genAI, nor doubt its potential to enable digital transformation. They take a balanced approach to genAI adoption, measuring the technology benefits and identifying and fixing the underlying issues. They also consider the challenges such as

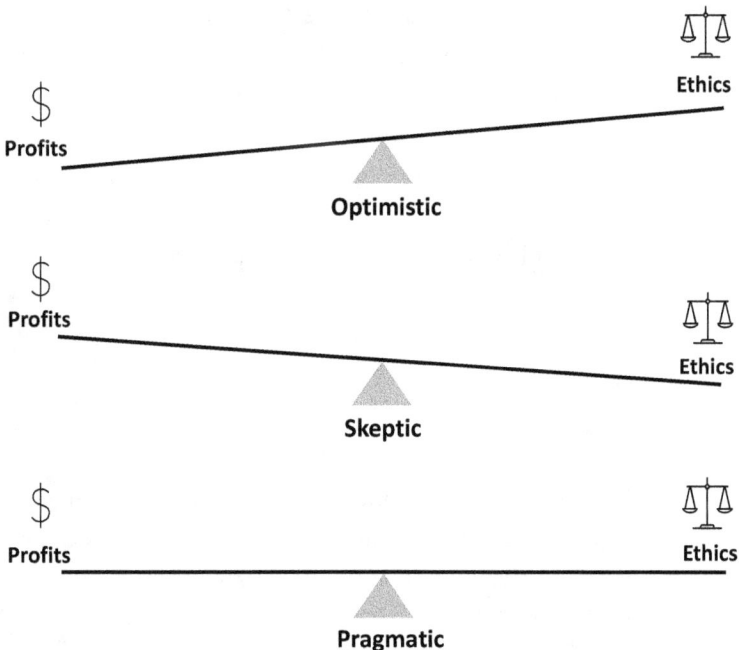

Figure 3.1 Firms with optimistic, skeptic, and pragmatic mindsets

bias and safety and invest in developing guardrails to ensure that genAI is used responsibly and ethically. They normally prefer to reserve their opinions about the speculations around the job prospects or job losses likely to be caused by it. They balance profits and ethics.

For a given business, the reactions can be different at different levels of hierarchy: upper, lower, and middle management. For example, in Lisa's story, Lisa demonstrated a pragmatic mindset. She took time to understand the technology, won her manager's and team's confidence, sought advice from external experts, analyzed ACC's current problems and pain points, and most importantly, measured the impact it might have on ACC's customers and employees. However, Dr. Rivera demonstrated an optimistic mindset. She prioritized profits over ethics. She saw the Air. ai demo, was impressed with its potential to replace customer care representatives, and believed that a similar solution should be implemented at ACC without even considering the opinions of her team.

As of the first quarter of 2024, majority of the 40 percent of the lagging companies comprise skeptic firms, and majority of 50 and 10 percent comprise both pragmatic and optimistic firms. Note that these percentages may change as we progress through the quarters and years.

The net reaction of a business to the genAI hype stems from the net mindset, which is determined by the weighted average of all the mindsets at different levels of hierarchy. Executives, influencers, key decision-makers, transformation drivers, and change agents carry higher weights. The value of the weights is proportional to the decision-making powers.

Lisa's story might have three possible next steps, either ACC:

- Does Dr. Rivera's way
- Does Lisa's way
- Does nothing

If we only combine Lisa's pragmatic and Dr. Rivera's optimistic mindset, we get a net optimistic mindset of the organization as Dr. Rivera carries a higher weight than Lisa, being the CEO with higher decision-making power.

For simplicity, let us imagine there are 10 employees at ACC: five in Lisa's team (Jane, Mark, Carlos, Sophia, and Layla), Lisa, David,

Dr. Rivera, one influencer named Ida, and one transformation driver named Taby. Lisa's team makes up the lower management. Lisa, David, and Taby comprise the middle management. Ida and Dr. Rivera are the executives.

Let us categorize each mindset into low, medium, and high and assign scores 1, 2, and 3, respectively. For example, low optimistic gets a score of 1, medium optimistic gets a score of 2, and high optimistic gets a score of 3. The following table shows the mindset, mindset level, and weight for each of ACC's employees:

Employee name	Mindset	Mindset level	Weight
Dr. Rivera	Optimistic	3	0.9
Ida	Skeptic	2	0.8
David	Pragmatic	3	0.7
Lisa	Pragmatic	3	0.4
Taby	Pragmatic	3	0.6
Jane	Pragmatic	1	0.1
Mark	Skeptic	3	0.1
Carlos	Optimistic	1	0.1
Sophia	Optimistic	1	0.1
Layla	Skeptic	1	0.2

The net optimistic score is given by,

Weighted average = [(Mindset level$_{Dr.Rivera}$ × Weight$_{Dr.Rivera}$) + (Mindset level$_{Carlos}$ × Weight$_{Carlos}$) + (Mindset level$_{Sophia}$ × Weight$_{Sophia}$)] / (Weight$_{Dr.Rivera}$ + Weight$_{Carlos}$ + Weight$_{Sophia}$)

= [(3 × 0.9) + (1 × 0.1) + (1 × 0.1)] / (0.9 + 0.1 + 0.1)

= 2.63

The net skeptic score is given by,

Weighted average = [(Mindset level$_{Ida}$ × Weight$_{Ida}$) + (Mindset level$_{Mark}$ × Weight$_{Mark}$) + (Mindset level$_{Layla}$ × Weight$_{Layla}$)] / (Weight$_{Ida}$ + Weight$_{Mark}$ + Weight$_{Layla}$)

= [(2 × 0.8) + (3 × 0.1) + (1 × 0.2)] / (0.8 + 0.1 + 0.2)

= 1.909

The net pragmatic score is given by,

Weighted average = [(Mindset level$_{David}$ × Weight$_{David}$) + (Mindset level$_{Lisa}$ × Weight$_{Lisa}$) + (Mindset level$_{Taby}$ × Weight$_{Taby}$) + (Mindset level$_{Jane}$ × Weight$_{Jane}$)] / (Weight$_{David}$ + Weight$_{Lisa}$ + Weight$_{Taby}$ + Weight$_{Jane}$)

= [(3 × 0.7) + (3 × 0.4) + (3 × 0.6) + (1 × 0.1)] / (0.7 + 0.4 + 0.6 + 0.1)

= 2.88

We see that the pragmatic mindset prevails. Note that this is just an example of how to determine an organization's genAI mindset. It doesn't necessarily imply any *action*. An organization with a high skeptic mindset score may still implement a GenAI solution, while an organization with a high optimistic mindset score might choose to do nothing. In this example, the net pragmatic mindset score was the highest. However, it doesn't necessarily mean that the ACC's next steps will be as per Lisa's way. Even though the optimistic mindset score is lesser than the pragmatic mindset, Dr. Rivera can use her CEO's prerogative and do things her way. Or she might decide to do nothing.

If as per the above example, ACC decides to do Lisa's way, still the chances of successful adoption of genAI are less. It is because less than the majority–40 percent of employees have pragmatic mindsets, whereas 60 percent of employees still have a combined optimistic mindset and skeptic mindset. There would be conflicts over choosing ethics over profits or vice versa. Hence, it is important to bring the mindset of a larger percentage of employees in an organization, including the heavyweights, to the *pragmatic* category.

A pragmatic mindset is the first booster for the scaled adoption of genAI.

Cultivating Pragmatic Mindset

Enterprises can cultivate a pragmatic mindset using the following two-step process:

1. Assessment
2. Targeted development programs

Step 1: Assessment

It can be conducted for a specific targeted group, an entire organization, or a specific function. The weights should be assigned in proportion to decision-making power. It is up to the business to decide the weights.

1. Make sure participants complete the AI/GenAI mindset assessment on the website www.digiculum.com/assessment.
2. Ask them to select the most relevant option based on their choice as per the given scenarios.
3. Ensure that they do not skip any case scenario.
4. Based on the legend, identify the predominating mindset for each participant.
5. Identify the mindset level for each participant.
6. Calculate the net mindset score for optimistic, skeptic, and pragmatic using the weighted average formula:

$$\text{Net mindset score} = \sum_{i=1}^{n} (w_i . x_i) \Big/ \sum_{i=1}^{n} w_i$$

where:

- w_i represents the weight of ith employee.
- x_i represents the mindset level of ith employee.
- n is the total number of employees in a given mindset category.

7. Compare the weighted average scores for all mindsets. The one with the highest score becomes the mindset of the targeted group, either the entire organization, or a specific function.

Step 2: Targeted Development Programs

1. Fill in the numbers in the table below based on assessment results:

Head counts	Executives	Middle management	Lower management	Total
Optimistic				
Skeptic				
Pragmatic				

2. Calculate the percentage in each category:

Percentage	Executives	Middle management	Lower management
Optimistic			
Skeptic			
Pragmatic			

3. Define the overall target pragmatic score to be achieved.
4. Visit www.digiculum.com/reskilling and sign up for the instructor-led course: Cultivating AI/GenAI Mindset. This course is offered to different target groups: executives, middle management, and lower management.

Summary

- Different enterprises reacted differently to the genAI hype based on their organizational mindsets.
- The organizational mindsets can be grouped into three categories: optimistic, skeptic, and pragmatic.
- Within an organization, mindset can be different at different levels of hierarchy.
- The net mindset is determined by the weighted average of all the mindsets at different levels of hierarchy.
- Executives, influencers, key decision-makers, transformation drivers, and change agents carry higher weights.
- The value of the weights is proportional to the decision-making powers.
- It is important to bring the mindset of larger percentage of employees in an organization, including the heavyweights, to the pragmatic category.
- *Pragmatic mindset is the first booster for the scaled adoption of genAI.*
- A certain mindset doesn't necessarily imply a specific action.
- Enterprises can cultivate a pragmatic mindset using the following two-step process:
  1. Assessment
  2. Targeted development programs

CHAPTER 4

Leveraging AI Maturity

DBS Bank Limited (DBS), a Singapore-based banking incumbent and one of the few early adopters of genAI, can be placed in the category of the 10 percent scaling enterprises. It introduced "DBS-GPT," a version of ChatGPT designed for employees, to aid them in content creation and writing assignments within a secure setting. More than 5,000 employees in DBS Singapore have utilized DBS-GPT, and its implementation is gradually expanding throughout the bank. DBS is also using genAI to extract information from documents, analyze it, and then populate the data into templates for new trade loans. The relationship managers are using genAI to consolidate both structured and unstructured data for crafting client proposals and evaluating client portfolios. Another important use case focuses on software development, where DBS is exploring how it can help software developers speed up time to market, improve software quality, and detect bugs.[1]

Unilever, a 93-year-old London-based consumer packaged goods company, is another example of a top 10 percent scaling enterprise. Unilever's notable AI application "Alex" is powered by the GPT application programming interface (API). Alex functions within Unilever's consumer engagement center to sort through emails, distinguishing them between spam and authentic consumer messages. For genuine messages, Alex suggests responses to human agents, who can further customize them if necessary. The implementation of Alex has reportedly slashed the time agents spend composing responses by more than 90 percent at Unilever. Unilever has developed a tool known as "Homer," which relies on the GPT API for content creation for product listings on Amazon. Within its initial week, the tool garnered 80,000 users.[2]

Another example of the top 10 percent scaling enterprise ahead of others in genAI adoption is Toyota, a Japanese multinational automotive incumbent. The Toyota Research Institute introduced a new genAI method to enhance the capabilities of vehicle designers. For example, a designer can give a prompt—*show me futuristic sleek variations of my design while minimizing drag*. It generates an output containing three design variations that can be optimized simultaneously.[3]

> DBS, Unilever, and Toyota are all incumbents in their respective industries and have been in business for at least five decades. Why are they so successful in adopting genAI, while most of the other businesses are struggling?
> Answer: All three of them have high *AI maturity*.

They began building and deploying AI capabilities much earlier in the decade of 2010.

A business with high AI maturity is better positioned to implement genAI as compared to those that don't. In the study by BCG, out of 40 percent of firms who did not take any actions, 25 percent of them had high maturity of predictive AI, a type of traditional AI. Out of 50 percent of firms that began piloting, 46 percent of them had high maturity of predictive AI. And, out of 10 percent of the scaling firms, 61 percent of them had high maturity of AI. This shows that enterprises with a strong foundation of traditional AI can leverage it better toward scaled adoption of genAI.

In a global survey of 3,100 business executives conducted by MIT and Boston Consulting Group, based on the understanding and adoption of AI, the firms can be classified into the following AI maturity archetypes:

- Passives
- Investigators
- Experimenters
- Pioneers

Passives have a low understanding and a low adoption of AI. They have more myths and misinformation around AI and limited awareness and access to information on how it can impact their enterprises.

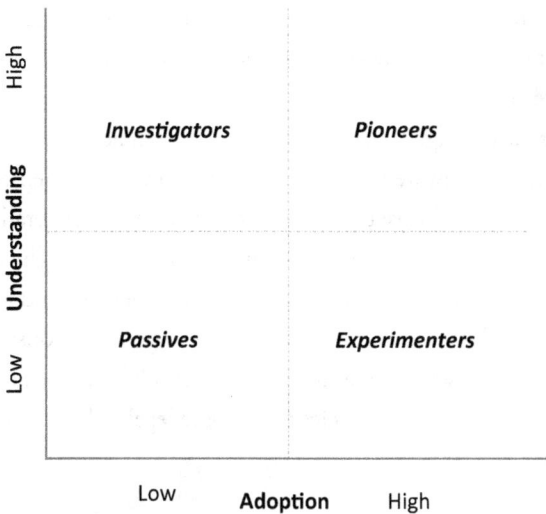

Figure 4.1 AI maturity archetypes

They have a shortage of AI skills and resources and do not have a strategy or budget to cultivate them. They have a rigid corporate culture, resistant to change due to the legal, ethical, security, and privacy concerns about AI.

Investigators have a high understanding but low adoption of AI. They have a good awareness and access to information on how AI can add value to their enterprises and positively impact their customers. They have a reasonable amount of AI skills and competencies and a strategy in place on how to cultivate them further. However, they lack a favorable culture with a low willingness to experiment and take risks due to legal, ethical, security, and privacy concerns about AI. There might be a shortage of budget for AI development due to the uncertainties regarding the return on investments.

Experimenters have a low understanding but high adoption of AI. They have limited awareness and access to information on how AI can impact their enterprises. Yet, they are willing to experiment and take risks. They have a shortage of AI skills but have a budget and strategy in place on how to cultivate them. They partner with AI vendors and external consultants who guide them through every developmental phase. They have an innovative and entrepreneurial culture, willing to adapt and exploit the benefits of AI, though they may still have legal, ethical, security, and privacy concerns about AI.

Pioneers have a high understanding and a high adoption of AI. They have a strong awareness of how AI can add value to their enterprises and positively impact their customers. They are generally the creators of AI assets and information and provide thought leadership to the industry. They have a strong AI competence and a favorable culture of learning and innovation with a good demonstration of a growth mindset. They either have policies in place or are continuously adapting their policies to mitigate legal, ethical, security, and privacy concerns about AI.

Combining three types of mindsets: optimistic, skeptic, and pragmatic, and four types of AI maturity archetypes: passives, investigators, experimenters, and pioneers, we have the following *AI maturity archetypes-mindsets* zones:

1. Passives- Optimistic (PO)
2. Passives- Skeptic (PS)
3. Passives- Pragmatic (PP)
4. Investigators- Optimistic (IO)
5. Investigators- Skeptic (IS)
6. Investigators- Pragmatic (IP)
7. Experimenters- Optimistic (EO)
8. Experimenters- Skeptic (ES)
9. Experimenters- Pragmatic (EP)
10. Pioneers- Optimistic (PiO)
11. Pioneers- Skeptic (PiS)
12. Pioneers- Pragmatic (PiP)

Most of the 10 percent leading firms are pioneers, with either optimistic, pragmatic, or skeptic mindsets, located in either PiO, PiP, or PiS zone. There is a heavy concentration of 40 percent "no action" firms in PS, PP, PO, IS, IP, and IO zones. The 50 percent "piloting" firms are most likely to be investigators, experimenters, or pioneers, with either

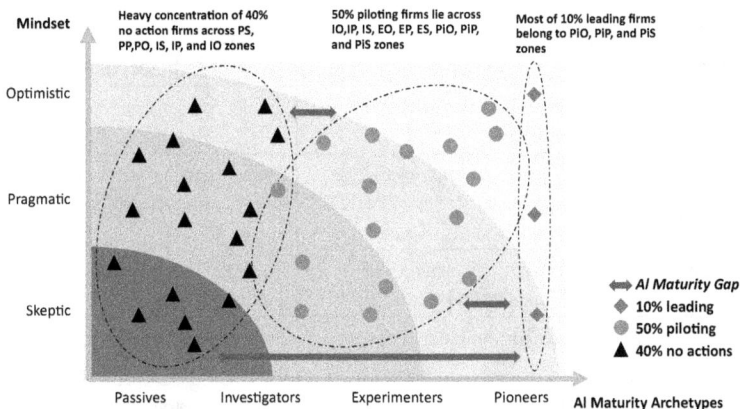

Figure 4.2 AI maturity archetypes-mindsets zones

optimistic, pragmatic, or skeptic mindsets. It is unlikely that they will be passives. They lie across IO, IP, IS, EO, EP, ES, PiO, PiP, and PiS zones. We see an AI maturity gap, which is relatively smaller between no actions and piloting firms, and between piloting and leading firms. It is huge between no actions and leading firms.

All the AI maturity archetypes: passives, investigators, experimenters, and pioneers, can launch genAI pilots. However, to drive scaled adoption of genAI, it is important to upgrade the AI maturity to the pioneers archetype.

Why is it so?

As seen earlier, genAI can be deployed in two modes: standalone mode and collaborative mode. Standalone mode involves only genAI deployment, whereas collaborative mode includes genAI deployment along with traditional AI and other technologies such as data, cloud, and automation.

The following table shows examples of some use cases on how genAI and traditional AI can be used collaboratively:

Industry	GenAI	Traditional AI
Automotive	Creates synthetic sensor data and simulations for safe testing	Identifies objects and makes decision
Software	Suggests code to enhance productivity	Assists in software development
Media	Generates new images, videos, music, and text	Analyzes content to improve patterns and biases

(*Continued*)

(*Continued*)

Industry	GenAI	Traditional AI
Healthcare	Creates synthetic patient data for model training	Predicts outcomes and analyzes medical data
Energy	Simulates new scenarios to optimize renewable energy grid performance	Monitors and predicts equipment failures in power plants using sensor data
Gaming	Generates game elements like environments and characters	Analyzes player data to optimize gaming experience
Manufacturing	Creates custom product designs	Refines designs based on data analysis and customer preferences
Marketing	Produces persuasive, targeted content	Analyzes customer data for personalized campaigns

Standalone mode can be used to drive genAI pilots. However, its chances of driving successful genAI scaled adoption are very less compared to the collaborative mode. The collaborative mode requires AI, and pioneers archetype offer the highest AI maturity.[4]

Hence, it is important to upgrade your current AI maturity to the pioneers archetype.

Pioneers AI maturity archetype is the second booster for scaled genAI adoption.

Upgrading Maturity to Pioneers

Enterprises can upgrade to pioneers using the following two-step process:

1. Assessment
2. Deployment programs

Step 1: Assessment

If you are a business incumbent or an entrepreneur, you can take the following assessment to know your AI maturity level.

Assessment

1. Distribute the assessment to all key stakeholders in your organization. It contains a total of 40 statements: 20 for AI understanding and 20 for AI adoption.

2. For each statement in the assessment, assign a score between 1 and 6, depending on the extent to which you agree or disagree, 1: strongly disagree, 2: disagree, 3: somewhat disagree, 4: somewhat agree, 5: agree, 6: strongly agree.

#	Statements	Your Score
	AI understanding	
1	We understand the differences between AI, machine learning, deep learning, and genAI	
2	We understand the fundamental difference between traditional AI and genAI	
3	We have more factual data and fewer myths and misinformation about AI	
4	We have a strong AI/ML technical competence	
5	We understand the legal, ethical, and social implications of AI	
6	We understand the security and privacy implications of AI	
7	We have good knowledge and understanding of natural language processing	
8	We have good knowledge and understanding of machine learning algorithms	
9	We have good knowledge and understanding of machine/computer vision	
10	We have good knowledge and understanding of predictive AI	
11	We have good knowledge and understanding of diagnostic AI	
12	We have good knowledge and understanding of generative AI	
13	We have good knowledge and understanding of neural networks architecture	
14	We are aware of the latest AI tools and vendors	
15	We believe that people with AI knowledge and application will replace those who don't	
16	We have a good understanding of data science and data analytics	
17	We have a good understanding of cloud	
18	We understand how AI, data, and cloud can work together	
19	We have a good understanding of cloud services and solutions	
20	We have a good understanding of data services and solutions	
a)	Total score	
	AI adoption	
21	We offer AI-based products, services, or solutions to our customers	
22	We often educate our customers on the latest AI trends and insights	
23	We constantly innovate new ways of engaging with customers regarding AI	
24	Our sales team is competent with the latest AI skills and knowledge	
25	We have strong business cases and proofs-of-concept (PoC)	

(Continued)

(*Continued*)

#	Statements	Your Score
26	We also engage with customers on data and cloud	
27	We offer personalized recommendation services to our customers based on AI	
28	We use AI tools to track customer behaviors	
29	We have a clear AI strategy	
30	We use AI in our internal operations	
31	We use AI-powered chatbots in customer support	
32	We have achieved significant cost reductions using AI	
33	We innovate continuously using AI	
34	We have sufficient AI learning assets and information	
35	We have easy access to AI learning assets and information	
36	People have a desire to learn new digital skills related to AI	
37	People are willing to invest time and effort in learning AI skills	
38	We offer AI learning plans and pathways for individuals	
39	We often share knowledge and reuse AI information	
40	Our leaders support a culture of AI learning	
b)	Total score	

3. Calculate the total score for AI understanding and compare it with the following legend:

   Between 20 and 40: low

   Between 41 and 90: medium

   Between 91 and 120: high

4. Calculate the total score for AI adoption and compare it with the following legend:

   Between 20 and 40: low

   Between 41 and 90: medium

   Between 91 and 120: high

5. Use the legend in the table below to map to your AI archetype.

AI types	AI understanding	AI adoption
Passives	Low	Low
Investigators	Medium/high	Low
Experimenters	Low/medium	Medium/high
Pioneers	High	High

Step 2: Deployment Programs

If your AI maturity is passives, then improve your maturity to investigators, and then pioneers. It is relatively easier to move from passives to investigators than from passives to experimenters, as it is easier to develop AI understanding than AI adoption. Tracks 1 and 2 are shown in Figure 4.3. Enterprises can customize the above tracks as per their business requirements.

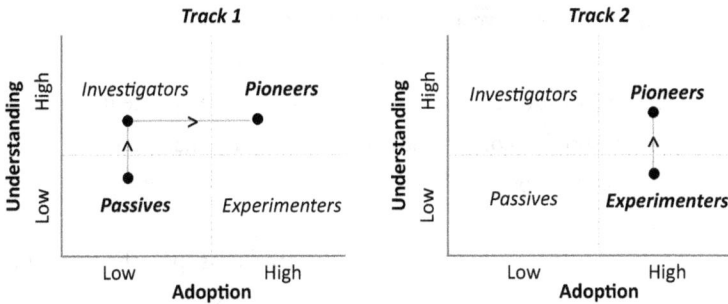

Figure 4.3 AI maturity development tracks

Track 1: Passives → Investigators → Pioneers

Passives to investigators

- Go to digiculum.com/reskilling to select courses on traditional AI.
- Encourage knowledge sharing.
- Promote a culture of learning.

Investigators to pioneers

- Go to www.digiculum.com/reskilling and sign up for the instructor-led course AI/GenAI Transformation Strategy.
- Build AI capabilities in customer-facing functions aligned with AI transformation strategy.
- Cultivate key AI roles and competencies such as AI developer, data scientist, machine learning (ML) engineer, AI product manager, and AI solution architect.

Track 2: Experimenters → Pioneers

- Go to www.digiculum.com/reskilling and sign up for the instructor-led course AI/GenAI Transformation Strategy.
- Break silos and work cross-functionally as one team.
- Seek assistance from external consultants and industry experts.

For Tracks 1 and 2

- Make sure you have an adequate budget for AI deployment.
- Ensure a buy-in from leaders and executives.
- Learn from success and failure stories of AI deployment.
- You can book a consultation at www.scalinggenai.com for additional support and guidance.

Enterprises can customize the above tracks as per their business requirements.

DBS—Success Story

DBS invested heavily to integrate AI across its operations, driven by stiff competition from fintech firms like Alipay, PayPal, Block, Grab, and Klarna, and due to shifting consumer preferences toward online banking during the pandemic. It had embarked on its digital transformation journey in the early decade of 2010. It had identified three strategic priorities:

- Embed in customer journey
- Digital to the core
- 30,000 startup culture

The first one involved making banking practically "invisible" to the customers and connecting with them more at a personal level. The second one involved making changes to the core of the bank's systems and processes using the latest digital technology. The third one meant creating a startup culture of learning, experimentation, and innovation with a workforce of 30,000. AI became the core capability driving these strategic objectives into reality.

The eight key implementation steps that enabled DBS to successfully adopt AI are:

Implementation steps	Description
1. Lessons from early failures	The three key lessons from failed AI lab development project with A*STAR and scaled pilot for wealth management with IBM Watson were: 1. Need for an agile methodology 2. Minimum viable product as starting point 3. Incremental development of solutions
2. Securing early wins	1. Preventive maintenance and cash replenishment at its ATMs, resulting in a significant reduction in ATM downtimes. 2. Interactive voice response and quantum image recognition applications to streamline customer queries, reducing call times, increasing satisfaction, and promoting human–bot collaboration in the contact center. 3. Anti-money laundering measures, including reducing false positives, 90-day hibernation for low-risk cases to focus on high-risk ones, network analysis to analyze relationship among potential criminals, and a streamlined case management system, improving efficiency and accuracy for analysts.
3. Building AI talent	DBS recruited experts in data and AI from top companies, implemented diverse training programs, including DigiFY, Data Heroes, and launched initiatives like hack2hire to enhance digital capabilities, fostering a culture of continuous learning and innovation.
4. Data first, cloud-centric approach	"Data first" organization had four main pillars: analytics capability, culture and curriculum, enablement of data usage, and technology platforms. 1. Analytics capability focused on accelerating and industrializing AI to reduce lead times and to deliver exponential outcomes. 2. Culture and curriculum focused on building a data-driven mindset, by enabling excellence in analytical and data science skills. 3. Enablement of data usage focused on enabling faster, responsible, and more informed decisions by getting the right data to the right people at the right time. 4. Technology platforms focused on providing analytical data science and business intelligence capabilities across DBS banking products and domains under one platform.

(Continued)

(*Continued*)

Implementation steps	Description
5. Experimenting with pilots	DBS prioritized AI integration through numerous experiments, infrastructure enhancement, and process refinement, aiming for a thousand annual trials, including data and AI, with CEO Piyush Gupta leading events showcasing innovative projects and empowering business units to explore AI solutions in their domains. Examples are HR division's Job Intelligence Maestro app and attrition prediction model.
6. Embedding AI in customer engagements	DBS rapidly implemented projects to digitize customer experiences, transitioning from traditional to digital banking by implementing strategies such as digital marketing, paperless processes, real-time analytics, and AI-driven nudges, resulting in a 10 to 12 percent increase in customer engagement and improved satisfaction indices.
7. Incorporating AI into internal operations	DBS implemented an organizationwide automation strategy, including robotic process automation and machine learning solutions within "intelligent automation" workflows, leading to the automation of over 100 complex processes by 2020. It developed the ADA data platform to streamline AI model creation, deployment, and management, alongside migrating AI and analytics systems to hybrid clouds for faster deployment and scalability.
8. Exploring new revenue streams with AI	DBS leveraged its AI expertise to diversify into new sectors, forming specialized teams, accelerating application releases through DevOps automation, establishing cross-referral agreements with lending platforms, and launching experimental projects like POSB Smart Buddy for financial literacy in schools.

By 2020, DBS achieved widespread adoption of the ADA platform, with over 90 percent utilization, alongside successful migration of applications and data to new environments, virtual private cloud, and data lakes, demonstrating exceptional progress in AI adoption metrics.

IBM Watson—Failure Story

IBM Watson is an example of a failed AI adoption. Developed by David Ferrucci, it showcased its potential beyond experimental stages with a triumphant victory on the game show Jeopardy in 2011, leading IBM to prioritize its advancement, especially in healthcare, and initiate collaborations with renowned institutions. By 2014, IBM invested over one billion dollars in Watson's technology, establishing the Watson unit and Watson Health, focusing on personalized cancer treatments and genomic sequencing partnerships. However, despite significant efforts, Watson's success in cancer treatment remained a challenge due to the complexity of genetic variations affecting outcomes.

The following are the six reasons why the adoption of IBM Watson for healthcare failed:

Failure reasons	Description
1. Misaligned purpose	IBM Watson was trained on a vast amount of generic datasets available publicly. After its success, IBM shifted Watson's focus to healthcare due to customer interest, despite objections from its creator, David Ferrucci. Healthcare is a specialized domain that requires high-quality specific data to be acquired from applications and systems and often validated by the experts. Watson, primarily built for Jeopardy, most likely would fail to serve the purpose of healthcare.
2. Gap between perception and reality	Watson showcased exceptional diagnostic abilities in identifying rare diseases, leveraging its extensive database and objective processing approach. Despite media hype suggesting its superiority over human doctors, challenges emerged in translating its laboratory success into practical patient care due to the complexities of medical decision-making and nuances in clinical data interpretation. While IBM oversold Watson's capabilities, real-world applications faced hurdles in adapting to medical professionals' workflows and handling the diverse and nuanced nature of clinical data.
3. No cooperation from key stakeholders	Watson's difficulty in engaging with doctors stemmed from a failure to manage their expectations and convey its role as a complementary tool, rather than a replacement. Doctors were hesitant to trust an AI system over their years of education and experience in patient care.
4. Inaccurate advice for cancer treatment	The oncology expert advisor faced criticism for frequently offering inaccurate cancer treatment suggestions, highlighting concerns among IBM's medical specialists and clients about the reliability of the product. IBM's reliance on synthetic training cases, instead of real patient data, for Watson's development hindered its effectiveness in oncology as cancer's complexity and variability made it difficult for AI to learn and apply treatment patterns effectively.
5. Loss of clientele	IBM Watson failed to meet client expectations due to ineffective integration of data assets and mismanagement, stemming from a lack of necessary skills and clear strategy, leading to frequent pivots and layoffs in IBM Watson Health.

(Continued)

(*Continued*)

6. Less commercial success	Between 2011 and 2017, IBM announced around 50 collaborations for healthcare AI solutions. Except for Watson for Oncology with Memorial Sloan Kettering, most didn't transition into commercial products.

Despite significant development and financial investment, IBM's Watson Health division faced rumors of a potential sale in 2021. These rumors became reality in 2022 when IBM divested the division, spinning it off into Merative, now owned by the private equity firm Francisco Partners.

Summary

- A business with high AI maturity is better positioned to implement genAI.
- Based on understanding and adoption of AI, the firms can be classified into the following AI maturity archetypes: passives, investigators, experimenters, and pioneers.
- Passives have a low understanding and a low adoption of AI.
- Investigators have a high understanding but low adoption of AI.
- Experimenters have a low understanding but high adoption of AI.
- Pioneers have a high understanding and a high adoption of AI.
- There are 12 AI maturity archetypes-mindsets zones: Passives-Optimistic (PO), Passives- Skeptic (PS), Passives- Pragmatic (PP), Investigators- Optimistic (IO), Investigators- Skeptic (IS), Investigators- Pragmatic (IP), Experimenters- Optimistic (EO), Experimenters- Skeptic (ES), Experimenters- Pragmatic (EP), Pioneers- Optimistic (PiO), Pioneers- Skeptic (PiS), Pioneers- Pragmatic (PiP).
- All the AI maturity archetypes: passives, investigators, experimenters, and pioneers can launch genAI pilots.
- *Pioneers AI maturity archetype is the second booster for scaled genAI adoption.*
- Enterprises can upgrade to pioneers using the following two-step process:
  1. Assessment
  2. Deployment programs

CHAPTER 5

Improving VITA Score

Imagine an Indian postal service company named Dak (it means post in Hindi) that has implemented genAI to revolutionize its delivery operations. GenAI analyzes a vast amount of historical delivery data, including parcel volumes, delivery locations, and traffic patterns, to generate optimized route plans. These routes are dynamically adjusted based on real-time factors such as weather conditions, traffic congestion, and delivery priorities. As a result, Dak has experienced a substantial reduction in fuel consumption and vehicle maintenance costs as the optimized routes minimize unnecessary mileage and idle time. This has translated into substantial cost savings for Dak, allowing it to allocate resources more efficiently and invest in other areas of its business. Moreover, genAI enables Dak to enhance customer satisfaction by ensuring timely and accurate deliveries, adapting quickly to new delivery demands, and providing customers with greater transparency and control over their shipments.

Imagine an Indian sportswear company named Khel (it means sports in Hindi), which sought to differentiate itself and increase its product value using genAI. By leveraging genAI capabilities, Khel revolutionized its content creation process by generating engaging marketing materials that included social media posts, promotional videos, and product descriptions. It successfully engaged its customers by conveying the advantages of playing the sport related to the specific sporting equipment they purchased. For example, to those customers who purchased swimming gears, Khel emphasized how swimming is a low-impact exercise that provides a full-body workout, improves cardiovascular health, increases muscle strength and endurance, enables weight loss, and enhances flexibility and coordination, through personalized blogs, posts, and emails. Additionally, it utilized user-generated content to showcase real-life stories and testimonials from individuals who experienced the positive effects of swimming on their health and lifestyle. GenAI enabled Khel to personalize its offerings and tailor them to individual customer preferences. By analyzing consumer data and behavior patterns, Khel developed customized product recommendations and marketing campaigns, further enhancing the perceived value of its products and driving sales. Internally, genAI was instrumental in optimizing Khel's operations. It implemented AI-driven algorithms to streamline inventory management, predict demand trends, and optimize supply chain logistics. This allowed it to reduce overhead costs associated with excess inventory and minimize product shortages, resulting in improved operational efficiency and profitability.

Imagine an Indian online education company named Shiksha (it means education in Hindi) that has revolutionized its offerings by integrating genAI to create new supplementary course content, enhance existing courses, and optimize internal operations. It offers two types of courses: standard and premium. A standard course comprises a series of lectures in the form of videos, readings, PowerPoints, notes, and quizzes. It is further enhanced by genAI, providing additional information to students, such as the types of jobs this course could help them find, additional courses they might need to take, real-world applications of the course, industry insights, and success stories of those who completed it. The premium package includes everything from the standard offering, along with an additional feature—a prompt window. This genAI-powered prompt window allows students to input prompts and generate new content dynamically based on their specific requirements. For example, students watching the standard video on biology could input a prompt about a specific topic such as cell division, and the system would generate relevant explanations, diagrams, and animations to help them understand the concept better. Similarly, a student learning a new language could input a phrase they wanted to practice, and the system could generate exercises, dialogues, and pronunciation guides based on that prompt. A finance student who wants to understand a particular concept, such as portfolio diversification, can type this prompt in the window enabling genAI to dynamically generate explanations, case studies, and interactive visualizations demonstrating the benefits and strategies of diversifying investment portfolios. Also, students can summarize the entire video or a particular concept in the video in the form of visual infographics, by providing related prompts in the window. Moreover, genAI has enabled Shiksha to streamline its internal operations by automating content creation processes, reducing manual workloads, and accelerating the production cycle. As a result, it has witnessed improved efficiency, reduced costs, and faster time-to-market for new courses and updates.

Out of the above three companies, which one do you think is extracting the most value from genAI?
Answer: Shiksha

Dak is using genAI only to optimize internal operations to reduce costs. Khel is using genAI not only to optimize internal operations but also to enhance the existing product value by providing additional information related to the product. Shiksha is using genAI not only to optimize internal operations and enhance the existing product value by providing additional information related to the product but also to generate new revenues through premium offerings that allow users to dynamically generate supplementary content.

How is Shiksha able to generate new revenue streams, that Dak and Khel cannot?
Ans: VITA

You were introduced to the acronym VITA in the introduction, and now it's being mentioned again. What exactly does VITA stand for? Let's uncover the mystery!
VITA stands for *Video, Image, Text, and Audio.*
Shiksha was able to generate additional revenue streams due to the presence of VITA or video, image, text, and audio in its products, the online courses. It has *video* in the form of animations and videos. It has *images* in the form of diagrams, pictures, and icons. It has *text* in the form of slide text, course descriptions, instructor bios, and transcripts. It has *audio* in the form of voiceovers by the instructors.

Khel's product sportswear goods and Dak's product (service) postal delivery do not have any VITA component. Note that operations supporting these products have VITA, but the products themselves do not. Dak's product is nontangible and non-VITA, Khel's is tangible and non-VITA, and Shiksha's is nontangible and VITA.

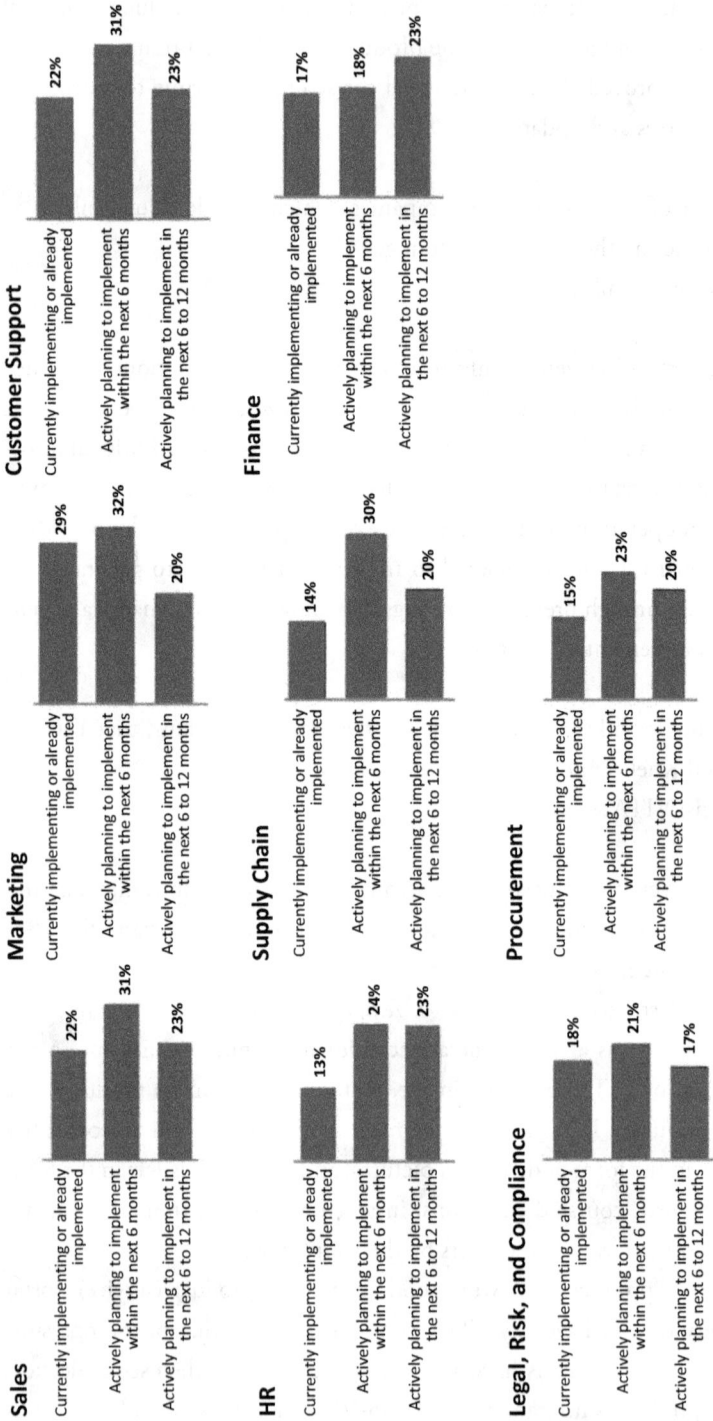

Customer Support

- Currently implementing or already implemented — 22%
- Actively planning to implement within the next 6 months — 31%
- Actively planning to implement in the next 6 to 12 months — 23%

Marketing

- Currently implementing or already implemented — 29%
- Actively planning to implement within the next 6 months — 32%
- Actively planning to implement in the next 6 to 12 months — 20%

Finance

- Currently implementing or already implemented — 17%
- Actively planning to implement within the next 6 months — 18%
- Actively planning to implement in the next 6 to 12 months — 23%

Sales

- Currently implementing or already implemented — 22%
- Actively planning to implement within the next 6 months — 31%
- Actively planning to implement in the next 6 to 12 months — 23%

Supply Chain

- Currently implementing or already implemented — 14%
- Actively planning to implement within the next 6 months — 30%
- Actively planning to implement in the next 6 to 12 months — 20%

Procurement

- Currently implementing or already implemented — 15%
- Actively planning to implement within the next 6 months — 23%
- Actively planning to implement in the next 6 to 12 months — 20%

HR

- Currently implementing or already implemented — 13%
- Actively planning to implement within the next 6 months — 24%
- Actively planning to implement in the next 6 to 12 months — 23%

Legal, Risk, and Compliance

- Currently implementing or already implemented — 18%
- Actively planning to implement within the next 6 months — 21%
- Actively planning to implement in the next 6 to 12 months — 17%

Figure 5.1 GenAI utilization functionwise

The higher the VITA component in a product, the higher is the value extracted from genAI.

As per the Gartner survey[1] in Figure 5.1, IT and customer-facing functions such as marketing, customer support, and sales have higher utilization than HR, supply, finance, procurement, and legal, risk, and compliance.

Functionwise VITA

The following table shows the functions in an organization ranked in descending order as per VITA components:

Rank	Functions	VITA analysis	VITA activities/ tasks/content	Utilization	VITA impact
1	Marketing	Video	Product demos, brand storytelling, testimonials, and reviews	Moderate	High
		Image	Graphics, logos, infographics, banners, display ads	High	
		Text	Web content, emails, newsletters, press releases, advertisements, reviews, testimonials	High	
		Audio	Podcasts, voiceovers, interactive voice response (IVR), music branding	High	
2	Sales	Video	Sales presentations, product demos, virtual tours, customer testimonials, training	Moderate	High
		Image	Brochures, flyers, case studies, diagrams, charts	High	
		Text	Proposals, contracts, agreements, sales scripts, emails	High	
		Audio	Sales calls, sales training	High	

(Continued)

(*Continued*)

Rank	Functions	VITA analysis	VITA activities/ tasks/content	Utilization	VITA impact
3	Customer support	Video	Troubleshooting guides, product setup and installation, live chat support	Low	Moderate
		Image	Screenshots, remote desktop sharing, visual guides, charts, diagrams	Moderate	
		Text	Knowledge base articles, FAQs covering common questions, troubleshooting steps, product information, email support, chat support	High	
		Audio	Call center support, IVR, voicemail support	High	
4	HR	Video	Videos on recruitment, training, employee engagement, onboarding	Low	Low
		Image	Infographics, organization charts, recruitment flyers	Low	
		Text	Job postings, employee communication and announcements, employee handbook, policy documents, performance appraisals, compensation and rewards guides	High	
		Audio	Conference calls, podcasts	Low	

Rank	Functions	VITA analysis	VITA activities/ tasks/content	Utilization	VITA impact
5	Supply	Video	Training videos, product demos, transport monitoring	Low	Moderate
		Image	Product images, damage documentation, packaging visuals	Moderate	
		Text	Purchase orders, inventory reports, compliance documents, customs documents, contracts, shipping notifications	High	
		Audio	Customer support	Moderate	
6	Finance	Video	Educational videos, market updates, client testimonials	Moderate	Moderate
		Image	Infographics, charts, graphs, visual diagrams	Moderate	
		Text	Financial reports, account statements, compliance documents, newsletters, articles	High	
		Audio	Customer support, IVR	Moderate	
7	Legal, risk, and compliance	Video	Training videos, compliance updates, case studies, audit reports	Low	Moderate
		Image	Infographics, charts, graphs	Low	
		Text	Legal documents, contracts, compliance manuals, risk assessments	High	
		Audio	Compliance support	Moderate	

(*Continued*)

(*Continued*)

Rank	Functions	VITA analysis	VITA activities/ tasks/content	Utilization	VITA impact
8	Procurement	Video	Supplier training videos, product demos	Low	Moderate
		Image	Supplier performance dashboards and metrics, charts, graphs	Low	
		Text	Request for Proposal (RFP), contracts, purchase orders, supplier agreements	High	
		Audio	Vendor hotline support	Moderate	

We can observe that the functions such as sales, marketing, and customer support, that have higher deployment of genAI have higher VITA components as compared to HR, finance, supply, procurement, and legal, risk, and compliance. This once again confirms the fact that higher the VITA, higher the scope of deploying genAI.

Industrywise VITA

The global survey by McKinsey in Figure 5.2, further shows the following industrywise combined usage of genAI tools: regularly for work, regularly for work and outside of work, and regularly outside of work:

- Technology, media, and telecom with 50 percent combined usage
- Healthcare, pharma, and medical products with 33 percent combined usage

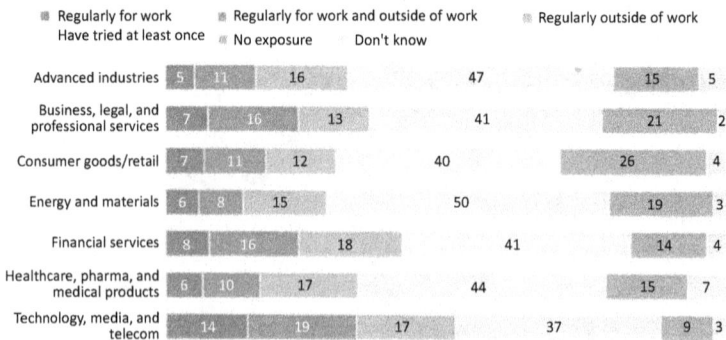

Figure 5.2 Industrywise usage of genAI tools

- Financial services with 42 percent combined usage
- Energy and materials with 29 percent combined usage
- Consumer goods/retail with 30 percent combined usage
- Business, legal, and professional services with 36 percent combined usage
- Advanced industries with 32 percent combined usage

The following table ranks industries in descending order based on VITA components in their commercial products or services:

Rank	Industries	VITA components	VITA impact	VITA activities/tasks/content
1	Entertainment	V I T A	High	Filming, script writing, sound recording, music, sound synthesizing, photography, storyboarding, editing
2	Media	V I T A	High	Writing, editing, proofreading, audio recording, advertising, content distribution through websites, social media, blogs, publications, audience engagement
3	Advertising	V I T A	High	Ad creation, promotional campaigns, branding, customer engagement
4	Education	V I T A	High	Lectures, e-books, notes
5	Journalism	V I T A	High	Articles, footage, photos, podcasts, news, blogs, interviews
6	IT, software, and technology	V I T A	High	Code, tools for video, images, text, and audio
7	Financial services	V I T A	High	Reports, articles, market analysis, graphs, charts, videos, investment advice, educational videos
8	Communications	V I T A	High	Voice and video calls, text messages, SMS, sharing images
9	Automotive	V I T A	High	Vehicle descriptions, safety manuals, reviews, photos, advertisement videos, tutorial videos, in-car entertainment, GPS navigation
10	Travel	V I T	Moderate	Destination pictures, videos, guides, travel blogs
11	Airlines	V I T	Moderate	Safety videos, inflight entertainment, flight bookings and schedules, safety cards containing images
12	Retail	I T	Moderate	Product images, reviews, descriptions
13	Healthcare	I T	Moderate	Medical imaging, patient records, informational texts

(Continued)

(*Continued*)

Rank	Industries	VITA components	VITA impact	VITA activities/tasks/content
14	Pharmaceutical	I T	Moderate	Product brochures, package inserts, drug labels, scientific publications, regulatory documents, patient information leaflets, graphs and charts showing clinical trial results, images or diagrams of drug formation
15	Banking	T A	Moderate	Text notifications, account summaries, customer support via phone, customer support via chatbots
16	Insurance	T A	Moderate	Policy documentation, claims report, customer support via phone, customer support via chatbots
17	Real estate	I T	Moderate	Property images, descriptions
18	Food and beverages	I T	Moderate	Food images, recipes
19	Consumer goods	I T	Moderate	Product descriptions, labeling, package/wrapper design
20	Industrial manufacturing	I T	Moderate	Technical documentation, diagrams
21	Fashion	V I	Moderate	Photography, brand promotional videos
22	Hotels and hospitality	I T	Moderate	Room images, reviews, menu displays
23	Oil and gas	I T	Moderate	Geographic and terrain maps, site photographs, operations and safety manuals, regulatory compliance documents
24	Aerospace and defense	I T	Moderate	Aircraft diagrams, product manuals, documents such as regulations, compliance, and protocols
25	Mining	I T	Moderate	Geological maps and images, mining manuals, technical reports
26	Utilities/energy	T	Low	Bills, invoices, utility guides
27	Supply, logistics, and delivery	T	Low	Documentation handling, barcode scanning, inventory reports
28	Public sector and government	T	Low	Documents, reports, and announcements to citizens
29	Construction	I	Low	Architectural diagrams, plans, site photos
30	Agriculture	T	Low	Manuals detailing crop cultivation practices

Comparing the data from the above table with McKinsey survey in Figure 5.2, we observe that industries, such as technology, media, telecom and financial services, that show high percentage usage of genAI also show a high VITA impact. Industries such as healthcare, consumer goods, retail, and advanced industries (industrial manufacturing), that show a medium percentage usage of genAI also show a moderate VITA impact. Utilities/energy, which shows the lowest percentage usage of genAI, also shows a low VITA impact.

We can conclude that enterprises and industries with higher VITA scores have better chances of adoption and value extraction from genAI. Thus,

Higher VITA score is the third booster for scaled genAI adoption.

VITA score is a measure of how much of your business, or its daily operational tasks, or products and services comprise video, image, text, and audio. If your organization shows a higher VITA score it means that you need to adopt genAI urgently. Otherwise, there is a high chance of being outperformed by your competition. If you haven't taken any action, it is important to begin piloting with convertible pilots.

The content created by genAI is categorized into the following six categories: text, image, audio, video, code, and synthetic data.

Code can be grouped under text and synthetic data can be text, image, audio, and video. Hence, we get the four broad categories of VITA: video, image, text, and audio, which can better position your organization and enable it to extract value from scaled adoption of genAI.

Enterprises can improve their VITA scores through the following two-step process:

1. Assessment
2. Improvement programs

1. **Assessment**

Measure the percentage of each of the VITA components in each customer product and/or service using the table below:

#	Products/Services	V	I	T	A
1	Name of product/service 1				
2	Name of product/service 2				
...	...				
n	Name of product/service n				
	Average percentages of each VITA				

Measure the percentage of each of the VITA components in each operational tasks or processes:

#	Operational tasks/processes	V	I	T	A
1	Operational tasks/processes 1				
2	Operational tasks/processes 2				
...	...				
n	Operational tasks/processes n				
	Average percentages of each VITA				

Use the following legend to assign a relevant percentage score:

VITA component	Percentage range (%)
Very high	81–100
High	61–80
Moderate	31–60
Low	11–30
Very low	0–10

2. **Improvement programs**
   1. Note down the current VITA score from the assessment.
   2. Specify the desired improved VITA score.
   3. Identify the lower and higher individual VITA components from the assessment based on the percentage.
   4. Make a relevant strategy on how to improve the level of a specific VITA component. Make sure you involve all the key stakeholders across functions and all hierarchical levels in the strategy planning workshop.

Summary

- VITA stands for video, image, text, and audio.
- The higher the VITA component in a product, the higher is the value extracted from genAI.
- *Higher VITA score is the third booster for scaled genAI adoption.*
- VITA score is a measure of how much of your business, or its daily operational tasks, or products and services comprise video, image, text, and audio.
- Enterprises can improve their VITA scores through the following two-step process:
  1. Assessment
  2. Improvement programs

SUMMARY OF PART 2

Boosters

- Cultivate pragmatic mindset
- Upgrade AI maturity archetype to pioneers
- Improve VITA score

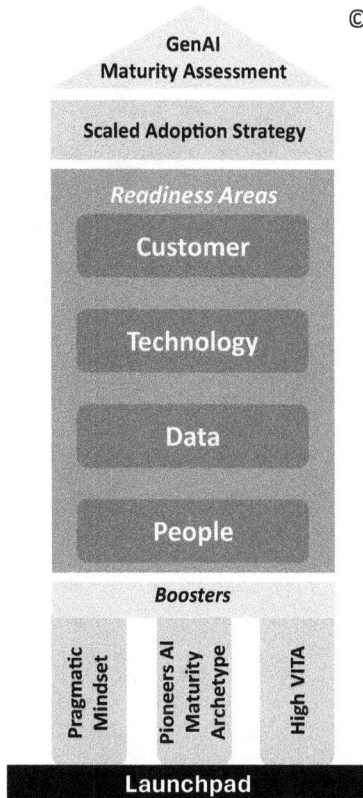

PART 3

Readiness Area

Customer

CHAPTER 6

Understanding Customer:

Readiness Audit, SPIN Engagement, Journey Maps

We begin with the story of two Asian-based IT system integrators, let us call them Ram Consulting and Shyam Consulting. Both started developing the most common pilot, the genAI-enabled chatbot for customer support. They both followed these steps:

- Defining objectives
- Selecting a specific use case sub-scenario
- Data acquisition and preparation
- Selecting LLM and genAI framework
- Designing workflows
- Backend integration
- Testing and validation
- Continuous improvement

Defining Objectives

Both Ram and Shyam had a common objective: To build a genAI-enabled chatbot to improve customer service efficiency and enhance user experience. The key metrics were:

Category	Metrics	Target
Customer service efficiency	Lead time reduction	25%
	Cost reduction	45%
	Inquiries escalated to humans	35%
User experience	Customer satisfaction index	Minimum 7 (scale of 1 to 10, 1: lowest, 10: highest)

Selecting a Specific Use Case Sub-scenario

There were three specific sub-scenarios: question and answering (Q&A), troubleshooting, and personalized recommendations. Q&A involves providing detailed information about products, features, specifications, and pricing to help customers make informed purchase decisions. Troubleshooting includes offering step-by-step guidance, diagnosing technical problems, and suggesting solutions to resolve customer issues efficiently. Personalized recommendations include analyzing user preferences, past interactions, and browsing history to deliver tailored product recommendations, promotions, and content that align with individual interests and needs. Ram chose two sub-scenarios: Q&A and troubleshooting. Shyam chose all three of them.

Data Acquisition and Preparation

Both Ram and Shyam follow the same three steps of data acquisition and preparation, which are as follows:

1. Data acquisition: identifying the data purpose, acquiring the right data, integrating and storing the data.
2. Data preparation: cleaning, annotating, and structuring the data.

More details on these steps are in Part 5.

Selecting LLM and GenAI Framework

Ram selected AWS Bedrock, a fully managed service that offers a choice of high-performing foundation models from leading AI companies like AI21 Labs, Anthropic, Cohere, Luma AI, Meta, Mistral AI, Stability AI, and Amazon via a single application programming interface (API). Shyam selected GPT-4 as LLM due to its language processing capabilities such as complex reasoning, chatbot-like abilities, Q&A, text summarization, creative writing, translation, and code generation, along with LangChain, a genAI framework aimed at simplifying the development of applications utilizing LLMs.

Designing Workflows

The chatbots by Ram and Shyam had the following workflows in common:

Workflow	Description
Welcome message	Upon initiation, the chatbot greets the user and offers assistance.
Information retrieval	Users inquire about specific topics, products, or services, and the chatbot provides relevant information or directs them to appropriate resources.
Task execution	Users request actions such as making reservations, placing orders, or scheduling appointments, and the chatbot facilitates these tasks.
Transaction assistance	Users seek help with completing transactions, such as making payments, tracking orders, or updating account information, and the chatbot guides them through the process step by step.
Troubleshooting	Users report issues or ask questions about products or services, and the chatbot guides them through troubleshooting steps.
Feedback collection	The chatbot solicits feedback from users to improve its performance or gather insights for future enhancements.
Escalation path	If the chatbot is unable to resolve an issue, it escalates the conversation to a human agent for further assistance.
Closing message	At the end of the interaction, the chatbot expresses gratitude, provides additional assistance options, or invites users to engage again in the future.

Shyam designed an additional workflow, personalization, which Ram did not.

Workflow	Description
Personalization	The chatbot remembers user preferences or previous interactions to provide personalized recommendations or responses.

Backend Integration

This process involves integrating the chatbot with backend systems and databases to access relevant information and perform actions enabling features such as user authentication, data retrieval, order processing, and third-party API integrations, as needed.

Testing and Validation

This procedure involves rigorous testing to ensure that the genAI chatbot consistently generates coherent and contextually relevant responses across diverse scenarios, incorporating real user feedback to improve performance and address any issues identified.

Continuous Improvement

The process involves improving the system performance based on continuous feedback from users.

Both Ram and Shyam completed the chatbot development almost at the same time. Both had a common customer named Retail X. Ram and Shyam presented the demos to Retail X. Ram's got accepted and Shyam's got rejected by the close of business.

How did things happen so fast?

Answer: Ram's pilot was customer-funded by Retail X.

Though both Ram and Shyam had aggressive sales plans with genAI, their near-term strategies were different. Shyam's strategy was:

Develop a pilot based on a use case and sell it to multiple customers.

Ram's strategy was:

One convertible pilot per customer.

In the first quarter of 2023, Shyam began developing the genAI chatbot based on approved funding from its executive leadership. However, around the same time, Ram began engaging with Retail X on genAI with various teams at various levels, with scaled adoption plan in mind. Though Ram's pilot development started two months after Shyam's, both completed it at the same time. Ram's pilot underwent very few changes and iterations as compared to Shyam's, because it had a clear and well-defined scope, agreed upon jointly with Retail X. Q&A and troubleshooting were the specific agreed use case sub-scenarios in the initial phase, with personalization to be added in the later ones along with other sub-scenarios. But Shyam started with all three of them together. Ram's pilot used live data from the customer for training the genAI model, whereas Shyam used synthetic data.

Thus, Ram's pilot provided better accuracy and confidence compared to Shyam's. Ram selected AWS Bedrock in consultation with Retail X, which already had its cloud infrastructure with AWS. Shyam went for GPT-4, an LLM suited for general-purpose deployments. Thus, Ram was able to successfully demonstrate the pilot and get approval for the next phase. Then, why did Retail X invite Shyam to present the demo? Because it wanted to do a comparative analysis with Ram's demo.

It is likely that some enterprises, in the race to implement pilots, might have overlooked the customer-first approach. And it is even likelier that those who were able to win a customer-funded pilot project did not discuss about scaling. The project Excalibur shows that 43 percent of the pilot projects were funded externally by the customers, whereas 57 percent were funded internally. A staggering 95 percent of the overall pilot projects lacked the scaled adoption engagements.

It is very important for enterprises to understand their customer requirements first before deploying genAI pilots or scaled solutions. Understanding of customer involves three steps:

1. Customer readiness audit
2. Engaging with customer
3. Preparing customer journey maps

Note that the readiness area:customer explained here, is applicable to B2B customers only. For B2C customers, book a consultation at www.scalinggenai.com.

Customer Readiness Audit

It would be incorrect to make assumptions about your customer's awareness and understanding of genAI. As seen earlier, different enterprises have reacted differently to the genAI hype, based on either their optimistic, skeptic, or pragmatic mindsets. Different customers are at different levels of genAI maturity. We segregate them based not only on average revenues and profits your business generates through them over a certain amount of years but also based on criteria such as genAI maturity level, VITA score, omnichannel engagements, and business relationships. It is done through a process known as *customer readiness audit*.

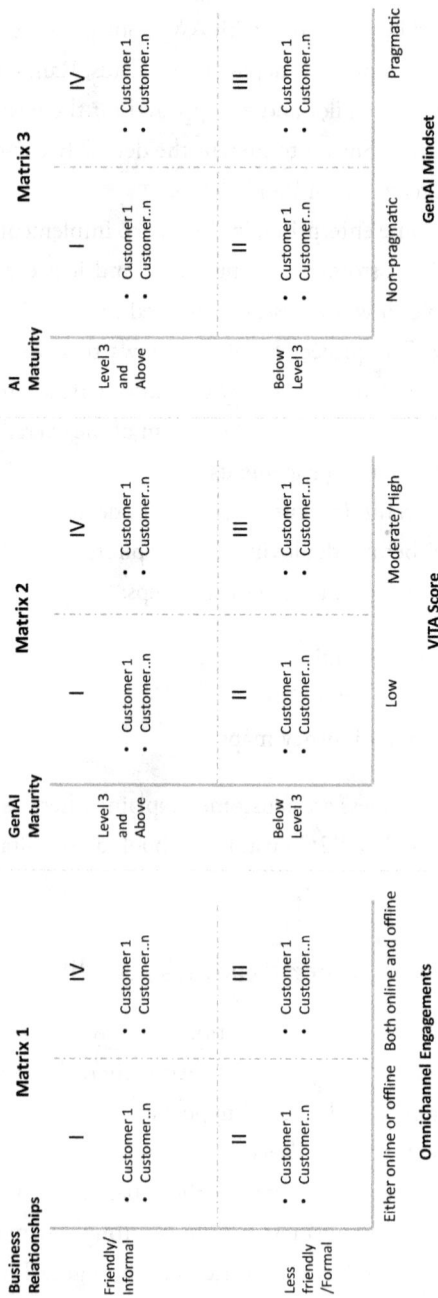

Figure 6.1 High-readiness customers selection matrices

From your customers list, shortlist the *high-readiness* customers using the following procedure:

1. Place all your customers in the Matrix 1: Business relationships versus Omnichannel engagements.
2. Filter out the customers in quadrant II of Matrix 1.
3. Move the ones in quadrant I, III, and IV to Matrix 2: GenAI maturity versus VITA score, after doing a genAI maturity and VITA assessment with them.
4. Place them in appropriate quadrants of Matrix 2.
5. Filter out the customers in quadrant II of Matrix 2.
6. Move the ones in quadrant I, III, and IV to Matrix 3: AI maturity versus GenAI mindset, after doing an AI maturity and GenAI mindset assessment with them.
7. Place them in appropriate quadrants of Matrix 3.
8. Filter out the customers in quadrant II of Matrix 3
9. The remaining ones in quadrant I, III, and IV of Matrix 3 are the high-readiness customers.
10. If no customers qualify under Matrix 3, prioritize those in quadrant IV of Matrix 2 as high-readiness customers. If none qualify, consider those in quadrants I and III of Matrix 2. If still none qualify, consider those in quadrant IV of Matrix 1. Finally, if necessary, select customers in quadrants I and III of Matrix 1.

Conducting a genAI mindset assessment for the entire organization may not be practical. Instead, it should be sufficient to assess the genAI mindset of executive leaders and key decision-makers at these customer organizations.

If there are many high-readiness customers and you need to select one or a few, you may select the ones with high revenues and profits your business generates through them.

Engaging With Customer

Before we select a convertible pilot with customers, it is important to understand their needs, perspectives, and concerns regarding genAI. For this, we use the popular SPIN methodology, used primarily for B2B sales. It is an approach focused on asking situation, problem, implication, and need-payoff (SPIN acronym) questions to understand the customer needs, uncover pain points, and provide tailored solutions. *Situation* questions aim to gather information about the customer's current circumstances or environment. *Problem* questions help identify specific challenges or issues the customer is facing. *Implication* questions explore the consequences or impact of the identified problems, highlighting the urgency or severity of the situation. *Need-payoff* questions focus on the benefits or value of addressing the customer's needs, helping them envision the positive outcomes of implementing a solution. By emphasizing active listening and empathetic engagement, SPIN selling aims to build rapport and trust with customers while effectively positioning the product or service as a valuable solution.

The following table shows some SPIN-related questions for engaging with genAI customers:

SPIN categories	Questions
Situation	- What is your current approach to genAI? Are you leveraging the AI technology? - What specific AI tools or platforms are you currently using, if any? - How do you currently handle tasks that could benefit from genAI capabilities? - How do you currently measure the success or effectiveness of your AI initiatives? - What is the size and composition of your AI development team?
Problem	- What challenges do you encounter when implementing AI solutions? - Can you identify inefficiencies in your current AI workflows? - What are the data challenges? - What limitations do you encounter with your current AI tools or platforms? - Have you noticed any recurring issues about the performance of your AI models?
Implication	- What impact do these challenges have on your business operations or outcomes? - How do these AI-related issues affect your team's productivity? - Are there any potential risks in not addressing these challenges? - How do the challenges impact your organization's ability to innovate? - What are the potential consequences if these AI-related issues worsen over time?

(Continued)

(*Continued*)

SPIN categories	Questions
Need-payoff	- What are the benefits of implementing genAI capabilities? - How do you foresee genAI enhancing creativity and innovation? - What specific efficiency gains or cost savings do you expect to achieve? - What are the new revenue streams? - How would genAI assist in personalizing customer experiences or loyalty?

Preparing Customer Journey Maps

Once you uncover the customer needs using SPIN, the next step is to develop the customer journey maps. *Customer journey maps* are visual representations of the entire experience a customer has with a company, product, or service. They detail every interaction the customer has across different channels and stages, from discovery to post purchase support. These maps enable enterprises to understand the customer's viewpoint, pinpoint areas of concern, and discover areas for enhancement. By mapping the customer journey, organizations can align their efforts to provide a smooth and enjoyable experience, enhancing customer satisfaction, loyalty, and retention. Developing customer journey maps involves several steps to ensure a comprehensive understanding of the customer experience:

Steps	Description
1. Define objectives	Clearly outline the objectives of creating the customer journey map, such as identifying pain points, improving touchpoints, or enhancing customer satisfaction.
2. Identify personas	Define the different customer personas or segments that will be represented in the journey map, considering factors like demographics, preferences, and behaviors.
3. Gather data	Collect qualitative and quantitative data from various sources, including customer feedback, surveys, interviews, sales data, and analytics, to understand customer interactions and experiences.
4. Map touchpoints	Identify all the touchpoints or interactions that customers have with your brand across different channels and stages of the journey, from initial awareness to post purchase support.
5. Create a timeline	Develop a timeline or framework that represents the chronological sequence of events and touchpoints in the customer journey, mapping out each stage from beginning to end.

Steps	Description
6. Document customer emotions and pain points	Capture the emotional highs and lows, as well as pain points or frustrations, that customers may experience at each touch-point along the journey.
7. Analyze and iterate	Analyze the customer journey map to identify patterns, trends, and opportunities for improvement. Iterate on the map based on feedback, insights, and changes in customer behavior or preferences.
8. Validate with stake-holders	Share the customer journey map with relevant stakeholders, such as marketing, sales, customer service, and product teams, to gather input and ensure alignment with business goals and objectives.
9. Implement changes	Use the insights from the customer journey map to implement changes and enhancements to the customer experience, addressing pain points, optimizing touchpoints, and enhancing overall satisfaction.
10. Monitor and update	Continuously monitor and update the customer journey map over time to reflect changes in customer behavior, market dynamics, and business strategies, ensuring that it remains a valuable tool for driving customer-centric initiatives.

Let us revisit Lisa's story from Chapter 3. She utilized customer journey maps, shown in Figure 6.2, to understand customer needs before developing the genAI solution, recognizing the necessity for specialized skills and seeking assistance from renowned consultant Alex Sanches. Through workshops organized by Alex, customer service representatives thoroughly explored each caller's experience, mapping emotional aspects and inquiries, resulting in comprehensive journey maps for potential patients, current patients, and patient's family members, providing a foundation for enhancing ACC's call experience.

Group Activity

Before meeting customers
1. Prepare a final list of high-readiness customers after passing them through the high-readiness customers selection matrices.

Engaging with customers
2. Use the SPIN methodology to gain deeper insights into their perspective on AI/genAI.

Customer Journey Map for a Current Patient Calling ACC

Need for Info/Support	The Call	Call Escalation	Conclusion	Post-Call
Decision to reach out to ACC for more information or to schedule an appointment.	Dialing the CHS helpline. Speaking with a representative.	Need to escalate the call for specialized queries or concerns.	Ending the call with the representative or department.	Reflecting on the call experience, waiting for follow-ups.

Positive: "CR was knowledgeable." · "I was able to speak directly with the right person." · "Courteous closing, promise of follow-up if needed."

Negative: "I was anxious and didn't know what to expect." · "CR said the system crashed. She couldn't check if I was in the system." · "I had to start all over, describing who I was." · "I didn't really know how to do the follow-up." · "I didn't receive any follow-up via email as promised."

Customer Journey Map for a Potential Patient Calling ACC

Discovery Phase	The Call	Call Escalation	Conclusion	Post-Call
Initial discovery of ACC through online search, referrals, or advertisements. Decision to reach out to ACC for more information or to schedule an appointment.	Dialing the ACC helpline. Speaking with a customer service representative.	Need to escalate the call to a higher authority or specialized department.	Ending the call with the representative or department.	Reflecting on the call experience, waiting for follow-ups.

Positive: "The CR was helpful and kind." · "I was able to speak directly with an RN." · "I received a follow-up email with some next steps."

Negative: "I was excited to find ACC." · "I didn't know what to expect." · "CR said the system crashed." · "I had to start from the beginning." · "I wasn't so clear on the next steps." · "It seemed like a generic email that wasn't personal."

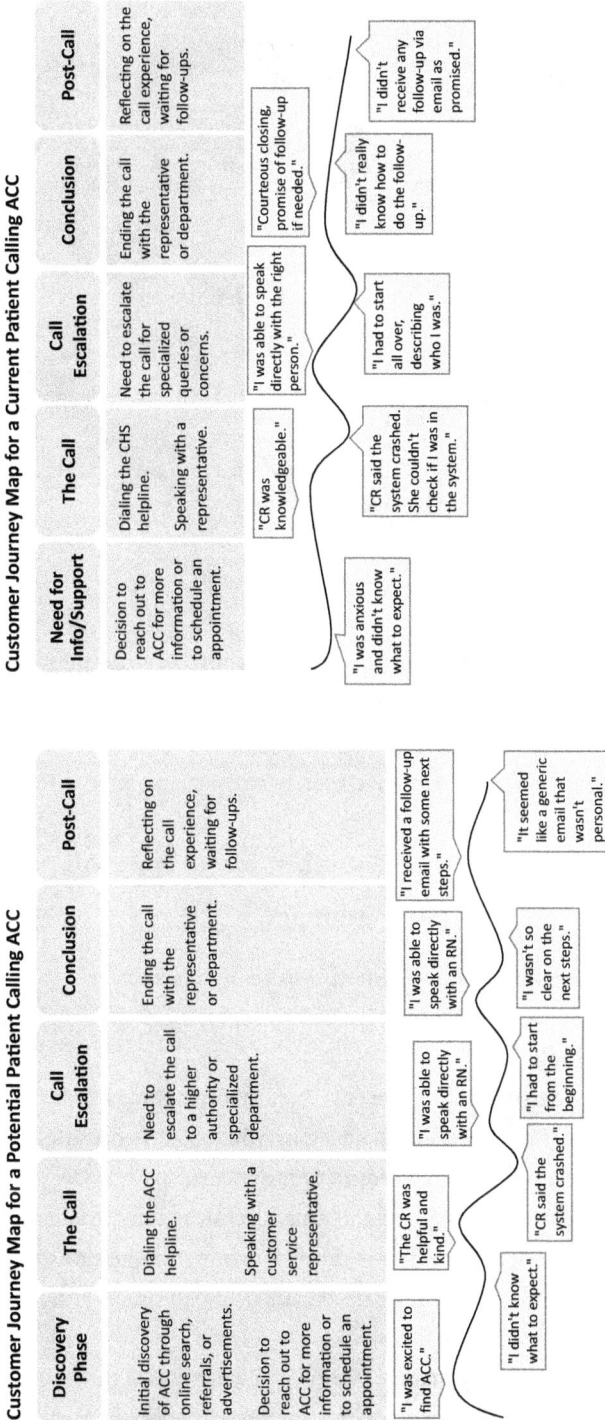

Figure 6.2 Customer journey maps[1]

Customer Journey Map for Patient's Family Members Calling ACC

Need for Info/Support	The Call	Call Escalation	Conclusion	Post-Call
Decision to call ACC for updates, support, or queries related to loved one's treatment.	Dialing the CHS helpline. Speaking with a representative.	Need to escalate the call for specialized queries or concerns.	Ending the call with the representative or department.	Reflecting on the call experience, waiting for follow-ups.

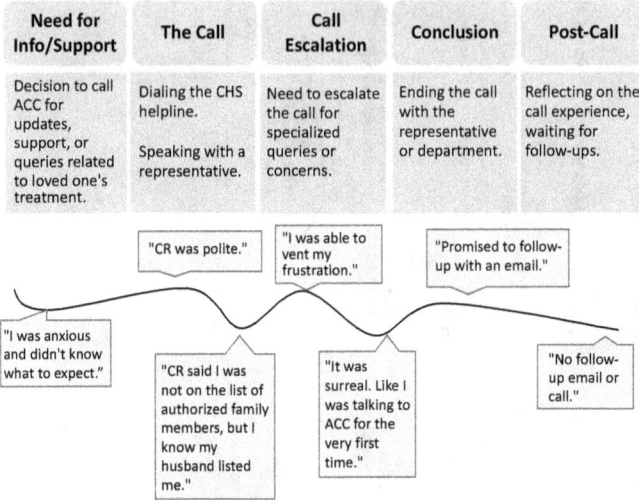

"CR was polite."

"I was able to vent my frustration."

"Promised to follow-up with an email."

"I was anxious and didn't know what to expect."

"CR said I was not on the list of authorized family members, but I know my husband listed me."

"It was surreal. Like I was talking to ACC for the very first time."

"No follow-up email or call."

Figure 6.2 (Continued)

Selecting the final customers

3. Choose one or a few customers from your high-readiness customers list to explore the possibility of co-developing either convertible pilots or a genAI solution.
4. Collaborate with them to create journey maps after interviewing their key stakeholders.

Summary

- It is very important for enterprises to understand their customer requirements first, before deploying genAI pilots or scaled solutions.
- The understanding of the customer involves three steps: customer readiness audit, engaging with customers using SPIN, and preparing customer journey maps.
- SPIN is an approach focused on asking situation, problem, implication, and need-payoff (SPIN acronym) questions to understand the customer needs, uncover pain points, and provide tailored solutions.
- Customer journey maps are visual representations of the entire experience a customer has with a company, product, or service.

CHAPTER 7

Positioning Business:
Value Chain, Use Cases, Products

In late 2020, AI21 Labs, headquartered in Tel Aviv, took its first step by transforming the writing and reading process through the launch of Wordtune, a consumer-oriented B2C writing application. This innovative tool utilized genAI software to suggest alternative text options, helping users enhance their writing. Following this success, Wordtune Read was launched in 2021, offering document summarization capabilities to users. Despite the various risks and challenges, the founders decided to build an in-house Large Language Model (LLM). Thus, in 2021, its LLM Jurassic-1 was launched with J1-Jumbo, a 178 billion parameter model, and J1-Large, a seven billion parameter model. AI21 Labs progressively began shifting its Wordtune app from OpenAI's LLM to Jurassic. In August 2021, AI21 Labs unveiled AI21 Studio, its NLP-as-a-service platform for developers and B2B businesses. In March 2023, it announced the launch of Jurassic-2, the latest generation of AI21 Studio's foundation models, alongside task-specific application programming interface (APIs) for third party developers. AI21 Labs had a deal with Amazon Web Services (AWS) to offer its LLM Jurassic as a fully managed service on AWS Bedrock. They also partnered with Google Cloud to build several genAI apps and capabilities leveraging various Google Cloud services.[1] Just 18 months after its launch announcement, AI21 Labs announced the end of the life cycle for Jurassic-2 foundation models, which will no longer be available after November 14, 2024. They were replaced by Jamba 1.5 models: mini and large, based on Mamba Structured State Space Model (SSM) technology.

We see that AI21 Labs has taken various positions in the genAI value chain, starting from being a B2C app provider, becoming an LLM provider, being a genAI platform provider for B2B enterprises, being a partner to an LLM curator and to a cloud hyperscaler, and then transitioning from a proprietary LLM provider (Jurassic) to an open-source one (Jamba). Going forward, there are several open options before the AI21 Labs founders: should they reconsider building an AI-powered chatbot like ChatGPT, an idea that they had dismissed earlier? What are the best opportunities to monetize LLMs? Should they concentrate on B2C applications like Wordtune or capitalize on larger prospects in the B2B? Should they allocate substantial resources to develop a platform for third-party innovation with its LLM, or should they prioritize building their own specialized applications? Should they consider licensing their technology, similar to OpenAI's arrangement with Microsoft?

Every decision AI21 Labs makes will impact its positioning in the genAI market.

How should your business position itself in the genAI value chain: should it adopt single positioning or take multiple positions?

Value Chain

Figure 7.1 shows the generative AI value chain. The main players are:

1. Customers: There are two types of customers, individuals and enterprises, which consume the content generated by genAI applications through text, image, audio, video, code, and synthetic data.
2. GenAI app providers: They develop specific genAI applications to generate one or more than one type of VITA content, typically designed for end-users with user-friendly interfaces. Examples are DALL-E, Synthesia, and RunwayML.
3. AI copilot providers: They provide AI copilots, a special type of genAI apps that play the role of virtual assistants, offering real-time guidance and feedback to enhance your work. They are infused into your existing enterprise product or service. The AI copilots can be developed internally or sourced through a third party. Examples are Microsoft Copilot and Salesforce Einstein.
4. Framework providers: There are some genAI app development frameworks that provide best practices and standardization to some extent. The popular ones are LangChain, TensorFlow, and PyTorch.
5. LLM providers: The major LLM providers are OpenAI, Google, Microsoft, and Meta.

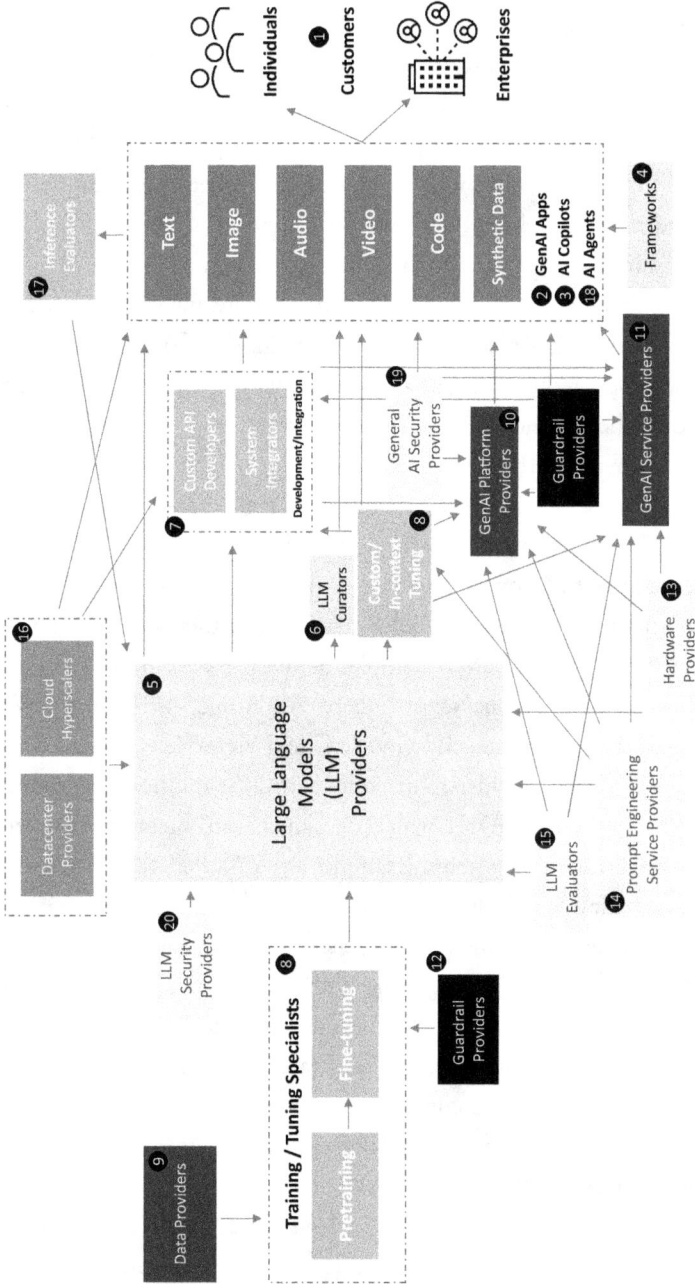

Figure 7.1 GenAI value chain

6. LLM curators: They offer a platform that provides users an access to a variety of LLMs based on their requirements. AWS Bedrock is a good example.

7. System integrators/custom API developers: The genAI apps can be either developed by LLM providers in-house or custom API developers and system integrators, who can develop and integrate them into the IT environments for enterprise customers. The examples of custom API developers and system integrators are Accenture, Tata Consultancy Services, Infosys, Wipro, and so on.

8. Training/tuning specialists: LLMs need to be pretrained, fine-tuned or custom/in-context tuned with business-specific data for business-specific genAI applications. Examples of training/tuning specialists are Hugging Face, Cohere, SambaNova, and Entry Point AI.

9. Data providers: The datasets for pretraining and fine-tuning are provided by data providers such as Scale AI, Kaggle, and Common Crawl.

10. GenAI platform providers: They provide customers a platform for developing their own genAI apps, based either on their own or external LLMs. They can either custom tune their LLMs in-house or through a third party. Examples of genAI platform providers are Hugging Face, SambaNova, Cohere, Anthropic, AI21 Labs, AWS SageMaker, MS Azure, and Google Cloud Vertex AI.

11. GenAI service providers: They offer genAI capabilities or functionalities via APIs or SDKs, which developers can integrate into various applications or systems. Examples are AWS Bedrock, MS Azure, Google Cloud, and OpenAI.

12. Guardrail providers: To avoid the generation of toxic or irrelevant content by generative AI for customers, it's essential to implement guardrails. Examples of guardrail providers are Moderation API by OpenAI, Perspective API, Azure Content Moderator, and Hugging Face.

13. Hardware providers: Companies such as NVIDIA, Intel, and AMD provide Graphics Processing Units (GPUs), whereas Groq provides Language Processing Units (LPUs).

14. Prompt engineering service providers: We know that crafting well-designed prompts helps guide the LLMs to produce more accurate and relevant responses, which makes prompt engineering an important function. There are companies such as KeyTalk AI and Promptly AI that offer prompt engineering services.

15. LLM evaluators: They measure a given LLM's performance using AI and data observability, and then benchmark it against others. Examples are companies like MosaicML, Moveworks, and Arthur, with its tool Arthur Bench.

16. Datacenter providers: LLMs can either have their private datacenters or lease them from datacenter-as-a-Service providers or can use the cloud infrastructure from the hyperscalers such as AWS, Azure, or Google Cloud. Examples of datacenter-as-a-Service providers are Equinix and Digital Realty.

17. Inference evaluators: They measure the quality and effectiveness of the generated outputs as per the prompts. Examples include companies such as Arize, Arthur, WhyLabs, Fiddler AI, and TruEra.

18. AI agents providers: AI agents are the autonomous entities that sense the environment, make independent decisions to achieve goals, adapt dynamically, and proactively learn over time. AI agent providers could be LLM providers such as Google, OpenAI, Anthropic; specialized startups such as Sana Labs, Amelia; and traditional system integrators such as Accenture, Tata Consultancy Services, Infosys, and Wipro.

19. General AI security providers: They focus broadly on safeguarding diverse AI platforms and applications from cybersecurity threats, infrastructure vulnerabilities, and data breaches. Examples are Microsoft Defender, Palo Alto Networks, and Crowdstrike.

20. LLM security providers: They specialize in protecting large language models from unique risks such as prompt injections, toxic outputs, and data leakage. Examples are Lasso Security, LLM Guard by Protect AI, and Vigil, an open-source LLM security scanner.

Group Activity

You need to discuss with your key stakeholders if you want to adopt a single-positioning or multi-positioning strategy. You can consider the following questions for discussion:

- What role does our business play in the current genAI value chain?
- What role do we want to play in the future?

- What do our customers expect from our business?
- What kind of products do they expect?
- How do our competitors position themselves within the genAI value chain, and how does that impact our strategic decisions?
- What are the market trends and emerging opportunities in the genAI industry, and how should we position ourselves to capitalize on them?
- What are the potential risks and challenges associated with each positioning strategy, and how can we mitigate them?
- How will our chosen positioning strategy impact our relationships with existing partners, customers, and other stakeholders?

Use Cases

The genAI use cases have two dimensions: content and capability. We know that the six main types of genAI content are text, image, audio, video, code, and synthetic data. The main capabilities of genAI are creation, summarization, and augmentation. *Creation* includes generating new content. *Summarization* includes producing a condensed version of the content. *Augmentation* includes modifying or adding more content to the existing one.

We see from the content-capabilities map in Figure 7.2 that creation capability is applicable across all the content types. Summarization maps with text, code, and synthetic data. Augmentation is applicable for all

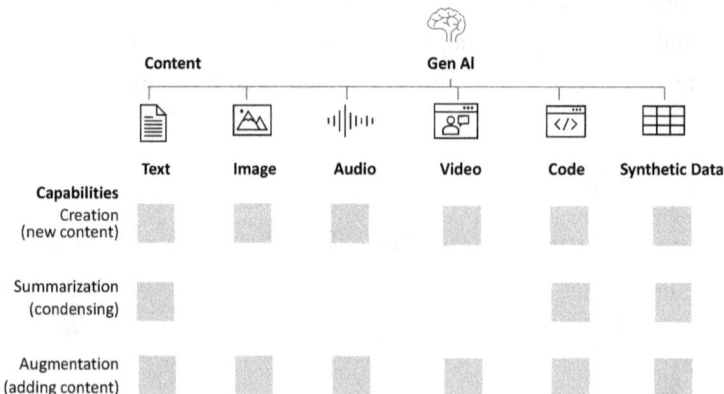

Figure 7.2 Content–capabilities map

contents. Based on the content-capabilities map we develop a use case. The use case is of three types:

1. Standalone
2. Collaboration
3. Infusion

Standalone use case involves the development of a new product, service, or solution with genAI content and capabilities. *Collaboration* use case involves using the content and capabilities of genAI product, service, or solution in collaboration with current systems to accomplish a specific task. *Infusion* use case involves embedding genAI content and capabilities into an existing product, service, or solution to enhance its performance. This is also known as *AI copilots*. An example of a standalone use case is a video generator by Synthesia. It is a new standalone genAI product where the user needs to prompt in a text to generate a video. This use case incorporates video as the content, and creation and augmentation as capabilities from the content-capabilities map.

An example of a collaboration use case is ChatGPT used in collaboration with an external system such as web searcher, email generator, calculator. You can type in an initial prompt into ChatGPT. For example, email Anna and ask if we can move today's meeting to Monday 11 am. ChatGPT generates the email with sender's and receiver's email ID, subject, and body and sends a request to a routing system. The routing system recognizes it as an email and sends it to an email-sending system.

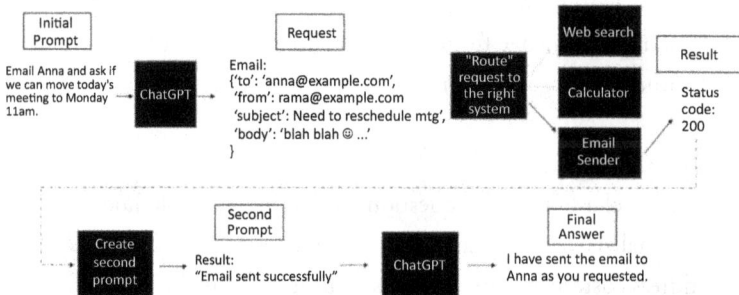

Source: LinkedIn post by Prof. Rama Ramakrishnan, MIT

Figure 7.3 Collaboration use case

The email-sending system sends an email and returns a status code if successful. This status code is converted into a second prompt. ChatGPT receives this prompt and generates the final answer.

An example of infusion use case is the Microsoft 365 copilot, which contains the genAI content and capabilities infused into Microsoft 365 apps such as Word, Excel, and PowerPoint. It also has a feature called Business Chat, which works across the LLM, the Microsoft 365 apps, and your data, such as your calendar, emails, chats, documents, meetings, and contacts, where you can give prompts such as "Prepare me for my upcoming meeting," and it will generate an output for you suggesting how to prepare for the meeting.

Functionwise Use Cases

Use cases can be classified as per the corporate functions and they can be either standalone, collaboration, or infusion. Figure 7.4 shows the list of top five functionwise use cases as per Gartner generative AI planning survey for 2024.

Top Industry-Agnostic Use Cases

Over the years 2023 and 2024, the following five genAI use cases became popular across different industries across the globe:

1. GenAI chatbots
2. Content creation for marketing
3. Agentic workflows
4. Creating knowledge from customer support interactions
5. Synthetic data generation

1. GenAI chatbots
   GenAI chatbots offer question answering, troubleshooting, and personalized recommendations, enabling enterprises to promptly address customer inquiries across multiple channels. They offer benefits such as reduced wait times, increased satisfaction, and lower service costs. Adopting conversational AI and generative AI in

Sales

Use Case	%
Generative Business Intelligence	34%
Pipeline & Forecast Intelligence	25%
AI Seller Assistant	20%
Generative Value Messaging	17%
Sales Decision Intelligence	17%

Marketing

Use Case	%
Channel Chatbots & Digital Humans	38%
Search & Advertising Optimization	32%
Content Copilot	29%
Localization	17%
Analytics Accelerator	16%

Customer Support

Use Case	%
Real-time Speech and Text Translation	40%
Virtual Customer Assistant	38%
Content Analytics	35%
Virtual Agent Assistant	30%
Call Summarization	27%

HR

Use Case	%
Job Descriptions & Skills Data	29%
Administrative Tasks, Policies Generation	25%
Search for Content	24%
Marketing Messages, Email Communications	24%
Employee Facing Chatbot	23%

Supply Chain

Use Case	%
Staff Assistance Chatbots	30%
Code Generation	30%
Interface with Tech Solutions	26%
New Hire Onboarding	26%
KPI Discovery and Diagnostics	23%

Legal, Risk, and Compliance

Use Case	%
Conduct Legal Research and Analysis	17%
Draft Contracts and other Legal Documents	16%
Conduct Due diligence	15%
Review and Compare Contracts	15%
Streamline Intake and Self-service Systems	15%

Finance

Use Case	%
Coding Assistance	22%
Revenue/Spend Data Classification	18%
Management Reporting Draft Creation	17%
Financial/Regulatory Reporting Draft Creation	17%
Contract and Document Review	16%

Procurement

Use Case	%
Sourcing and Contract Lifecycle Management	18%
Supplier Information Discovery & Mngmt.	17%
Supplier Communications	15%
Sourcing Advisory Desk Chatbot	14%
Summarization of Proposal Reviews	10%

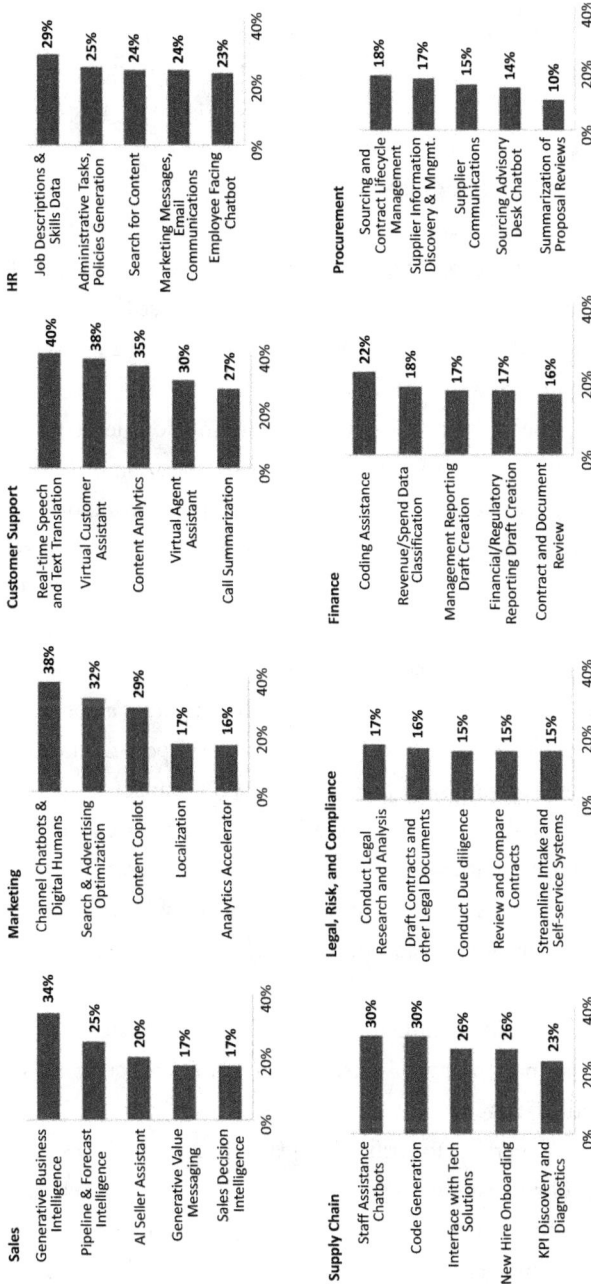

Figure 7.4 Top five functionwise use cases as per Gartner generative AI planning survey 2024

customer service could lead to cost reductions of up to 30 percent across industries.[2] For example, Expedia Group integrated ChatGPT into its app for AI-powered travel advice, offering destination, hotel, and transportation recommendations, with users able to bookmark suggestions and check availability. Most of the genAI chatbots use cases were based on RAG architecture.

2. Content creation for marketing

Some of the key tasks of genAI marketing content creation use case include writing descriptions and creating images, videos, audios for products; creating new content for social media posts, blogs, and articles; enhancing recommendation engines; and improving ad placement.

3. Agentic workflows

They represent the next evolution in automation, leveraging intelligent AI agents that can autonomously manage complex, multi-step processes. Unlike traditional automation, these workflows adapt in real-time, make context-aware decisions, and interact seamlessly with users, enabling more dynamic and efficient task execution. By integrating natural language understanding and learning capabilities, agentic workflows can significantly enhance productivity, reduce manual intervention, and deliver personalized outcomes across industries.

4. Creating a knowledge base from customer support interactions

Customer support systems, such as AWS Connect or ServiceNow, capture valuable insights during interactions with customers, especially during critical incidents, with most interactions recorded. GenAI processes these recordings to create a knowledge base for incident management and problem-solving within IT teams. Voice, tone, and sentiment analysis can improve service delivery by automating incident documentation for future reference and training purposes, enabling hyper-personalized services for customers.

5. Synthetic data generation

Synthetic data refers to artificially created data that mimics the characteristics of real data but is generated algorithmically rather than being obtained from actual observations. Synthetic data generation offers several advantages, such as privacy preservation, data augmentation for training machine learning models, and the ability to generate data for scenarios where real data may be limited or expensive to obtain.

Group Activity

Once you determine your positioning in the genAI value chain, you need to discuss with your stakeholders the key use cases to be developed. You can consider the following questions:

- Should we replicate any of the top five industry-agnostic use cases in our business?
- Should we replicate any of the top five functionwise use cases in our business?
- Are there any additional use cases besides the above two categories?
- Should the use cases be standalone, collaborative, or infused?
- Do we have the necessary capabilities to develop the use cases?
- How do the identified use cases align with our overall business objectives and strategic goals?
- What are the potential challenges and barriers to implementing each use case, and how can we overcome them?
- How will the adoption of these use cases impact our existing workflows, processes, and resources, and how can we ensure a smooth transition?

Products

GenAI products are classified into two types: single modal or multimodal products. The single modal products can have either of the following six genAI-generated contents: text, image, audio, video, code, and synthetic data. Multimodal products contain a combination of two or more of the above contents. These products could be existing products infused with genAI capabilities or completely a new product that has never existed before. We can plot a 2 × 2 matrix as shown in Figure 7.5.

An example of a single modal new product is Microsoft Generative Erase, an inpainting tool that allows you to remove unwanted objects from your photos with ease without disrupting the background behind them. It predicts what pixels would look like without the object in place, based on the surrounding area.

An example of a single modal current product is copy.ai, a genAI powered tool designed to generate marketing and creative content such as

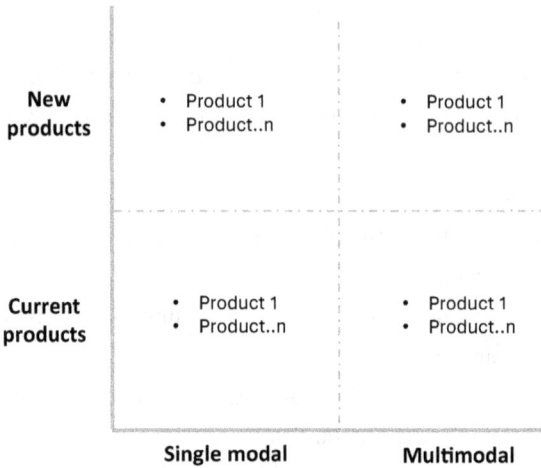

	Single modal	Multimodal
New products	• Product 1 • Product..n	• Product 1 • Product..n
Current products	• Product 1 • Product..n	• Product 1 • Product..n

Figure 7.5 2 × 2 matrix for genAI products

media captions, blog introductions, product descriptions, and advertisement. It helps businesses save time by automating content creation with user-friendly prompts.

An example of a multimodal current product is Microsoft 365 AI copilot, which contain the genAI capabilities infused in Word, Excel, and PowerPoint.

An example of a multimodal new product is Sora, a genAI text-to video product by OpenAI. Users can input textual descriptions of what they want to see in a video, and Sora generates corresponding videos based on those descriptions.

As shown in Figure 7.6, a product comprises multiple use cases, which can be either standalone, collaborative, or infused, leveraging content and capabilities.

The product can be offered to the customers using either one or more of the popular business models listed below:

1. Subscription: You can offer access to your AI products or services through a monthly, quarterly, or annual subscription fee. Clients can select an appropriate plan based on their requirements.
2. Pay-per-use: It involves charging users based on the volume of content generated, processing power used, or the number of input prompts. It is ideal for users with on-demand usage needs.

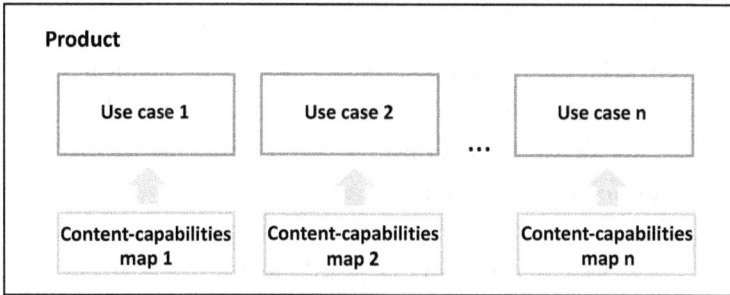

Figure 7.6 Product composition

3. Freemium: Offer a basic version of your genAI product for free, with premium features available through a paid subscription. This allows users to try out your product before deciding to upgrade. It can also help you build a dedicated user base.
4. Licensing: Allow other companies to license your AI products for integration into their own products or services. The licensing can be either annual, quarterly, or monthly.
5. Platform based: You can be the owner of the genAI platform or a marketplace where you can connect buyers and sellers. For example, the genAI app developers can connect with the customers through the platform. They can either sell off-the-shelf products, customize the existing ones to meet customer requirements, or develop a new product altogether.

OpenAI used a combination of the above-listed business models. They adopted a freemium business model to give users access to its advanced AI technologies. Initially, users received free tokens for a three month period, allowing them to use OpenAI's API. After the tokens were used up or the free trial ended, users had to choose a paid membership to keep using the API, with a "pay-as-you-go" system ensuring they only paid for the resources they consumed. In addition to the free version of ChatGPT, OpenAI introduced a subscription option called ChatGPT Plus, priced at $20 per month, which offers access to GPT-4 (more specifically, GPT-4-turbo), faster response times, and priority access during high demand.

Group Activity

Once you decide on the use cases, you can decide with your team, which products to develop. You can go the other way too—first decide on a product to be developed and then develop the use cases later. You can consider the following questions:

- Do we want to develop a new genAI product or add genAI capabilities to an existing one?
- Do we want to develop a single modal or multimodal product?
- What benefits would the product bring for my customers?
- Which business model should we use?
- Should it also include a service?
- Is there a similar product available in the market?
- How many products do we want to develop?
- Do we have sufficient budget?
- How do we market this product?

Summary

- GenAI use cases are of three types: standalone, collaboration, and infusion.
- Each use case comprises a content-capabilities map.
- There are six content types: text, image, audio, video, code, and synthetic data.
- There are three main capabilities: creation, summarization, and augmentation.
- A product comprises two dimensions: 1) single modal or multimodal 2) new or current.
- A product can comprise one or more than one use case.
- Customers can select between the five types of business models: subscription, pay-per-use, freemium, licensing, and platform based.

## CHAPTER 8

Quantifying Value:

Productivity Gains, Business Case, Key Metrics

Erik Brynjolfsson and his colleagues conducted a study with 5,000 customer support agents using an AI tool built on Large Language Model (LLM) by OpenAI. The tool was introduced gradually to different agents, allowing for comparison between users and non-users. Agents utilizing the AI tool handled 13.8 percent more customer inquiries per hour, with less-skilled and less-experienced agents experiencing a significant 35 percent improvement. The top-performing agents saw marginal or possibly no improvement, suggesting potential stagnation in gains.

Shakked Noy and Whitney Zhang's study involved 444 business professionals who used ChatGPT to write business documents. The participants were divided into two groups tasked with producing documents with and without AI assistance. In the first round, participants produced documents without AI assistance, yielding similar results in both groups. In the second round, those using ChatGPT finished their tasks in 17 minutes on average, compared to 27 minutes for those without AI support, representing a 59 percent productivity improvement. Quality assessment on a scale of 1 to 7 by independent graders showed higher scores for documents with ChatGPT assistance, with an average rating of 4.5 compared to 3.8 without AI. These differences were statistically significant, highlighting the potential of ChatGPT to enhance both productivity and quality, especially considering most users had no prior experience with the tool.

Sida Peng and collaborators from Microsoft Research, GitHub, and MIT conducted a study involving 70 programmers tasked with implementing an HTTP server in JavaScript. Half of them used the GitHub Copilot AI tool, while the other half did not use any AI tools. Participants had an average coding experience of six years and spent about nine hours per day coding, demonstrating their proficiency. The key finding revealed that programmers without AI assistance took an average of 160.89 minutes (2.7 hours) to complete the task, while those using AI completed in 71.17 minutes (1.2 hours).

The results show significant productivity increases across different tasks with AI assistance—support agents handled 13.8 percent more inquiries per hour, business professionals wrote 59 percent more documents per hour, and programmers coded 126 percent more projects per week, suggesting that tasks with higher cognitive demands benefited more from AI support.[1] The above three experiments were widely cited and were often used by consultants and sales executives to demonstrate the productivity of genAI to clients.

But do higher productivity gains necessarily indicate a good business case?

Once we have selected a genAI product catering to the needs of the customer, it is important to quantify its value. This is done with the help of productivity gains and business case.

Productivity Gains

Productivity gains due to genAI refer to the increase in efficiency and output achieved by enterprises when using genAI-powered tools to automate tasks, generate content, or assist in decision-making processes, compared to efficiency without genAI-powered tools. This increase in productivity can manifest as a reduction in time required to complete tasks, an increase in the volume of work accomplished within a given time frame, or improvements in the quality of output produced.

Consider an analyst working at a financial services company who uses genAI tools to generate a daily one-page report per stock for its two premium clients, each with five stocks in the portfolio. Without the genAI tool, the time taken is 12 minutes per report. For five stocks, it takes 60 minutes. GenAI can generate one report in one minute, which includes the time to write a prompt and generate the output. It then takes five minutes to proofread the report for errors manually. Total time per report is 6 minutes, and total time per client is 30 minutes.

Productivity gain (%) is calculated as:
Reduction in time / original time × 100

= (60 – 30) / 60 × 100

= 50%

Now, the analyst can generate reports for four clients in two hours, assuming each takes 30 minutes.

Productivity gain (%) is calculated as:

Increase in the volume of work / original volume × 100

= (4 – 2) clients / 2 clients × 100

= 100%

The quality rating, including spelling, grammar, and syntax, increases from 5 to 7.

Productivity gain (%) is calculated as:

Increase in quality / original quality × 100

= (7 – 5) / 5 × 100

= 40%

Thus, depending on what parameters we consider for measuring productivity gains, either reduction in time, increase in volume of work, or increase in quality of work, we get different productivity gains.

Consider another task of coding at the same company, where the programmer takes 30 minutes to write certain lines of code. With the genAI tool, the time is reduced to 10 minutes.

The productivity gain (%) is calculated as:

Reduction in time / original time × 100

= (30 – 10) / 30

= 66.67%

Combined productivity can be calculated as:

Total time saved / Total original time × 100

= (time saved on Task 1 + time saved on Task 2) / Total original time × 100; where Task 1 is generating reports and Task 2 is coding

= (30 + 20) / (60 + 30) × 100

= (50) / (90) × 100

= 55.55%

It is proven that genAI shows high productivity. However, it doesn't necessarily mean a good business case. Productivity gains are task-specific, whereas a business case is a projectwide exercise comprising multiple tasks.

Business Case

The three experiments at the beginning of the chapter show a drastic quantitative improvement in productivity gains. However, they do not reflect the quality of the output product. The genAI tools are good at producing the first draft. However, they cannot guarantee the output accuracy. A human should be in the loop to manually verify the output's accuracy. If the cost of fixing errors exceeds the cost of producing the output, then it does not make a good business case.

For each task that is evaluated for productivity gains, we can calculate a simple business case using the following steps:

Step 1: Calculate the cost of the task without genAI.
Step 2: Calculate the cost of the genAI app + the cost of detecting and fixing errors in genAI's attempt at completing a task.
Step 3: Compare Steps 1 and 2.
If Step 2 is less expensive then go to Step 4. If Step 2 is more expensive, we do not have a good business case.
Step 4: Assess error impact or the maximum tolerable inaccuracy.
a. If it is within the threshold, then go ahead with the task.
b. If it is high and exceeds the threshold, then hold on with the task and subject it to further evaluation.

The above calculations might work well enough for a pilot. But for a scaled adoption, a detailed business case needs to be worked out enterprisewide.

In Chapter 1, we saw that enterprises are not able to produce a compelling business case for scaled adoption of genAI, like the one they developed for cloud during its hype phase. This is due to the following reasons:

1. Inability to estimate from pilots
2. Unjustifiable budget
3. Inability to estimate the cost drivers

1. Inability to estimate from pilots

   Most enterprises are in the piloting phase. Nearly half of the pilots are funded externally by the customers (43 percent) and the others (57 percent) internally by the enterprises. These pilots are mostly developed by a specific function such as sales, customer support, or the AI/GenAI center of excellence. The wider cross-functional teams are mostly excluded. Legal has limited involvement. From a project management standpoint, involving too many resources in a pilot project is not feasible. There is a limit to the number of users using the pilot. Customers are hardly able to generate any new revenue streams or achieve cost efficiencies from it. The development costs are much more than the cost savings. Estimating scaled adoption costs required in developing a business case from pilot development costs is difficult due to:

   a. Small scale in controlled environment: This environment might not reflect the complexities and challenges of real-world scaled adoption.

   b. Specific scope: Pilots often target specific tasks or use cases. The costs associated with these specific tasks might not translate well to the broader range of tasks genAI could be applied to in a large-scale deployment.

   c. Exclusion of key cost drivers: Pilots do not include important cost drivers such as data, infrastructure, workforce training and reskilling, and operations and maintenance.

   d. Exclusion of hidden costs: Pilots do not account for hidden costs related to legal compliance, regulations, data privacy, and security, which may become prominent in the future.

2. Unjustifiable budget

   The cost of developing pilots is only a few hundred thousand U.S. dollars. The scaled adoption would require millions of U.S. dollars and most of the lagging enterprises do not have budgets for its development. This is because they have either taken "all talks, no actions" (discovery) or "few talks, more actions" (piloting) approach. Why would a business allocate a budget for millions of dollars for scaled adoption when the plan is only to develop pilots worth thousands? It is very unlikely that the executive leadership would approve the budget without a clear roadmap. Another reason why it is difficult to approve a budget is that all the funds won't be channeled toward scaling genAI. A major chunk, around 80 percent would be needed to develop the foundational infrastructure, such as cloud, security, storage, data, platform, and AI—to maximize genAI's value. First, this may raise concerns among stakeholders about immediate return on investment, especially if it means delaying or reducing resources for other critical initiatives important to running business as usual. Second, stakeholders may question whether the proposed allocation aligns with the organization's strategic objectives and risk tolerance, particularly if it involves a substantial upfront investment with uncertain outcomes.

3. Inability to estimate the cost drivers

The genAI scaled adoption would include technologies such as data, AI, cloud, and automation, in addition to genAI. It is very difficult to estimate the costs required for data acquisition, cleaning, storage, and processing because most enterprises do not have an awareness of what type of data is required in the first place. They fail to understand which data is important, where is it located, and how to access it. As a result, estimating the amount of data required for fine-tuning LLMs is difficult, making cost estimation nearly impossible and hindering the development of a compelling business case.

Business Case Development: Case Study

Imagine there is a home furnishing retail company that wants to implement a genAI solution to provide a unique online shopping experience to the customers helping them make quick and easy buying decisions. The customers can select which products best fit their home using a genAI app. They need to upload the pictures of different home areas such as living room, bedroom, kitchen, bathrooms, corridors, balcony, storage, backyard, basement, and garage. The customers should give a prompt: Tell me which products can decorate my living room within a budget of EUR 2,500. Or, tell me where this lamp would fit the best in my home. And genAI app gives its best suggestions and recommendations. Advanced features of the app would provide the customers with a new and unique interior design for the home such as paint on the wall, flooring, ceiling, and placement of furniture—either customer's own furniture, furniture from the current retail company, furniture from any other vendor, or completely new furniture design based on their preferences. To do so, the retail company needs to fine-tune an existing LLM not only with its product inventory but also with the inventory of other vendors. It also needs to acquire and store a large amount of data containing the individual preferences of its customers. It needs a robust data solution to ensure data is acquired, cleansed, stored, and processed. It needs an AI solution that can provide recommendations to customers based on their preferences, such as brand, furniture color, price, and size, and optimize its internal business processes. It might need automation to ensure the business processes are automated and cost-effective. Finally, it needs cloud technology that can provide adequate infrastructure to store data such as product inventory, vector databases, and host AI and genAI applications.

The business case consists of five parts:

1. As-is costs—not using genAI solution
2. GenAI development costs
3. GenAI operational costs
4. Cost comparison
5. Value analysis

The value drivers for the company are:

- Increased sales revenues from enhanced customer experience
- Increased revenue from reselling other vendor products
- New revenues from partnerships with new players such as interior designers and architecture firms

The table below is only a guiding template. Feel free to add more or remove any items as per your business requirements.

1.	As-is	Costs
1.1	*Datacenter costs (on prem)*	
1.1.1	Facilities: power supply, cooling, backup	
1.1.2	Lease term remaining	
1.1.3	Lease term penalties	

(Continued)

(Continued)

1.	As-is	Costs
1.1.4	Connectivity—leased lines to the datacenter	
1.1.5	Datacenter maintenance and support	
1.2	**Infrastructure costs**	
1.2.1	Server costs	
1.2.2	Storage costs	
1.2.3	Networking costs	
1.2.4	Operations and maintenance costs	
1.3	**Application costs**	
1.3.1	Existing licenses	
1.3.2	Application development	
1.3.3	Application operations and maintenance	
1.3.4	Regulations and compliance	
1.3.5	Security	
1.3.6	Disaster recovery	
1.3.7	Decommissioning	
1.4	**People costs**	
1.4.1	Direct people costs (employees)	
1.4.2	Third-party costs (contractors, consultants)	
1.5	**Cloud migration costs**	
1.5.1	Center of excellence + people (employees, consultants)	
1.5.2	Migration planning and design	
1.5.3	Development	
1.5.4	Testing	
1.5.5	Acceptance	
1.5.6	Deployment	
1.5.7	Landing zone configuration	
1.5.8	Licensing	
1.5.9	Training and certification	
1.6	**Cloud operational costs**	
1.6.1	Billing	
1.6.2	Center of excellence + people (employees, consultants)	
1.6.3	Training and certification	
1.7	**Miscellaneous costs**	
	Total as-is costs (annual)	

For the above table, we assume that there is an ongoing cloud migration.

2.	GenAI development	Costs
2.1	**LLM development costs**	
2.1.1	Planning and designing	
2.1.2	Pretraining	
2.1.3	Fine-tuning	
2.1.4	Custom tuning	
2.1.5	Inference testing and evaluation	
2.2	**GenAI platform costs**	
2.2.1	Planning and designing	
2.2.2	Development	
2.2.3	Installation and integration	
2.3	**GenAI app/agents costs**	
2.3.1	Planning and designing	
2.3.2	Development	
2.3.3	Testing	
2.3.4	Deployment	
2.3.5	Maintenance and support	
2.4	**Costs to integrate cloud, data, AI, etc. with genAI**	
2.5	**Infrastructure upgrade costs**	
2.6	**Training and certification**	
2.7	**People costs (employees, consultants)**	
2.8	**Miscellaneous costs**	
	Total development costs (annual)	

3.	GenAI operations	Costs
3.1	**Licensing/subscription costs**	
3.1.1	LLM licensing/subscription	
3.1.2	Platform licensing/subscription	
3.1.3	Application licensing/subscription	
3.2	**Data operational costs**	
3.2.1	Acquisition	
3.2.2	Cleaning and preparation	
3.2.3	Storage	
3.2.4	Migration to cloud	
3.2.5	Center of excellence + people (employees, consultants)	

(Continued)

(Continued)

3.	GenAI operations	Costs
3.2.6	Training and certification	
3.3	***Traditional AI operational costs***	
3.3.1	Infrastructure	
3.3.2	Platform	
3.3.3	Application	
3.3.4	Center of excellence + people (employees, consultants)	
3.3.5	Training and certification	
3.4	***Cloud operational costs***	
3.4.1	Billing	
3.4.2	Center of excellence + people (employees, consultants)	
3.4.3	Training and certification	
3.5	***Training and certification***	
3.6	***People costs (employees, consultants)***	
3.7	***Miscellaneous costs***	
	Total operations costs (annual)	

4.	Cost comparison	Costs
4.1	As-is costs	
4.2	GenAI development costs	
4.3	GenAI operations costs	
4.4	Total development and operational costs (4.2 + 4.3)	
4.5	Cost savings—delta between 4.1 and 4.4	

5.	Value analysis	Value
5.1	Revenues from genAI solution	
5.2	Revenues from reselling other vendor products	
5.3	Revenues from partnerships with new players	
5.4	Cost savings from internal operations	
	Total value (annual)	

	Year 1	Year 2	Year 3	Year 4	Year 5	Year 6
As-is costs (1.)						
GenAI costs (2. + 3.)						
Cost savings						
Value						

Note that the business case development template shown above is relevant to GenAI solutions, and a similar version can be created for convertible pilots—book a consultation at www. scalinggenai.com for details.

Key Metrics

The final step in the readiness area: customer is to define the key metrics. By tracking key genAI metrics, organization can identify gaps in implementation and make corrections to improve outcomes. Metrics also aid in resource allocation decisions, allowing organizations to prioritize initiatives based on their impact. Continuous monitoring of metrics facilitates ongoing improvement and innovation in genAI implementation over time. Enterprises can select key metrics aligned with their business requirements to scale both GenAI solutions and convertible pilots. The following table shows the list of key metrics:

#	Name	Description
1	Number of active users	The number of active users using the genAI app
2	Frequency of usage	The number of times the active users use the app
3	Session duration	The average length of the session per user
4	Customer satisfaction	Feedback from customers regarding their satisfaction with the genAI app, often measured through surveys, ratings, or net promoter score
5	Conversion rates	The percentage of users who take a desired action, such as making a purchase, completing a form, or subscribing to a service, after interacting with the genAI app
6	Retention rate	The percentage of customers who continue to use the genAI app over time, indicating its ability to retain users and provide ongoing value
7	Increased sales	New sales due to genAI app
8	Cost savings	Cost savings due to genAI app
9	Ease of use	The ease of learning and interacting with genAI app
10	Output accuracy	The percentage of accurate outputs
11	Error rates	The frequency of incorrect or misleading outputs produced by genAI
12	Speed	The average time taken by genAI to complete tasks
13	Training time	The time required to train the model to achieve desired performance
14	Performance	The number of issues reported
15	Integration	The ease of integration of genAI app with other tools and workflows

Group Activity

Once you agree with the product or service to be developed with the customer:

1. Calculate productivity gains per task along with your key stakeholders across different functions.
2. Get productivity gains calculations approved from the customer.
3. Make your best attempt to develop a business case together with the customer. Involve your executive leadership too, if possible.
4. Agree on key metrics with your customer. You may choose from the above table or define new key metrics as per requirements.

Summary

- Productivity gains due to genAI refer to the increase in efficiency and output achieved by individuals or organizations when using AI-powered tools to automate tasks, generate content, or assist in decision-making processes.
- Higher productivity gains do not necessarily imply a good business case.
- A business case has the following five components: as-is costs, genAI development costs, genAI operational costs, cost comparison, and value analysis.
- By tracking key genAI metrics, organization can identify gaps in implementation and make corrections to improve outcomes.

SUMMARY OF PART 3

Readiness Area

Customer

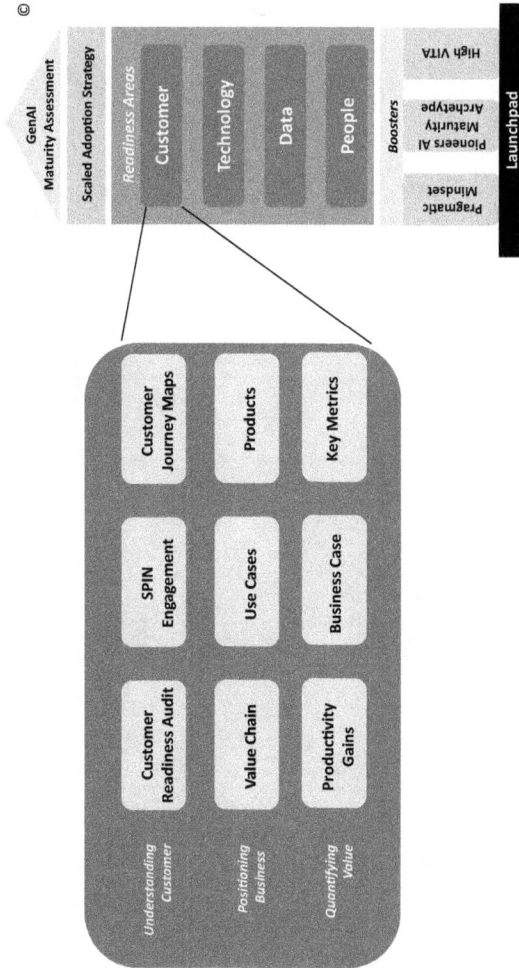

Readiness Rocket

PART 4

Readiness Area

Technology

CHAPTER 9

Large Language Models:

Selection, Fine-Tuning Versus RAG, Curation

At the CIO summit in Nordics, the Chief Information Officer (CIO) of a leading automotive company in Europe was narrating her experience about selecting large language models (LLMs). She said, "We regularly interact with different LLM providers because we learn something new with every interaction. However, everyone tries to push their product on us. That's where we are left with no clue about what next step we need to take."

Another CIO said:

It is important to stay updated on the latest advancements in LLM technologies, as the landscape is rapidly evolving. Market is very competitive, where each LLM provider claims superiority for its product. Despite the overwhelming amount of information, every business must carefully evaluate each offering against its specific needs and objectives. But the challenge is that we do not have clarity on what our needs are.

"The regulations expect the AI to be explainable. Business should be able to explain what went into training and why AI is producing a certain output. LLMs are a *black box*. It is hard to understand what goes inside them. It is very difficult to explain and interpret the single modal text LLMs. And now we have multimodal ones. Imagine the level of complexities we must deal with," said the third one.

It's the year 2025. Current single modal LLMs can generate text from text. The current single modal models can generate image from image, audio from audio, and video from video. The current multimodal LLMs such as GPT-4, can generate only image from text besides text from text. The current multimodal models can generate image from text, text from image, video from text, audio from text, video from image, image from video, text from audio, and text from video.

Modes such as audio and video are currently under research and development. Soon, it is likely that we will see LLMs offering all four modes or VITA: video, image, text, and audio.

Though the terms LLM and models are often used interchangeably, there is a distinction between them. An LLM is associated with natural language processing (NLP) and is typically used when the task primarily involves text-to-text processing. This is because text constitutes about 90 percent of natural language compared to other VITA forms such as video, image, and audio. When tasks do not involve text-to-text processing, *model* is used instead of LLM.

Is your business ready to handle this complexity and uncertainty?

LLM Selection Assessment

The first major technological decision on the genAI scaled adoption journey is selecting an LLM, which is based on the following factors:

- Business requirements
- Core model characteristics
- Model performance
- Ethical considerations
- Business architecture

Business Requirements

The following are the key business requirements to be considered before selecting a model:

Business requirements	Questions
Primary goal	- What specific problem are you addressing with the LLM? - Are you aiming to improve customer engagement, internal operations, or corporate culture?

Business requirements	Questions
Expected tasks	- What kinds of tasks do you intend for the LLM to perform: text generation, sentiment analysis, summarization, translation, question answering, or something else? - Do you require a model that can handle multiple tasks simultaneously (multitask learning)? - Would your tasks include any one or more of the VITA: video, image, text, and audio? - Is there any specific industry or domain you would like to develop your model for?
Expected scale	- What is the expected volume of data and traffic that the application will handle? - Are you deploying the model for a small-scale project, a medium-sized business application, or an enterprise-level deployment? - Will the application need to scale dynamically to accommodate fluctuations in demand?
Computational resources	- What are the computational resources available for model training, inference, and deployment? - Do you have access to high-performance computing resources such as GPUs or TPUs? - Are there limitations on memory, storage, or processing power that may influence your choice of model? - Are the resources energy efficient?
Data availability and quality	- What is the availability and quality of data for pretraining and fine-tuning the LLM? - Do you have access to labeled datasets relevant to your use case, or will you need to collect and annotate data? - Are there concerns about data privacy, bias, or representativeness that need to be addressed?

Core Model Characteristics

The table below shows the questions to be considered while determining the core model characteristics:

Core model characteristics	Questions
Transformer architecture	- Which transformer architecture do you consider: encoder–decoder, decoder only, or encoder only?
Model size	- How many parameters does the model comprise?
Model interpretability and explainability	- How important is it for the model's predictions and decisions to be interpretable and explainable? - Do you need tools or techniques to provide insights into how the model arrives at its conclusions?

(Continued)

(*Continued*)

Core model characteristics	Questions
Robustness, privacy, and security	- How robust and generic does the model need to be across different domains, languages, or data distributions? - Are there specific edge cases or challenging scenarios that the model must handle effectively? - Is the model compliant with privacy and security standards such as General Data Protection Regulation (GDPR), EU AI Act, and Health Insurance Portability and Accountability Act (HIPAA)?
Fine-tuning and customizability	- Can we fine-tune or tailor the model to specific needs? - How feasible is transfer learning? Is it possible to transfer data from one domain to another when it is limited?
Integration with existing systems and workflows	- How seamlessly can the LLM be integrated with your existing systems, applications, and workflows? - Are there APIs or interfaces available for integrating the model with other software components? - Will there be a need for custom development or modifications to existing systems to support the LLM?
Cost and licensing considerations	- What are the upfront and ongoing costs associated with acquiring, deploying, and maintaining the LLM? - Are there licensing agreements or usage fees that need to be considered?
Knowledge cutoff	- Is the knowledge cutoff date recent? - How often is the cutoff date updated?
Open source	- Is the model open source? - What are the pros and cons of an open-source model compared to a proprietary one?
Modality	- Do you require a single modal or multimodal model / LLM? - In case of multimodal requirements, which specific VITA modes are you looking at?

Model Performance

The table below shows some of model's performance considerations:

Performance	Questions
Accuracy	- What is the accuracy level of output desired? - What is the model's tolerance to noise, misspellings, grammatical errors, or incomplete sentences?
Performance versus resource trade-off	- How do you find the desired level of balance between accuracy and resource efficiency?

Performance	Questions
Latency and throughput	- What is the desired model latency?
Consistency	- How consistently is the model able to produce desired output?
Deployment	- Where would the model be hosted, on-premises or cloud?
Real-time adaptation or continuous learning	- Is the model able to learn and improve on an ongoing basis, either through fine-tuning on new data or other adaptation techniques?
Multilingual capabilities	- Is the model able to support multiple languages, which can be beneficial for diverse applications?
Support and maintenance	- What are the support and maintenance Service Level Agreements (SLAs)? Is there community support available? - What is the frequency of updates and upgrades? - How good is the documentation?

Ethical Considerations

The table below shows some of model's ethical considerations:

Ethical considerations	Questions
Bias assessment and mitigation	- Do you have a good procedure to assess the biases in the model? - Do you have an effective bias mitigation strategy in place? - How frequently do you reassess and update your bias assessment and mitigation procedures?
Ethical guidelines	- Does the model adhere to established ethical principles for AI development such as fairness, transparency, and accountability? - Have you conducted comprehensive audits to ensure that the model's decision-making processes align with ethical standards and legal regulations?

Business Architecture

Based on the building blocks of generative AI shown in Figure 9.1, we can develop five types of genAI business architectures: prompt based, application based, fine-tuning based, pretraining based, and development based.

In a *prompt based* business architecture, LLMs are developed, pretrained, and fine-tuned with built-in applications provided by the vendor. A user just needs to write prompts to generate the required inference. In *application based* business architecture, LLMs are developed, pretrained,

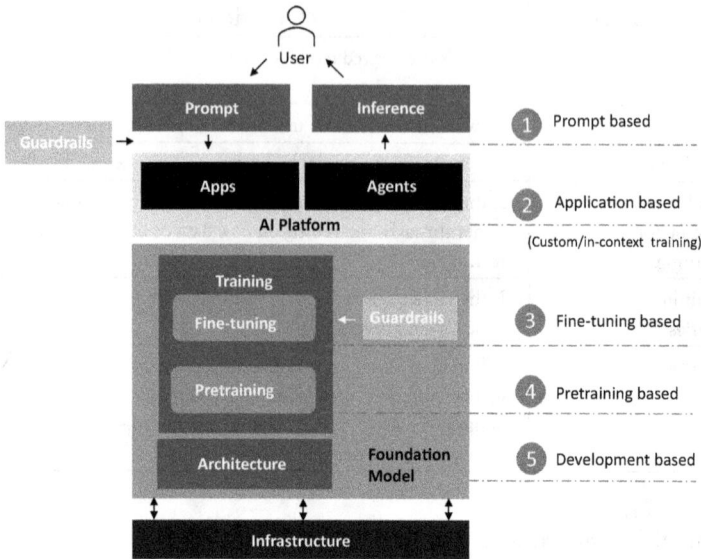

Figure 9.1 Building blocks of generative AI

and fine-tuned by the vendor. But the applications need to be developed by the business before starting to prompt them. In *fine-tuning based* business architecture, LLMs are developed and pretrained on a large corpus of unlabeled data by the vendor. But the model needs to be fine-tuned and applications need to be developed by the enterprises before applying prompts on them. In *pretraining based* business architecture, only the LLM frameworks are developed by the providers. Pretraining, fine-tuning, and application development need to be done by the enterprises before applying prompts to them. In *development based* business architecture, the enterprises build an LLM from the scratch, then pretrain and fine-tune it, and develop an application before starting to apply prompts to it.

The table below shows the model comparisons based on CAPEX/OPEX, lead times, and associated costs.

Business Architecture	CAPEX/ OPEX	Lead times	Costs
Prompt based	Subscription based	1–2 weeks	Subscription and minor customizations
Application based	Subscription based	1–3 months	Subscription, custom tuning, application development, application hosting, maintenance and support

Business Architecture	CAPEX/ OPEX	Lead times	Costs
Fine-tuning based	License based	3–6 months	All of above + fine-tuning
Pretraining based	License based	6 months to 1 year	All of above + pretraining
Development based	Upfront capital	1–2 years	All of above + LLM datacenter hosting including hardware and electricity

Your business is most likely to use a commercially available model trained on huge corpus of public data and then further train it with your organization's bespoke data. Usually, the development based models show the best performance with high accuracy compared to other models as they are trained, pretrained, and fine-tuned on business-specific datasets. If there are cost constraints, limited parameters to train, and scarcity of training datasets, a small language model (SLM) could be a viable option. SLMs use fewer computational resources, might take shorter training times, perform at higher speeds, and produce less latency than LLMs.

Fine-Tuning Versus RAG

Fine-tuning is the process of taking a pretrained model, trained by the LLM provider on a large corpus of data in the public domain, and further training at least one of its internal parameters such as weights, biases, or hyperparameters such as temperature, learning rate, top-K sampling threshold.

The challenges with the knowledge that an LLM is trained on are, first, it is static. It has a certain training cutoff period. An LLM is not dynamically updated with the latest events and available knowledge. Second, LLMs are trained on a massive corpus of text. As a result, they are good at general knowledge but lack specialized information or niche knowledge related to your specific use case or business. One way to overcome this issue is to prepare specific niche datasets and fine-tune your model. However, fine-tuning is an expensive process and needs people with special expertise and skillsets that are rare to find in the market.

In the RAG approach, rather than directly inputting a prompt to the LLM to generate a response, the process involves first parsing the user

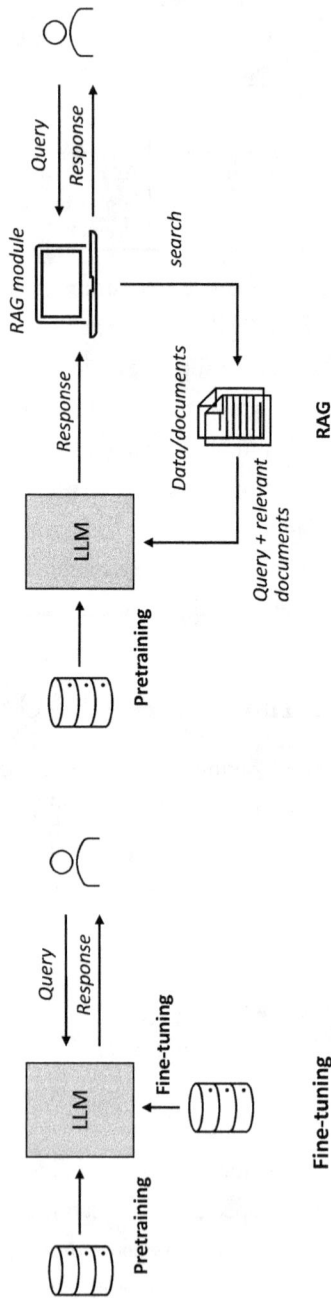

Figure 9.2 Fine-tuning and RAG

query through a RAG module. This module comprises a retriever and a knowledge base. The retriever uses the query to search the knowledge base for relevant information, which is then extracted to form an input prompt for the LLM. The knowledge base consists of a stack of documents that need to be prepared in four steps: loading the documents, chunking them into smaller pieces to fit the LLM's context window, translating the chunks into text embeddings, and finally storing these embeddings in a vector database for efficient retrieval during the search process. This approach ensures that only relevant information is used to generate responses; thus improving system performance.

When to Select RAG Over Fine-Tuning?

RAG is more suited for developing chatbot-based applications for your business, which includes customer support, Q&A, and troubleshooting. The most important condition is that there should be an available documentation for these processes. For RAG, we need to acquire an off-the-shelf LLM. We can save the costs and the energy consumption associated with fine-tuning it. Some empirical studies suggest that RAG is better than fine-tuning for use cases that require more specialized domain knowledge. RAG has limitations and will only provide information within the context of the documents it retrieves at inference time. For example, you give the following prompt to RAG—Help me plan my summer vacation. It will process your profile, retrieve the relevant information, determine the number of vacation days remaining, and review your company's vacation policies. Using the LLM it is integrated with, it can suggest vacation destinations based on your available days, offering the best price deals and logistical options.

Imagine you have a B2C business where you must continuously collect data by tracking the number of visitors on your website and monitoring their online behavior. You have implemented RAG. You give a prompt—tell me why the number of users spiked at 2 pm yesterday. RAG will not be able to answer the prompt as it is out of scope and context of the information it is provided with. For such use cases, you need a fine-tuned LLM, which is continuously trained on the newly generated data about the number of visitors.

If you have a convertible chatbot pilot developed on RAG, you can scale it with RAG as long as it satisfies your use case by enabling you to prompt and retrieve information for you within the context of documentation you provide. Otherwise, it is advisable to switch to fine-tuning.

The following are the benefits of fine-tuning your LLM:

- Performance: Fine-tuning enhances performance by reducing hallucinations, improving consistency in generated output, and minimizing unwanted information. By training the model on specific data relevant to the task or domain, it can produce more accurate and contextually appropriate responses.
- Privacy: Fine-tuning allows for greater control over data privacy and security. By training the model on-premises or within a virtual private cloud, organizations can mitigate the risk of data leakage or breaches associated with sharing sensitive information with external services. It ensures that sensitive data remains within the organization's infrastructure, reducing the exposure to external threats.
- Cost savings and energy efficiency: Fine-tuning enables cost savings and energy efficiency through techniques such as Parameter Efficient Fine-tuning (PEFT) and Low-rank Adaptation (LoRA).
- Transparency: Fine-tuning can give you better control over datasets, which can provide greater transparency into the model's behavior and performance, allowing organizations to optimize resource allocation and budgeting effectively.
- Reliability: Fine-tuning improves the reliability of the LLM by providing better control over uptime, reducing latency in generating responses, and enabling content moderation. It can consistently produce high-quality and reliable output, meeting the organization's expectations for performance and reliability.

LLM Curation

LLM curation is a service that curates different LLMs onto a single platform with the sole purpose of providing the best and most accurate output to the users in response to their prompts. Imagine there is a single user and five LLMs, as shown in Figure 9.3. User gives the same prompts P1, P2, and P3 to all five LLMs, which produce different outputs given by Ranks 1 to 5. It is observed that LLMs 3 and 4 give the best outputs to the prompts P1, P2, and P3. If the user had subscribed to LLM 1, it would always get the lowest quality output. But if the user subscribes to the LLM curation service, the prompt will be routed to the LLM that will always provide the user with the best quality output.

This curation service comes with two options:

1. The system automatically selects the best LLM response for a given user prompt.
2. Users can provide the LLM preference. For example, the user can prefer to route the prompts only to LLMs 3, 4, or 5 and not to LLMs 1 and 2. Or the user can also select a single LLM 3 only.

An example of such a curator is AWS Bedrock, which gives users the flexibility to select their LLMs. Users can easily experiment with and evaluate top LLMs for their use case, privately customize them with their data using techniques such as fine-tuning and RAG, and build agents that execute tasks using their enterprise systems and data sources. Since Amazon Bedrock is serverless, users don't have to manage any infrastructure and can securely integrate and deploy genAI capabilities into their applications using the AWS services.[1]

Another example is Accenture, who launched its foundation model services, based on a proprietary switchboard framework, which allows users to toggle between a combination of models as per their business requirements based on factors, such as cost, accuracy, and size.[2]

Activity

Use the flowchart shown in Figure 9.4 to select the best LLM option.

	LLM 1	LLM 2	LLM 3	LLM 4	LLM 5
P1	Output-LLM1-P1 *Rank 5*	Output-LLM2-P1 *Rank 3*	Output-LLM3-P1 *Rank 1*	Output-LLM4-P1 *Rank 2*	Output-LLM5-P1 *Rank 4*
P2	Output-LLM1-P2 *Rank 5*	Output-LLM2-P2 *Rank 4*	Output-LLM3-P2 *Rank 2*	Output-LLM4-P2 *Rank 1*	Output-LLM5-P2 *Rank 3*
P3	Output-LLM1-P3 *Rank 5*	Output-LLM2-P3 *Rank 3*	Output-LLM3-P3 *Rank 1*	Output-LLM4-P3 *Rank 2*	Output-LLM5-P3 *Rank 4*

User Prompts

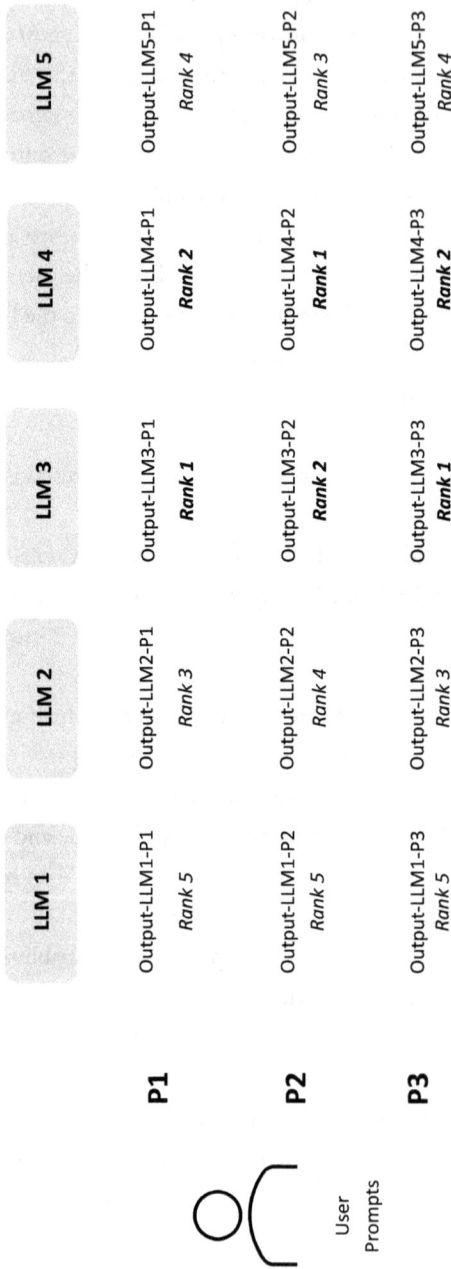

Figure 9.3 LLM curation

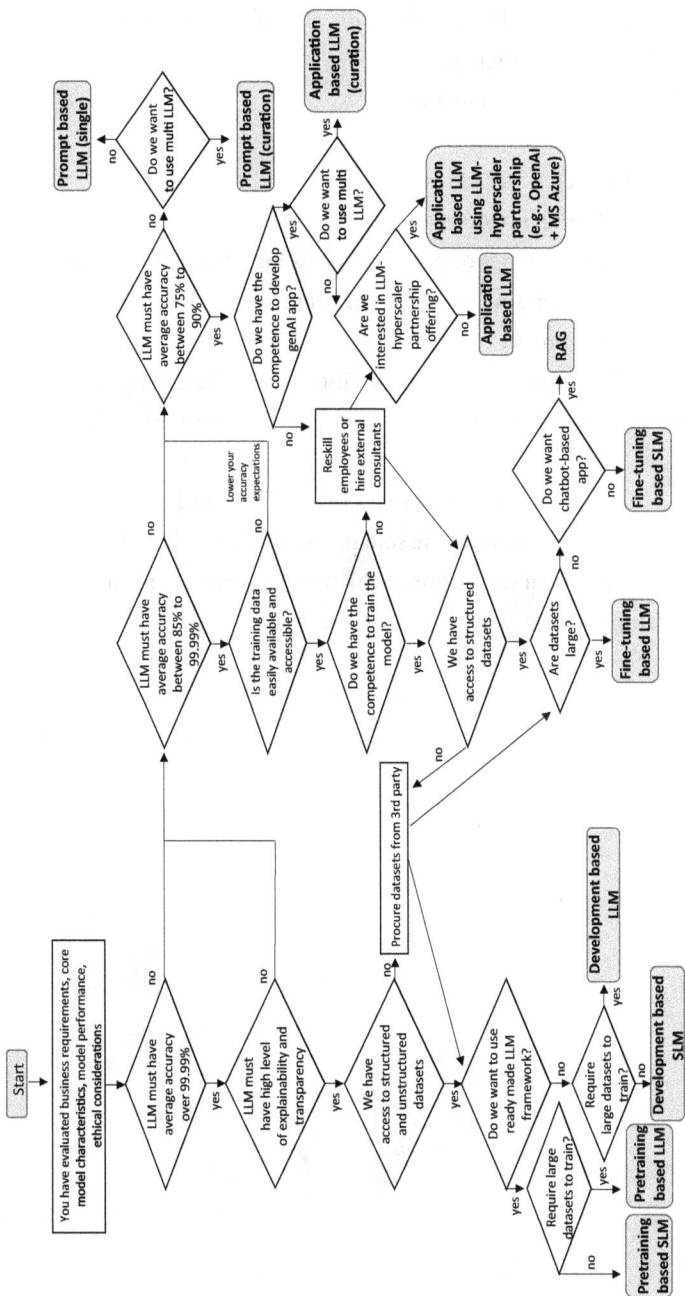

Figure 9.4 Flowchart

Summary

- The selection of LLM is based on the following factors:
  1. Business requirements
  2. Core model characteristics
  3. Model performance
  4. Ethical considerations
  5. Business architecture
- There are five types of genAI business architectures: prompt based, application based, fine-tuning based, pretraining based, and development based.
- RAG is more suited for developing chatbot-based applications for your business, which includes customer support, Q&A, and troubleshooting.
- LLM curation is a service that curates different LLMs onto a single platform with the sole purpose of providing the best and most accurate output to the users in response to their prompts.

CHAPTER 10

Manage Assets:

Capabilities, Infrastructure, Technical Debt Reduction

DBS has leveraged advanced analytics and machine learning to enhance its capabilities in financial crime prevention. Its transaction surveillance group developed a machine learning model that utilizes a broader range of data to prioritize suspicious cases based on risk scores. It also implemented a network link analysis capability to examine relationships among potential fraudsters and identify suspicious networks.

Shell utilizes predictive maintenance to improve the efficiency and reliability of its equipment across its facilities. Data from various equipment are aggregated into a central platform, leveraging Microsoft's Azure cloud service and Databricks' Delta Lake software. It can monitor over ten thousand pieces of equipment daily with support from engineers who are skilled in both machine learning and equipment operations.

Airbus has expanded its ecosystem within its defense and space division by introducing the OneAtlas satellite imagery and analytics service. It utilizes satellites to capture images and couples them with deep learning models to detect, classify, and monitor objects and changes over time with high precision. OneAtlas offers comprehensive geospatial analytics, supporting diverse applications like land use analysis, change detection, and economic activity monitoring, serving as the basis for sector-specific services in defense, mapping, agriculture, forestry, and oil and gas industries.

Ping An, a diverse Chinese conglomerate spanning insurance, banking, asset management, healthcare, and technology sectors, integrates facial recognition technology into various services. Customers utilize facial recognition for identity verification when submitting insurance claims through Ping An's mobile app or website, expediting the verification process and facilitating swift claim payouts. In financial services, facial recognition aids identity verification for loan applications; thereby enhancing security and expediting credit approval by analyzing facial data against existing records.

Bank of America offers a virtual financial assistant called Erica, accessible through its mobile banking app. Users can interact with Erica using natural language speech or text commands to perform various banking tasks, such as checking account balances, transferring funds, paying bills, and getting account information. Erica uses speech recognition to understand the user's voice commands and convert them into text. Then, based on the user's request, Erica provides responses or executes actions, which are converted back into speech using text-to-speech technology, allowing the user to hear the responses audibly. This service enhances the user experience by providing convenient and hands-free access to banking services through voice interaction.

Kroger, one of the largest retail companies in the United States, delivers personalized recommendations by leveraging customer data and insights gathered through its loyalty programs, shopper behavior analysis, and other data sources. Using advanced analytics and artificial intelligence algorithms, Kroger processes this data to understand individual preferences, shopping habits, and purchasing patterns. Based on this information, Kroger tailors personalized recommendations for each customer, suggesting products and promotions that are likely to be of interest to them. These recommendations are often delivered through various channels, including digital platforms, mobile apps, email newsletters, and in-store promotions, enhancing the overall shopping experience for customers.[1]

Firms need to build long-term AI capabilities to transform themselves as AI or genAI based enterprises. An AI capability building requires these six essential ingredients:

1. Strategy: It should address the purpose—why do we want to build an AI capability?
2. Competence: It should be developed using reskilling and upskilling programs or hiring external consultants.

3. Funding: A sufficient annual budget should be allocated for building a capability.
4. Support from leadership: It can be provided through regular governance meetings.
5. Communication plan: It involves regular internal and external communications that can position and brand your firm as an AI company.
6. AI monetization: AI should be sold as a standalone product or service, a value enhancer, or a process optimizer.

As shown in Figure 10.1, AI technologies form the building blocks. A capability can be developed based on one or more technologies. Use cases are built by combining one or more capabilities. Products or user applications can be developed by combining use cases.

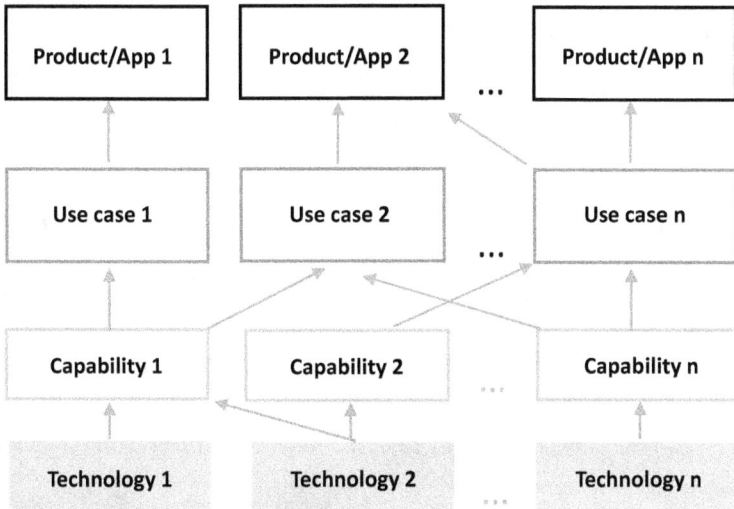

Figure 10.1 Product/App composition

Build Capabilities

Figure 10.2 shows four main building blocks and seven fundamental capabilities of AI.

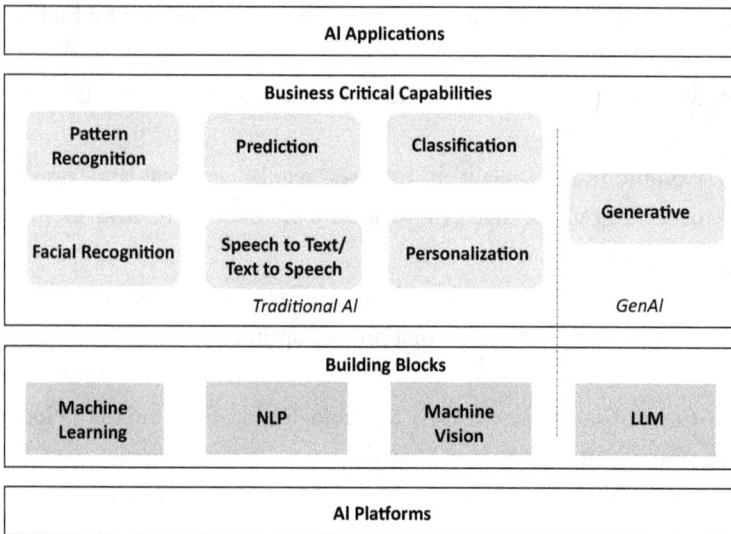

Figure 10.2 Capabilities of traditional AI and generative AI

The main building blocks are:

1. Machine learning
2. Natural language processing (NLP)
3. Machine vision
4. Large language model (LLM)

Machine learning is the ability to learn from data without being explicitly programmed.

NLP stands for natural language processing, which is the ability to understand and interpret the intent behind the human language.

Machine vision is the ability to detect and recognize faces and objects in an image.

LLMs are deep learning algorithms that have the ability to recognize, summarize, translate, predict, and generate human-like content using very large datasets.

A *capability* is defined as the operational tasks to be performed by AI that add value to the business.

The fundamental capabilities of AI/genAI are:

1. Pattern recognition
2. Prediction

3. Classification
4. Facial recognition
5. Speech to text/Text to speech
6. Personalization
7. Generative

Pattern recognition is the ability to identify a consistent or repeatable pattern based on various data points.

Prediction is the ability to offer a forecast based on observed patterns or collected data points.

Classification is the ability to segregate the data or information objects based on certain characteristics.

Facial recognition is the ability to identify a person based on facial expressions and understand his/her emotional state based on the different facial expressions.

Speech to text/Text to speech is the ability to transform spoken words into text and written text into speech.

Personalization is the ability to offer personal recommendations to the user based on his/her preferences.

Generative is the ability to generate new text, image, or other form of content using generative models.

The six examples at the beginning of the chapter illustrate the six fundamental capabilities of traditional AI: DBS–pattern recognition, Shell–prediction, Airbus–classification, Ping An–facial recognition, Bank of America–speech to text/text to speech, and Kroger–personalization.

An AI application is built by combining one or more business capabilities based on the business problem to be solved.

Group Activity

1. Discuss within your group which AI/genAI capabilities you would like to build. Consider the following questions:
   a. Why do we want to build a capability?
   b. Do we have enough competence? If not, how do we plan to build it?
   c. Are there any reskilling and upskilling programs in place?

d. How much budget do we need to build a capability?

e. What support do we need from our leaders?

f. What is our communication plan?

g. How do we position and brand our business with regards to AI?

h. Do we have an AI/genAI monetization strategy?

i. How do we want to sell AI/genAI—standalone product or service, value enhancer, or process optimizer?

Add more questions to the list if needed.

Assess Infrastructure

Infrastructure evaluation before deploying genAI is important for the following reasons:

1. Scalability: GenAI systems often require significant computational resources. Evaluating infrastructure ensures that the deployment environment can handle the computational demands of the AI system, both in terms of current requirements and potential future scalability needs.

2. Performance optimization: Understanding the capabilities and limitations of the infrastructure allows for optimizations to be made. This includes optimizing hardware configurations, network setups, and software environments to ensure optimal performance of the genAI system.

3. Security: GenAI systems may process sensitive data or perform critical tasks. Infrastructure evaluation helps identify and address potential security vulnerabilities in the deployment environment, ensuring data integrity, confidentiality, and system resilience against cyber threats.

4. Resource management: Assessing infrastructure capabilities helps in effectively managing resources such as processing power, memory, storage, and network bandwidth. Proper resource allocation ensures smooth operation of the genAI system without resource bottlenecks or wastage.

5. Compliance and governance: Many industries have regulatory requirements and governance frameworks regarding AI deployment.

Infrastructure evaluation ensures that the deployment environment complies with relevant regulations and standards, mitigating legal and compliance risks.

6. Cost management: Understanding infrastructure requirements helps in estimating deployment costs accurately. It enables organizations to make informed decisions about investments in infrastructure and to optimize costs without compromising performance or security.

7. Integration: Evaluating infrastructure compatibility with existing systems and technologies is crucial for seamless integration and interoperability, ensuring that the genAI system can effectively interact with other components of the IT infrastructure and business processes.

Infrastructure Readiness Assessment Survey

Rate the following statements on a scale of 1 to 6, where 1: strongly disagree, 2: disagree, 3: somewhat disagree, 4: somewhat agree, 5: agree, 6: strongly agree.

#	Statements	Your score
1	Our current hardware infrastructure (e.g., CPUs, GPUs, AI accelerators) can support high computational workloads.	
2	Our organization has adequate licenses for AI software tools and frameworks.	
3	Our network infrastructure provides sufficient bandwidth and low-latency communication.	
4	Our current storage systems have adequate capacity to store large volumes of data.	
5	We have robust security measures to safeguard against cyber threats and unauthorized access.	
6	Our infrastructure is scalable and flexible enough to accommodate the growing computational requirements.	
7	Our infrastructure can process data at a speed necessary for real-time or near-real-time applications.	
8	Our infrastructure can efficiently train AI/genAI models within acceptable timeframes.	
9	Our infrastructure can support inference of AI/genAI models in production environments.	

(Continued)

(*Continued*)

#	Statements	Your score
10	Our infrastructure allows for easy integration of AI/genAI with existing IT systems and workflows.	
11	We have evaluated the cost implications of upgrading our infrastructure to support genAI solution.	
12	Our infrastructure complies with relevant regulations and standards governing the use of AI.	
13	Our infrastructure includes robust backup and disaster recovery mechanisms.	
14	We gather feedback from users regularly to optimize infrastructure.	
15	We have established guidelines and policies governing the responsible use of infrastructure.	
16	Our infrastructure includes tools for monitoring the performance and analytics.	
17	We provide dedicated user support for infrastructure.	
18	We understand the benefits of Infrastructure as code (IaC).	
19	We have achieved a high level of automation through IaC.	
20	IaC is well-integrated with our existing development and deployment workflows.	
21	Our infrastructure is designed with long-term sustainability considerations.	
	Average score	

Use the table below to map your infrastructure readiness level:

Average score	Level
Score ≥ 5	Very high readiness
4 ≤ score < 5	High readiness
3 ≤ score < 4	Medium readiness
2 ≤ score < 3	Low readiness
1 ≤ score < 2	Very low readiness

Group Activity

Evaluate your infrastructure readiness using the assessment. Answer the following questions in your group:

a. What do the assessment scores tell us?

b. How do we improve the infrastructure readiness?

c. Do we have necessary skills to do so?

d. What is our long-term infrastructure strategy?

e. Do we plan to move our infrastructure to cloud?

f. How is our adoption of IaC?

Add more questions to the list if needed.

Technical Debt Reduction

Managing technical debt for genAI is crucial for ensuring the long-term success and sustainability of AI initiatives within an organization. *Technical debt* refers to the accumulation of suboptimal design choices, shortcuts, and trade-offs made during the development and deployment of AI systems. In the context of genAI, where complex algorithms and large datasets are common, technical debt can quickly accumulate if not managed effectively, which can severely impact its performance. Therefore, organizations must adopt strategies to identify, prioritize, and address technical debt in their AI projects.

The following are the 10 best practices for managing technical debt:

1. Establish clear coding standards: Define and enforce coding standards and best practices specifically for genAI development. This includes guidelines for code readability, maintainability, and documentation to minimize technical debt accumulation.

2. Regular code reviews: Conduct regular code reviews to identify and address potential technical debt issues early in the development process. Encourage collaboration and knowledge sharing among team members to ensure code quality and consistency.

3. Automated testing: Implement automated testing frameworks and pipelines to validate the functionality, performance, and robustness of genAI models. This includes unit tests, integration tests, and end-to-end tests to catch regressions and prevent technical debt buildup.

4. Continuous integration/continuous deployment (CI/CD): Embrace CI/CD practices to automate the build, testing, and deployment of genAI models. This helps streamline development workflows, reduce manual errors, and ensure consistent quality across releases.

5. Modular design: Adopt a modular design approach for genAI systems, breaking down complex algorithms into smaller, reusable components. This promotes code reusability, scalability, and easier maintenance, reducing the risk of technical debt accumulation.

6. Version control: Use version control systems such as Git to track changes to code and configuration files. This allows for better collaboration, rollback capabilities, and traceability of code changes, helping to mitigate technical debt associated with code churn.

7. Documentation: Maintain comprehensive documentation for genAI models, including model architectures, data preprocessing steps, and experimental results. This facilitates knowledge transfer, troubleshooting, and future enhancements, reducing technical debt due to lack of understanding.

8. Monitoring and alerting: Implement monitoring and alerting systems to track the performance, health, and usage of genAI models in production. This allows for early detection of anomalies, performance degradation, and security vulnerabilities, enabling proactive management of technical debt.

9. Refactoring and optimization: Allocate time and resources for regular refactoring and optimization efforts to address accumulated technical debt. This includes identifying and eliminating code smells, performance bottlenecks, and architectural flaws to improve code quality and maintainability.

10. Continuous learning and improvement: Foster a culture of continuous learning and improvement within the genAI team. Encourage knowledge sharing, experimentation, and feedback loops to identify areas for optimization and innovation, reducing technical debt over time.

Group Activity

Discuss with your group the best practice to manage the technical debt with the help of the following guiding questions:

a. How do we rate our technical debt on a scale of 1 to 10, 1: lowest and 10: highest?

b. What is the impact of technical debt on our business?

c. Which best practices should we implement to manage it? Why?

Summary

- A *capability* is defined as the operational tasks to be performed by AI that add value to the business.
- Machine learning, NLP, machine vision, and LLM are the four main building blocks of AI.
- The seven fundamental capabilities of AI/genAI are pattern recognition, prediction, classification, facial recognition, speech to text/text to speech, personalization, and generative.
- It is important to have a long-term and sustainable infrastructure strategy.
- Choose the best practices to manage and mitigate technical debt.

CHAPTER 11

Right Selections:
Ecosystems, Vendor, Green AI

A 2023 study in the Nordics explored the benefits of ecosystem for genAI development, involving 10 senior management employees from various enterprises divided into two groups. One group collaborated regularly, sharing best practices and attending workshops, while the other worked independently without interaction. After six months, the collaborative group learned three times faster, had clearer visions for genAI deployment, and demonstrated higher innovation levels compared to the stand-alone group. These results underscore the importance of collaboration and knowledge sharing in fostering learning and innovation within the ecosystem.

To succeed in the digital age, it is sometimes important for the firms to collaborate or partner with one another. That's where the ecosystems play a very important role. An *ecosystem* is defined as a group or cohort with certain business objectives, where people seek and share knowledge and information from one another. The future of work will be largely dependent on a firm's ability to work in ecosystem.[*] A McKinsey report suggests that by 2025, ecosystems will generate $60 trillion in revenue, which will constitute 30 percent of global sales in that year.[1] Boston Consulting Group found that the use of the word *ecosystem* in annual reports of large enterprises had grown 13-fold over the last decade, and that firms using and acting on it grew much more rapidly than those that didn't.[2]

---

[*] www.digiculum.com/ (accessed April 24, 2025).

Ecosystem Selection

In any ecosystem, there are typically two main types of participants: pioneers and followers, each offering unique strengths and benefiting from collaboration. *Pioneers* take on leadership roles, bringing together firms with diverse expertise and business models, while *followers* contribute their own expertise to enhance the ecosystem's value. Ecosystem can span multiple industries or exist within a single industry, with participants collaborating to create shared value. Across industries, collaboration between pioneers and followers drives mutual benefit, while within an industry, firms may collaborate with competitors, partners, or customers to maximize value extraction and creation.

In a genAI landscape, there are various ecosystems to consider:

- Business incumbents across industries—that can share best practices and experiences about genAI. Make sure that no competitors fall in one ecosystem group or cohort. You can put competitors in another ecosystem.
- LLM providers—they can discuss the common challenges such as sales, sustainability, and scarcity of competence.
- GenAI platform and app developers—they can share and seek best development practices and learnings from one another.
- Data training experts and data providers—they can address the common challenges of data acquisition and preparation.

How do you know which ecosystem is beneficial for you? Should you be a follower or a pioneer? First, you must find out who are the pioneers and followers in the ecosystem. Second, you must assess if they can bring any value to your business or if you can provide any value to theirs. You must know your digital strategic priorities very well and then do due diligence on an ecosystem available using the following five criteria:

- *Objective* involves finding the main purpose of the pioneers and followers to join the ecosystem.
- *Differentiation* involves understanding the unique capability each player is bringing to the ecosystem.

- *Trust* explores the amount of mutual confidence and respect each player has for one another. Your firm must decide how well you would trust each of the members of the prospective ecosystem.
- *Governance* describes how all the players can solve issues with utmost cooperation and monitor the progress and performance of the ecosystem.
- *Flexibility* means how quickly can each player adapt to the changes.

Group Activity

1. Using the sheet below, list down all the ecosystems that you want to be a part of or want to initiate.

Ecosystem	Objective	Differentiation	Trust	Governance	Flexibility	Score
Ecosystem 1						
Ecosystem 2						
...						
...						
Ecosystem n						

2. Rate each of the criteria with the following rating, 1: very low, 2: low, 3: moderate, 4: high, 5: very high.
3. Add the final score for all the ecosystems. Select the one with the highest score.

Vendor Selection

Selecting the right vendor for genAI is a critical decision that can significantly impact the success of AI initiatives within an organization. A vendor with deep domain knowledge and experience can provide tailored solutions that align with an organization's goals, ensuring successful implementation and deployment of genAI systems. Conversely, choosing an inexperienced vendor may lead to project delays, subpar results, and wasted resources, hampering the organization's AI efforts.

Selection Procedure

The first step in vendor selection is to thoroughly assess the organization's requirements and objectives. This includes understanding the specific use cases for genAI, the desired outcomes, and any regulatory or compliance considerations that may apply.

It is important to begin with the following two vetting questions:

1. Is the vendor compliant with AI regulations such as the EU AI Act?
2. Is the vendor compliant with data, privacy, security, and ethics regulations?

Your procurement or sourcing team, responsible for vendor selection, must conduct due diligence on vendors with regard to their compliance with regulations. This includes submission of their compliance certificates, interviewing, and so on. Your legal team should also be involved in this process.

Once the vendor clears this step, you can consider the following questions to determine the vendor type—multi-value vendor or niche vendor. A multi-value vendor is the one that specializes in multiple value areas in the genAI value chain. A niche vendor is the one that specializes in a specific value area in the genAI value chain. Refer to Figure 7.1 for more details.

Questions to evaluate a multi-value vendor:

1. Across how many value areas does it operate?
2. How many pilot projects were deployed? What is the success rate?
3. How many large-scale adoption projects were deployed? What is the success rate?
4. How many customers does it have?
5. Across how many industries has it deployed projects?
6. What is the average customer feedback rating received?
7. How many employees does it have?
8. What is the estimated AI competence level?
9. What are the estimated levels of the adjacent technologies?
10. How are its products or services reviewed in the market?
11. Can it offer customizable solutions tailored to specific industry needs or use cases?

12. What level of customer support and post implementation services, including response times, escalation procedures, and availability of training resources, would you consider for internal teams?

13. Can it demonstrate successful case studies or testimonials from clients in similar industries or with comparable requirements?

14. What are the common challenges you observe in deploying your products?

15. What are the risks associated with deploying your products or services?

16. What partnerships or collaborations do you have with other technology vendors, research institutions, or industry organizations in the field of genAI?

17. How do you ensure clean and quality data?

18. How do you handle model drifts in genAI deployments?

Questions to evaluate a niche vendor:
All the above questions plus,

- How is the vendor's track record, experience, and domain knowledge in a given niche?
- What technology stacks or frameworks, including the availability of pretrained models, and customization options, does it use for development?
- Does it have any built-in capabilities or use cases specific to the niche?
- Which tools or systems does it use?

Vendor checklist (for both the types)

Items	Yes or no
Compliance with relevant standards and regulations for ethical AI and data protection	
Adequate measures for data privacy and security in handling sensitive data	
Approach to transparency, explainability, and bias mitigation in genAI models	
Maintenance and support, versioning, and update procedures for products	
Adequate data storage and data migration practices and procedures	

(Continued)

(*Continued*)

Items	Yes or no
Metrics to evaluate product performance	
SLAs in place for services	
Adequate training and documentation	
Pricing and other contractual terms and conditions	
Cloud deployments: public, private, or hybrid	
Compatibility of their product with your existing IT environment	
Roadmap for product development	
Handling of issues, incidents, breaches, or vulnerabilities	
Adequate security measures for handling adversarial attacks	
Adequate disaster recovery measures	

Green AI

When assessing the environmental impact of a genAI model, there are two key factors to consider:

1. Carbon emissions during model training
2. Energy consumption during inference

Models with a large number of parameters and training datasets typically consume more energy and generate higher carbon emissions. Recent genAI models require significantly more computing power for training compared to previous generations, with demands doubling every six months, according to research. Researchers have highlighted the significant environmental impact of training large language models like GPT-4 or PaLM, estimating their carbon emissions at approximately 300 tons of CO_2. To put this into perspective, the average person generates around 5 tons of CO_2 annually, while a medium-sized genAI model produces CO_2 emissions equivalent to 626,000 tons.

Inference consumes less energy per session than training. However, as these models are deployed in the cloud for inference and used by millions of users, the cumulative energy consumption becomes significant. NVIDIA estimates that a large portion, 80 to 90 percent, of the energy cost of neural networks occurs during ongoing inference processing.

The following steps can help make genAI greener:

1. Fine-tune existing models rather than training new ones from scratch.
2. Use energy-conserving computational methods such as TinyML, which enables the execution of ML models on small, low-power edge devices such as microcontrollers, eliminating the need to transmit data to servers for processing.
3. Reuse models and resources.
4. Include AI/genAI activity in your carbon monitoring, utilizing tools such as CodeCarbon and Green Algorithms.

Group Activity

Discuss in your group the current and future environmental impact of using genAI with the help of the following guiding questions:

a. How do we measure carbon emissions during training a model?
b. How do we measure energy consumption during inference?
c. What is the overall carbon emission of our business?
d. What will be the carbon emission in future with genAI?
e. What steps are we going to take to make genAI greener? Why?

Summary

- In any ecosystem, there are typically two main types of participants: pioneers and followers, each offering unique strengths and benefiting from collaboration.
- We do due diligence on all the ecosystems using the following five criteria:
  o Objective
  o Differentiation
  o Trust
  o Governance
  o Flexibility

- There are two types of genAI vendors: multi-value vendor and niche vendor.
- A multi-value vendor specializes in multiple value areas in the genAI value chain.
- A niche vendor specializes in a specific value area in the genAI value chain.
- When assessing the environmental impact of a genAI model, there are two key factors to consider:
    1. Carbon emissions during model training
    2. Energy consumption during inference

SUMMARY OF PART 4

Readiness Area

Technology

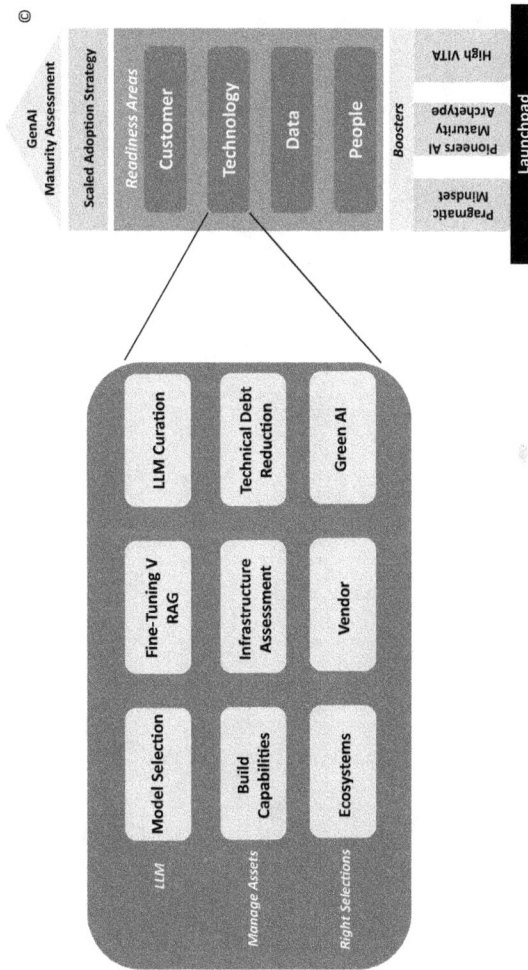

Readiness Rocket

PART 5

Readiness Area

Data

CHAPTER 12

Data Acquisition:
Purpose, Identify, Acquire

A European e-commerce analytics and personalized marketing solutions company, recognizing the value of data-driven insights in today's competitive market, made huge investments in improving data. The customer data was acquired from online behaviors, social media engagements, and purchase histories. The internal operations data was acquired from various tools, systems, and processes. The acquired data was stored in data lakes. A data lake is a big storage pool where a company keeps loads of data, such as text, documents, images, and videos, in its original, unprocessed form. Unlike traditional data storage systems, such as a data warehouse that organizes data into folders, a data lake uses a flat architecture, which adds tags and unique IDs to each piece of data to make it easier to locate and access.[1]

Over a period, the data lake became a data swamp. Piles of data kept on pouring into the data lake without any governance, control, or quality audit. There was duplication of efforts, conflicting analyses, and wasted resources. It was challenging to separate useful data that could provide actionable insights. The company struggled to determine which metrics were most relevant to their business goals. It faced significant costs related to storing, processing, and managing the vast volumes of data they had accumulated. This was due to a lack of well-defined *purpose*. If they had established clear objectives, aligned their data initiatives with business goals, and implemented robust data governance practices, they could have avoided many of the challenges they faced and positioned themselves for long-term success in the ever-evolving digital landscape.

The data readiness is divided into three phases:

- Data acquisition
- Data preparation
- Data production

The data acquisition phase is divided into purpose, identify, and acquire.

Purpose

Data readiness at an organization always begins with a purpose: why is data strategy essential for genAI? What is our data purpose?

The relationship between data and genAI models is unique. The input to a genAI model is data. And the output from the model is also data. The relationship can be described with the statement:

Need data to generate data

The data purpose can be broadly categorized into the following two categories:

- Monetization
- Non-monetization

Monetization can be further divided into:

- Direct monetization
- Indirect monetization

Direct monetization involves selling the data generated as-is or with some minor customizations.

Indirect monetization involves wrapping the data around a product or a service to enhance its value and customer willingness to pay.

Non-monetization includes cost savings due to efficient internal operations driven by genAI.

An example of direct monetization is subscription to Bloomberg news. It offers subscription-based access to its comprehensive financial news and information services, catering to individual investors, financial professionals, corporations, and institutions. Another example is IBM's Weather Company, which leverages a combination of data sources, including traditional weather data, satellite imagery, and advanced analytics, to provide accurate and reliable weather forecasts and insights.

An example of indirect monetization where data is wrapped around a product or a service is Schindler, an elevator manufacturer. The company enhances its elevators with a performance dashboard, enabling building managers to monitor elevator operations effectively. Another example involves intergovernmental organizations such as the World Bank, offering platforms for participating governments to showcase how their contributions support their philanthropic objectives.

One example of non-monetization is United Parcel Service. It utilized vehicle route data to optimize delivery routes, resulting in annual savings of U.S. $400 million. Another example is Columbia Sportswear, which leveraged historical package-tracking data to address root causes in their supply chain, mitigating both out-of-stock and overstocking issues and saving over U.S. $27 million in inventory expenses.[2]

Thus, the relationship statement between genAI and data can be remodified as:

Need data to generate data, either to monetize or non-monetize.

The data purpose can be linked to either one or more of the following four business objectives, which are also the key decision levers of genAI investment as seen earlier:

1. Increased revenue
2. Reduced costs
3. Increased customer satisfaction
4. Increased employee satisfaction

Direct and indirect monetization maps to increased revenue and increased customer satisfaction, respectively. Whereas non-monetization maps to reduced costs and increased employee satisfaction.

Group Activity

Following are some of the key basic questions that you need to discuss internally within your team:

Data purpose	Questions
Increased revenue	1. What percentage increase in the current revenue stream are we expecting? 2. Are we going to offer a new product or service? 3. How do we enable increased revenue—direct or indirect monetization?
Reduced costs	1. What percentage of cost reduction are we expecting? 2. How much costs can we reduce by improving the process efficiency and streamlining the data flows? 3. How much costs can we reduce by collaborating with a partner from genAI value chain?
Increased customer satisfaction	1. What is the current customer satisfaction rating? What future rating are we expecting? 2. Does it improve delivery lead times and product or service complexity? 3. Does it improve customer support?
Increased employee satisfaction	1. Can the employees easily access the data? 2. Does it contribute to employee learning and development? 3. Does it reduce employee workload?

Identify

Before acquiring data, it's essential to understand its role within the organization. This involves mapping out processes and workflows to identify what data serves as input and what becomes output. There are three types of data flows:

1. Data flow at customer touchpoints
2. Data flow between functions
3. Data flow within a function

The data flow at customer touchpoints can help a firm generate valuable insights about the customers, which its competitors may not have access to. The data flow between and within functions can provide valuable business insights for making important decisions. This practice is known as *data-driven* decision-making.

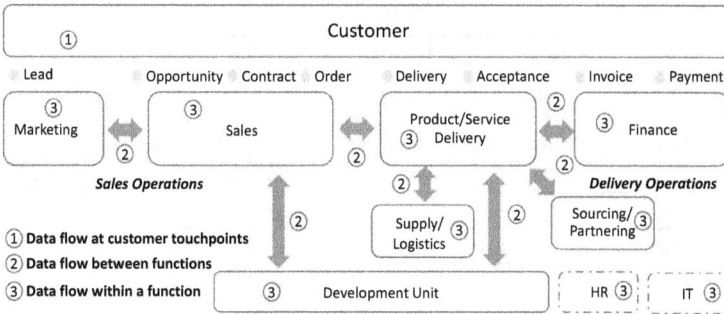

Figure 12.1 Three types of data flows

Group Activity

1. Using the sheet below, note down all the data flowing IN and OUT of the firm at various customer touchpoints.

Customer touchpoints	Data flowing IN	Data flowing OUT
Lead		
Opportunity		
Contract		
Order		
Delivery		
Acceptance		
Invoice		
Payment		

2. Using the sheet below, note down all the data flowing between various functions. Add or remove functions if needed.

Data flowing between functions	Delivery	Supply/ logistics	Development unit	Finance	Marketing	Sourcing	HR	IT
Sales								
Delivery								
Supply/ logistics	X							
Development unit	X	X						

(Continued)

(*Continued*)

Data flowing between functions	Delivery	Supply/ logistics	Development unit	Finance	Marketing	Sourcing	HR	IT
Finance	X	X	X					
Marketing	X	X	X	X				
Sourcing	X	X	X	X	X			
HR	X	X	X	X	X	X		

3. Using the sheet below, note down all the data flowing within functions. Add or remove functions if needed.

Functions	Data flow
Sales	
Delivery	
Supply/logistics	
Development unit	
Finance	
Marketing	
Sourcing	
HR	
IT	

If the required data for a certain AI application or project cannot be identified internally within the organization, then the fourth method is to check if it is available with any of the external vendors.

Acquire

Once the data sources are identified, the next step is to acquire it. Data can be at rest or in motion. *Data at rest* refers to data that is stationary, residing in storage systems like databases, data warehouses, or cloud repositories. *Data in motion* refers to data actively in transit between different locations, typically facilitated by data pipelines. This process, known as *data ingestion*, involves transporting data from diverse sources to a storage destination where it can be accessed, utilized, and analyzed by organizations. Throughout this journey, the data undergoes various transformations based on the specific business needs and the intended destination, ranging from basic extraction and loading to more advanced processes like predictive analytics or machine learning in data warehouses.

The acquired data needs to be stored. Organizations can use cloud storage solutions provided by hyperscalers such as AWS, Microsoft Azure, and Google Cloud. Selecting a specific cloud storage service involves considering several factors such as data type, performance requirements, durability and availability, cost, access control and security, integration with other services, scalability, data lifecycle management, compliance requirements, and support and documentation.

Let's continue with the story of Ram and Shyam consulting from Chapter 6. Ram used the real customer data. The data *purpose* for Ram was non-monetization—to feed the chatbot with the right data so that it can perform the desired tasks.

For the Retail X, the right data was *identified* at the following three locations:

1. Product databases containing product manuals and product descriptions.
2. Knowledge bases containing policies, support manuals, standard operating procedures, FAQs, customer service logs, website analytics, customer surveys and feedback, conversational data, and social media interactions.
3. Customer relationship management (CRM) tool containing information on new and existing clients, track record of previous, current, and future deals and purchases, key stakeholders, account planning, and allocated operational expenditure budget.

As product databases, knowledge bases, and CRM tools are owned by sales and marketing teams, it is an example of data flows between functions and within a function.

For simplicity, assume that Retail X has three products: prod#1, prod#2, and prod#3, and three customers: cust#1, cust#2, and cust#3. All the products have a user manual and customer reviews.

Assume that:

The data related to prod#1, prod#2, and prod#3 are hosted by two databases: db_p1 and db_p2.

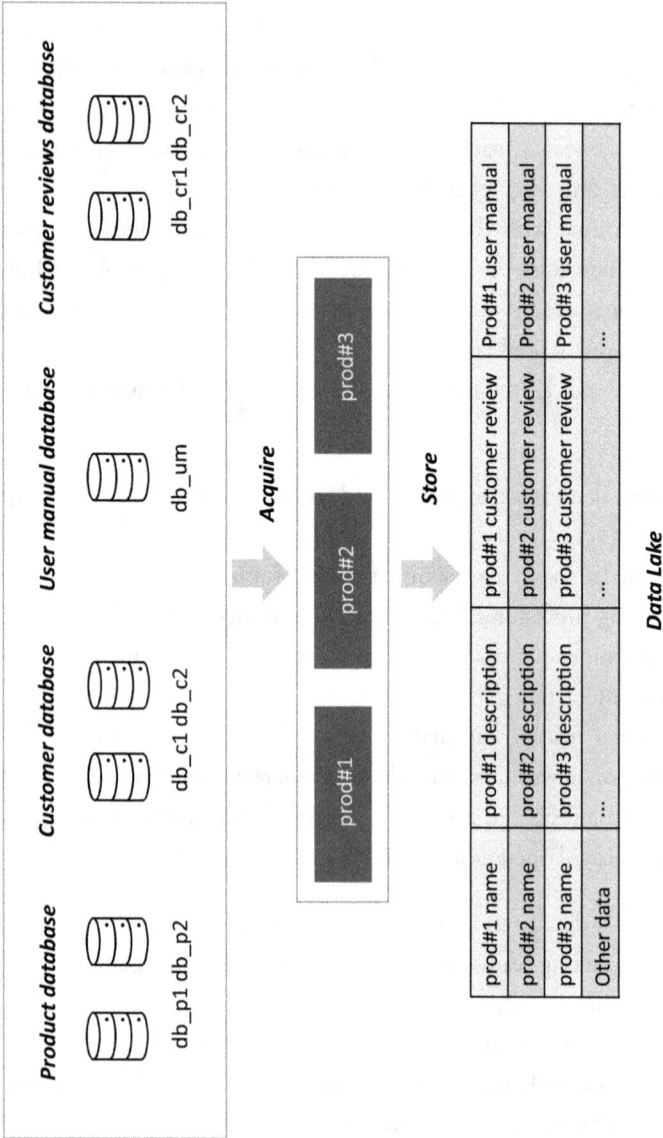

Figure 12.2   Acquisition process

The data related to cust#1, cust#2, and cust#3 are hosted by two databases: db_c1 and db_c2.

The user manual data is hosted by the database db_um and the customer reviews data are hosted by two databases: db_cr1 and db_cr2.

The *acquire* process involves gathering the data from the right databases for the products, customers, user manuals, and customer reviews. The collected data is stored in a data lake.

The acquisition process is shown in Figure 12.2. It can be automated or done manually.

Summary

- The data readiness is divided into three phases: data acquisition, data preparation, and data production.
- The data acquisition phase is divided into purpose, identify, and acquire.
- The data purpose can be broadly categorized into two categories: monetization and non-monetization.
- Monetization can be further divided into direct monetization and indirect monetization.
- There are three types of data flows:
  1. Data flow at customer touchpoints
  2. Data flow between functions
  3. Data flow within a function
- Data at rest refers to data that is stationary, residing in storage systems like databases, data warehouses, or cloud repositories.
- Data in motion refers to data actively in transit between different locations, typically facilitated by data pipelines.

CHAPTER 13

Data Preparation:

Clean, Annotate, Structure

The product development team of a European-based global IT company, with operations across Europe, Asia, and America, had developed an AI-based hiring and selection tool. The purpose of the tool was to evaluate job candidates for a leadership and talent management program and shortlist them for the next rounds of personal interviews, which included interviews with HR, hiring manager, and an executive. The motive behind this program was to onboard and cultivate leaders who can lead AI-driven transformations within the company. There were five open consulting positions in each of the five industry verticals: financial services, communications, healthcare, retail, and public sector. Over a thousand applications were received. The hiring manager was keen on selecting the best and brightest talents for these positions across the globe. The candidates were asked to submit their CVs along with a questionnaire to assess their personalities and culture fit. The tool shortlisted around 50 candidates for the HR interview. Out of which, the first batch of top 10 was passed over to the hiring manager; let us call him Per. Per interviewed all of them but was unable to shortlist a suitable candidate. He interviewed the next batch of 10. The result was the same. Per interviewed all 50 candidates. He was unable to find the right one. Per was surprised and wanted to investigate the AI selection tool.

After investigation, it was discovered that the tool contained biases that severely impacted the shortlisting of candidates. It gave more weightage to the candidates with a master's degree, and among them, more weight was given to the candidates with an MBA than MS, MSE, or MTech.

The candidates with educational backgrounds from elite and reputed business schools were given more preference. Those with more than seven years of work experience were considered more qualified. There was no limit on the maximum work experience. Thus, overqualified candidates with more than 15 years of work experience were also shortlisted by the tool. The candidates living in the same city or country in Europe were given higher preference over those from other parts of Europe, America, or Asia. The CVs that showed more experience with genAI or had more genAI-related keywords were given higher ratings. In the personality test, candidates with more social and extrovert profiles were given more consideration. In the culture fit assessment, the candidates who adhered to the culture were given more weight. And the most surprising finding was that the candidates who did not submit the cover letter along with their application were filtered out immediately, though the submission of cover letter was optional.

The tool was designed by the head of product development; let us call her Petra. She was not properly communicated with the objectives of the program. She had her own ideas and expectations about it, which biased the tool design. The tool was temporarily suspended for the program. The company had to resort to the traditional method of shortlisting the CVs. A team of additional HRs was called in to go through the tedious process of manually screening around a thousand CVs. In total, 75 were shortlisted for the HR round, out of which 35 were selected for the interview with Per. Out of which, 10 were selected for the interview with the executive, and the final five candidates were offered the position after a group discussion with the HR, Per, and the executive.

Among the final five selected ones, two held MBA; one graduated from an elite business school. Three had submitted cover letters along with their application. Two were from Europe, two from Asia, and one from America. Two had analytical and introvert personalities. Three had prior experience with AI. One out of the three who had prior experience with AI, also had experience with genAI, and all of them had scored less on the culture fit test. And interestingly, none of them had been shortlisted by the AI tool in the first round.

Biases can severely impact the performance of tools and systems. Can we completely eliminate them?

Biases

Biases refer to systemic preferences or prejudices embedded within the data or algorithms used to train AI models. These biases can lead to unfair or discriminatory outcomes in AI-generated content or decisions. It is not possible to have an AI model completely free of bias, but it is possible to control and mitigate it.

Biases stem from human instincts. There are five major instincts that cause bias in genAI models:[1]

1. Generalization and categorization instinct
2. Gap instinct
3. Single-perspective instinct
4. Size instinct
5. Fear instinct

1. Generalization and categorization instinct

We humans tend to generalize people, data, facts, or information, often without realizing it. For instance, encountering a lawyer proficient in public speaking may lead to the assumption that all lawyers excel in this skill, overlooking the diverse specialties and capabilities within the legal profession. We humans also have a natural tendency to categorize individuals, information, data, and facts into various groups based on shared characteristics or attributes. For example, people are often grouped into socioeconomic strata such as income, education level, occupation, and wealth, or grouped based on common interests and beliefs.

Petra felt that the candidates with an MBA were more suitable for leadership roles than those with technical degrees. She herself had an MBA degree, and most leaders she met so far had MBAs. So, she generalized that all candidates with an MBA are a good fit for the program. She showcased her categorization instinct by setting a hard selection category for the candidates above and below seven years of experience.

2. Gap instinct

We have an irresistible temptation to divide all kinds of things into two distinct and often conflicting groups, with an imagined gap. By demonstrating gap instinct, we are basically categorizing. But the main difference between the gap instinct and categorization is that in the gap instinct, the disparity is much larger and wider as compared to categorization. Due to this, we may miss out on the ones that lie in the middle of two polarized ends. For example, in society, individuals frequently categorize themselves and others into distinct social classes, such as the wealthy and the poor class, often leaving out the middle class that comprises a majority of the population. Another example of this instinct is that individuals often categorize themselves and others into distinct national groups, such as local citizens and immigrants, where they tend to exclude those immigrants who are citizens and residing in that country for many years.

Petra had an optimistic mindset about genAI and thus felt it to be a key competence in the candidates to be selected for the leadership program. With her gap instinct, she categorized the candidates into experience with genAI and no experience with genAI, which excluded the majority of candidates with current or potential competence on AI and adjacent technologies such as data and cloud.

3. Single-perspective instinct

Humans have the tendency to favor simplicity, which is driven by the desire for clarity and comprehension. We tend to choose options that are more common and less complicated. For instance, someone might pursue a traditional career in medicine, law, or engineering because it's deemed more prestigious, while overlooking their passion for less conventional fields such as entrepreneurship, digital marketing, or social media influencing.

Petra, due to her single-perspective instinct, designed the selection tool to be simple and straightforward, exactly as per the job description and the expected roles and responsibilities that did not favor the candidates demonstrating different skills, extracurricular interests, or scoring low on the culture fit assessment. One of the five candidates, who was screened out by the AI tool in the first round and later selected by Per with the traditional hiring process, was a part-time faculty at an online business school; in addition to being full-time employee at the competitor IT consulting company. She also had created a few courses on learning platforms such as Udemy. While applying, she wrote a note in the comments section questioning whether being a part-time faculty or a content provider on Udemy had any legal implications or could impact the hiring process. The writing of her note made her application to be perceived a bit different and complicated by the algorithm in the AI tool.

4. Size instinct

Distorting the scale of things or misperceiving their significance is a common human trait. It's natural for us to magnify the importance of lonely figures, such as numbers, without considering their broader context. We tend to overestimate the negative information and underestimate the positive ones. One example where we instinctively misjudge the importance of a lonely number is in the context of social media metrics, such as the number of likes on a post. Individuals often place excessive emphasis on the numerical value of likes, equating it with the significance or quality of the content. However, a post with a low number of likes may still hold considerable value or meaning to certain individuals, while a high number of likes does not necessarily indicate the content's true impact or relevance.

Petra's size instinct gave higher priority to candidates from elite business schools, which she perceived as more valuable than other schools. It was also because she was herself from one of the top-ranked business schools across the globe. She overlooked the fact that there could be candidates from lesser ranked business schools with similar or better potential.

5. Fear instinct

The fear instinct in people can lead to biases when individuals perceive certain groups or situations as threatening, even in the absence of objective evidence. People fail to differentiate between the "frightening" and "dangerous," which are two different things. Something frightening poses a perceived risk. Something dangerous poses a real risk. Frightening things that capture our attention may not be necessarily risky.

Petra gave more weight to the candidates from same city or country, to those who submitted cover letters, and to more social and extrovert personality profiles. She had mostly worked with people from her own country, culture, and background all throughout her career and was apprehensive about working with those from other countries. She normally recruited people with cover letters, as she considered it to be a mark of professionalism and attention to detail. She feared that analytical and introvert personality type leaders would slow down the growth of the organization. She was frightened by the unreal risks.

Hallucinations

Hallucinations are the outputs generated by the LLMs that distort the interpretation of data and generate misleading outcomes. They can be classified into the following five categories:

1. Irrelevant
2. Illogical
3. Inaccurate
4. Inconsistent
5. Injurious

1. Irrelevant hallucinations

   They deviate from the context or query provided to the model, providing off-topic information. They may be logical, accurate, consistent, and non-injurious but just not relevant to the context.

   For example, when an LLM was prompted—Tell me something about the NBA Commissioner. The response was:

   In the world's most popular basketball league, the NBA Commissioner, Adam Silver, has long been regarded as a leader and decision-maker. First, Silver has claimed his dedication for maintaining fairness and competitiveness in the game. Second,

Silver has repeatedly emphasized his concern for players' health and well-being. In this case, *Stern's* words and actions clash with his stated goal of caring for player welfare.

Here, the LLM initially mentioned Silver but then randomly switched to Stern.[2]

2. Illogical hallucinations

They lack coherence or logical reasoning. They may be relevant, accurate, consistent, and non-injurious, but just not logical.

For example, during the reinforcement learning of GPT-3, for the instruction: explain the moon landing to a six-year-old in a few sentences, GPT-3 hallucinated and gave some vague, illogical answer: explain the theory of gravity to a six-year-old.[3]

3. Inaccurate hallucinations

They contradict known facts or fabricate entirely new content. They may be relevant, logical, consistent, and non-injurious but just not accurate.

For example, Google Bard was prompted with "What new discoveries from the James Webb Space Telescope or JWST can I tell my nine-year-old about?" Bard responded with a number of answers, including one suggesting that the JWST took the very first picture of a planet outside of our own solar system. These distinct worlds are called "exoplanets." *Exo* means from outside. This was inaccurate, as the first pictures of exoplanets were taken by the European Southern Observatory's very large telescope in 2004, as confirmed by NASA. This mistake was identified hours prior to Google's launch event for Bard in Paris, during which a senior executive from Google praised Bard as the company's future direction.[4] This costed Alphabet, the parent company of Google, a loss of market value of around U.S. $100 billion.[5]

4. Inconsistent hallucinations

They are different from the input data used to train the model, providing misleading information. They may be relevant, logical, accurate, and non-injurious but just not consistent. For example, Microsoft Bing's chatbot provided misleading information when asked basic questions about elections in Germany and Switzerland, often misquoting its sources.[6]

5. Injurious hallucinations

They spread false information, potentially causing harm to others. They may be relevant, logical, accurate, and consistent but just not non-injurious. For example, Google Gemini produced a malicious response against the Indian Prime Minister Narendra Modi, calling his policies "fascist," provoking a confrontation between Google and the Indian government. Google immediately responded by saying, "Gemini is built as a creativity and productivity tool and may not always be reliable, especially when it comes to responding to some prompts about current events, political topics, or evolving news."[7]

Biases in training data used to train the genAI models can lead to hallucinations that can erode trust in genAI systems. There are three levels of hallucinations: alarming, moderate, and mild. Injurious ones are always alarming. Others can be any of the three categories.

The data preparation phase is divided into clean, annotate, and structure.

Clean

Data cleaning is the process of removing:

1. Irrelevant data
2. Duplicate data
3. Erroneous data
4. Missing data
5. Data outliers
6. Biases in data

Figure 13.1 shows the survey response of 90 data scientists and data engineers to understand the main causes of model inaccuracy.

It shows that the lack of data preparation is the main cause of inaccurate responses.

Let us visit the story of Ram and Shyam consulting from Chapter 6.

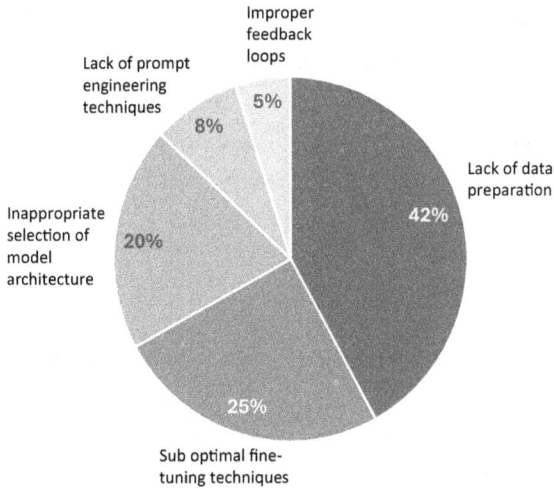

Figure 13.1 Main causes of model inaccuracy

The following table contains the data for the three customers of Retail X.

Cust#1	Cust#2	Cust#3
Emily Johnson	John Smith	Sarah Patel
35	45	72
Female	Male	Female
Marketing manager	IT consultant	Nurse
Married	Single	Married
Bachelor's degree	Master's degree	Diploma
$80,000/year	$10,000,000/year	$65,000/year
New York City, NY	San Francisco, CA	Austin, TX
reading, yoga, reading	technology, hiking, cooking	photography, yoga, cooking
Email	Text message	Social media
Occasional splurges on luxury items	Practical spender, prioritizes savings	Early adopter of gadgets
Apple, Lululemon	Samsung, Columbia	Google, Nike
2 (Emily and her spouse)	1 (lives with a cat)	4 (Sarah, spouse, 2 children)
Owns a condominium	Rents an apartment	Owns a house
Good health	Excellent health	Average health
Drinks:	Drinks:	Drinks:
Smokes: No	Smokes: Yes	Smokes: Yes

The irrelevant data here could be the personal habits of the customers, such as smoking. The duplicate data is "reading," which has appeared twice for Emily Johnson. The erroneous data here is age 72 for Sarah, which is past the traditional retirement age for nurses. The missing data is whether the customers drink or not. The outlier data is the salary of $10 million for John Smith, who is employed as an IT consultant.

Removing Biases

Biases arising from human instincts can be removed as shown in the table below:[8]

Instincts	Bias removal techniques
Generalization and categorization instinct	1. Look for differences within groups. 2. Look for similarities across groups. 3. Look for differences across groups. 4. Avoid generalizing from one group to another.
Gap instinct	1. Look for the data in the middle when presented with data showing a distinct gap. 2. Eliminate extreme cases if they represent the minority, as they do not reflect the general trend.
Single-perspective instinct	1. Test your ideas: collect examples from people who disagree with you. 2. Be open to ideas from others. 3. Beware of simple ideas and simple solutions.
Size instinct	1. Compare the sizes or numbers: large numbers may appear significant on their own, but without comparison, their true importance may be misleading. 2. Follow the Pareto's 80/20 rule: usually 20% of the large sizes or numbers in a dataset are more important than the remaining 80%.
Fear instinct	1. Differentiate between frightening and risky. 2. Calculate the risk using the equation: Risk = danger × exposure. How dangerous is it? How much are you exposed to it?

Mitigating Hallucinations

To mitigate hallucinations, it is recommended to use a guardrail. A guardrail can be deployed at both the input and output of an LLM. How robust one wants to create a guardrail depends on the business requirements and should be compliant with the responsible AI and ethical guidelines.

Figure 13.2 contains the flowchart showing steps to be considered in designing a guardrail.

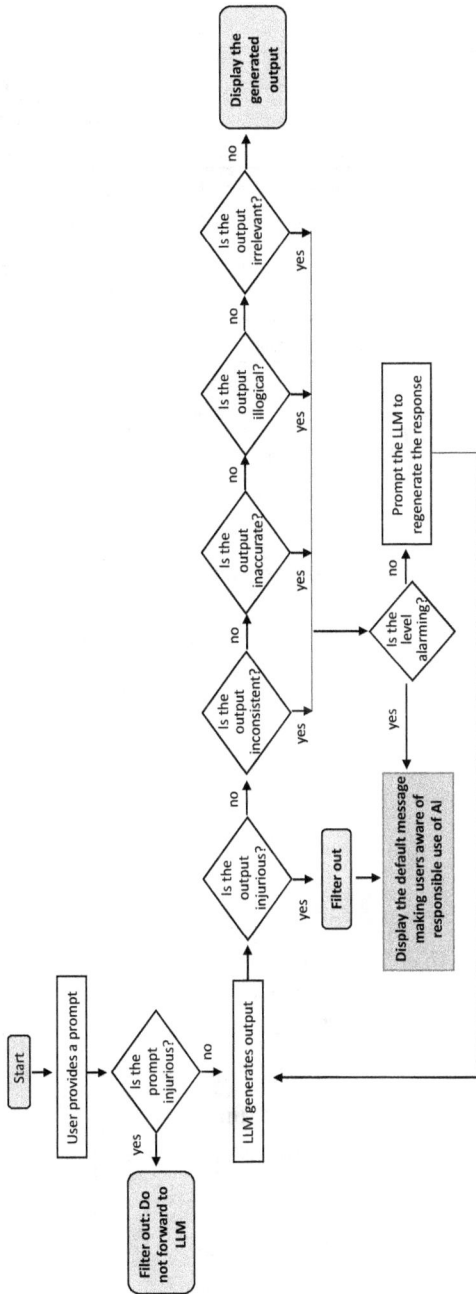

Figure 13.2 Designing a guardrail

The following table shows the guardrail success metrics:

Metrics	Description
Bias detection accuracy	It measures the accuracy of the guardrail in detecting biases present in the LLM's training data or outputs.
False positive rate	It indicates the proportion of instances where the guardrail incorrectly flags outputs as biased.
Failed detection rate	It measures the proportion of instances where the guardrail fails to detect biases or inaccuracies in the LLM's outputs.
Guardrail activation rate	It measures the frequency of guardrail activation in response to potential biases or inaccuracies in the LLM's outputs.
User feedback and satisfaction	It measures the effectiveness of the guardrail from the perspective of end users.
Adherence to compliance standards	It assesses the guardrail's effectiveness in ensuring ethical and responsible AI practices.

Annotate

Once the data is cleaned, the next step is to annotate, which includes two steps:

1. Classification
2. Labeling

1. Classification
   There are seven main classifiers:
   1. Internal (int) versus External (ext)
   2. Confidential (c) versus Non-confidential (nc)
   3. Sensitive (s) versus Non-sensitive (ns)
   4. Real-time (r) versus Non-real-time (nr)
   5. At rest (ar) versus In motion (im)
   6. Insightful (ins) versus Non-insightful (ni)
   7. Measurable (m) versus Non-measurable (nm)
   Users can add more classifiers.
2. Labeling
   Labels are user-defined and play a crucial role in structuring datasets. Labeling is essential for creating organized data and is typically

conducted during fine-tuning and custom tuning. By default, labeled datasets inherently include classifiers.

The following tables show the labels and classifiers of the data for the three customers of Retail X.

Labels	Cust#1	Cust#2	Cust#3
Name	Emily Johnson	John Smith	Sarah Patel
Age	35	45	72
Sex	Female	Male	Female
Occupation	Marketing manager	IT consultant	Nurse
Marital status	Married	Single	Married
Education level	Bachelor's degree	Master's degree	Diploma
Income level	$80,000/year	$10,000,000/year	$65,000/year
Geographic location	New York City, NY	San Francisco, CA	Austin, TX
Interests/hobbies	reading, yoga, reading	technology, hiking, cooking	photography, yoga, cooking
Preferred communication	Email	Text message	Social media
Buying behavior	Occasional splurges on luxury items	Practical spender, prioritizes savings	Early adopter of gadgets
Preferred brands	Apple, Lululemon	Samsung, Columbia	Google, Nike
Household size	2 (Emily and her spouse)	1 (lives with a cat)	4 (Sarah, spouse, 2 children)
Home ownership status	Owns a condominium	Rents an apartment	Owns a house
Health status	Good health	Excellent health	Average health
Drinks			
Smokes	No	Yes	Yes

Classifiers	int versus ext	c versus nc	s versus ns	r versus nr	ar versus im	ins versus ni	m versus nm
Name	int	c	ns	nr	ar	ni	nm
Age	int	c	ns	nr	ar	ni	nm
Sex	int	c	ns	nr	ar	ni	nm
Occupation	int	c	ns	nr	ar	ni	nm
Marital status	int	c	ns	nr	ar	ni	nm

Label: Industry

Aerospace Automotive Banking Capital Comms. Consumer Chemicals Energy Healthcare HiTech Industrial Insurance Life Natural Public Retail Software/ Travel Utilities
markets and media goods   equipment   sciences resources services   Platforms

Label: Function

Sales Marketing Service Product Finance HR IT Customer
                   delivery development   support

Label: Category

- Industry specific
- Benchmarks and survey
- Macroeconomics
- Web browsing and traffic

- Company jobs
- Company news and financials
- Company information
- ESG

- Geospatial
- Consumer demographic
- Consumer transaction
- Product info

- Consumer targeting
- Transport
- Entertainment
- People

- Social media
- Mobile apps
- Sales & commerce
- Process

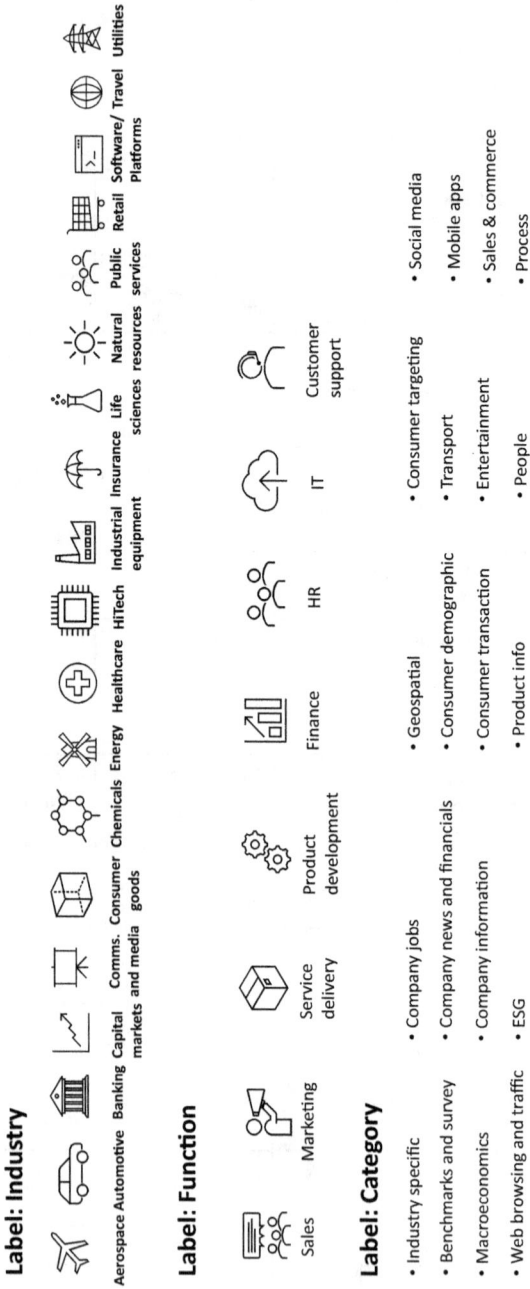

Figure 13.3 Labeling

Classifiers	int versus ext	c versus nc	s versus ns	r versus nr	ar versus im	ins versus ni	m versus nm
Education level	int	c	ns	nr	ar	ni	nm
Income level	int	c	s	nr	ar	ins	m
Geographic location	int	nc	ns	nr	ar	ins	nm
Interests/ hobbies	int	nc	ns	nr	ar	ins	nm
Preferred communica-tion	int	nc	ns	nr	ar	ni	nm
Buying behavior	int	c	ns	r	im	ins	m
Preferred brands	int	c	ns	nr	ar	ins	m
Household size	int	nc	ns	nr	ar	ins	m
Home owner-ship status	int	c	ns	nr	ar	ni	nm
Health status	int	c	s	nr	ar	ni	nm
Drinks	int	c	ns	nr	ar	ni	nm
Smokes	int	c	ns	nr	ar	ni	nm

Classification and labeling processes can be automated for large datasets.

Figure 13.3 shows a standardized labeling format. Label: Industry, Label: Function, and Label: Category describe the specific industry, function, and category, respectively, to which a given dataset belongs.

A label can be divided further into sub-labels. For example, within Label: Function, there are sub-labels such as Label: Function: Sales, Label: Function: Marketing, and so on. Users can define multiple levels in the label hierarchy.

Structure

Once data is annotated, it needs to be stored in a structured format. We have seen the data lake, which normally contains the raw data. For processed data, we use the following structures:

1. Data warehouse: This centralized repository integrates data from multiple sources for reporting and analysis. It primarily houses historical data organized in a structured format that is optimized for efficient querying and analysis.

2. Datasets: Collections of data points or observations designed for analysis and processing. Datasets vary significantly in terms of size, complexity, and content, and they may originate from various sources, including experiments, surveys, observations, or simulations.

3. Data products: These are tailored solutions that enhance a company's ability to fulfill its data requirements. Designed to serve the entire organization, data products facilitate multiple use cases across various functions. They include:

   • Datasets: Reusable data, data streams, data feeds, or APIs that cater to the needs of both the whole enterprise and individual business functions.

   • Code: Feature code and transformation snippets that streamline operations.

   • Analytics models: Reusable machine learning models that enhance predictive and analytical capabilities.

   • Dashboard reports: Reusable dashboards and other visualizations that support data-driven decision-making.

4. Knowledge graph: A sophisticated data structure that organizes knowledge in a graphical format. Entities (nodes) are interconnected by relationships (edges) to form a comprehensive network of information. Unlike traditional databases, which rely on tables and predefined schemas, knowledge graphs offer greater flexibility and the ability to capture complex interrelationships between entities in a way that is both intuitive and reflective of natural language contexts.

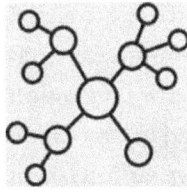

Knowledge Graph

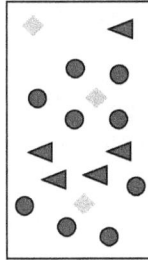

Datasets

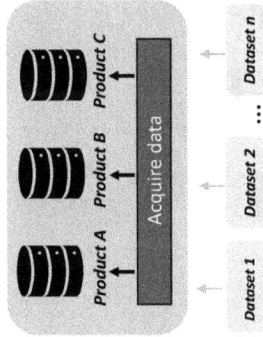

Data Products

Data 1	Data 2	Data 3	Data 4
...	...	...	...
...	...	...	...

Data Warehouse

Figure 13.4 Data structures

Summary

- *Biases* refer to systemic preferences or prejudices embedded within the data or algorithms used to train AI models.
- There are five major instincts that cause biases in genAI models: generalization and categorization instinct, gap instinct, single-perspective instinct, size instinct, and fear instinct.
- *Hallucinations* are the outputs generated by the LLMs that distort the interpretation of data and generate misleading outcomes.
- Hallucinations can be classified into the following five categories: irrelevant, illogical, inaccurate, inconsistent, and injurious.
- Data cleaning is the process of removing irrelevant data, duplicate data, erroneous data, missing data, data outliers, and biases in data.
- Data annotation includes two steps:
  1. Classification
  2. Labeling
- For processed data, we use the following structures: data warehouse, datasets, data products, and knowledge graph.

CHAPTER 14

Data Production:
Train, Evaluate, Democratize

At a U.S.-based genAI startup, a team of data scientists and engineers developed a state-of-the-art genAI model that aimed to revolutionize the way articles and blog posts were created, promising to generate high-quality content with minimal human intervention. Rigorous testing and validation were conducted to ensure its accuracy and reliability. However, shortly after its release, users began reporting inconsistencies and errors in the generated content.

Concerned about the performance, the team started a detailed investigation to uncover the root cause of these inference failures. They meticulously reviewed the model architecture, fine-tuning parameters, and training data, but no obvious flaws were found. They also explored the possibility of data corruption or hardware issues but found no evidence. Despite their best efforts, the team struggled to pinpoint the exact cause of the inference failures. The complexity of the genAI model made it challenging to isolate specific factors contributing to the errors. The tools available for debugging genAI models were insufficient to effectively trace and troubleshoot inference failures, leaving the team without adequate resources to address the issues.

As the investigation continued, frustration grew within the team. They experimented with various debugging techniques and consulted experts in the field, but progress was slow. Eventually, after months of exhaustive testing and analysis, the team reluctantly concluded that they were unable to identify the precise cause of the inference failures.

How difficult is it to pinpoint the cause of model inaccuracies? Are there any proactive measures to prevent them?

The data production phase is divided into train, evaluate, and democratize.

Train

There are three stages of training: pretraining, fine-tuning, and custom tuning. In the *pretraining* phase, LLMs are fed a large corpus of text data from the internet, from which they can understand the basics of human language, grammar, sentence structure, and basic facts about the world. The LLMs create their initial parameters for understanding that data, on which further and more specific capabilities are built. Generally, pretraining follows the *unsupervised* learning procedure, where the training data is unlabeled. In the *fine-tuning* phase, the model's initial parameters are updated to specialize in the business-specific task it is being fine-tuned to perform. Generally, fine-tuning follows the *supervised* learning procedure, where the training data is labeled. *Custom tuning* is an optional training step. The genAI model is fed with lots of business-related instructions that tell the system the best possible output. It is a method coupled with reinforcement learning through human feedback (RLHF). You can either create your own datasets, use the one commercially available, or customize the commercially available ones with your own instructions.

Data is required for pretraining, fine-tuning, and custom tuning the LLM. The most important step is to convert the text into numbers. This process is called vectorization. *Embeddings* are a special type of vectors that capture semantic relationships between words and are stored in a vector database. We have the following three options for training a model:

1. Retrain all the parameters
2. Transfer learning
3. Parameter-efficient fine-tuning (PEFT)

Retraining all the parameters, especially a model with billions of parameters, is not a good option from time, costs, energy or sustainability perspective. In *transfer learning*, a model trained on one task is reused as the starting point for a model on a second related task. Instead of retraining all the parameters, we freeze most of them and only fine-tune the important ones, primarily the last few layers of neural networks. In *PEFT*, we freeze all the parameters and augment the model with an additional model that is trainable and much smaller in size.

Evaluate

Inference refers to the process of using the trained model to generate outputs in response to the user prompts. Training and evaluating the model happen simultaneously and iteratively. It is very challenging to evaluate an LLM inference due to several reasons:

1. Subjectivity: The quality of the generated text or output from an LLM can be subjective and context-dependent, making it difficult to establish universal criteria for evaluation. What may be considered good or relevant output by one evaluator may not necessarily be perceived the same way by another.
2. Lack of ground truth: Unlike in tasks such as image classification or speech recognition, where there are clear ground truth labels for evaluation, assessing the correctness or relevance of text generated by an LLM often lacks definitive ground truth. This makes it challenging to objectively measure the accuracy of the model's outputs.
3. Context sensitivity: The quality of LLM inferences depends heavily on the context provided in the input prompt. Evaluators need to consider how well the generated text aligns with the given context, which adds another layer of complexity to the evaluation process.
4. Human-like inconsistencies: LLMs may produce human-like inconsistencies such as logical inconsistencies, exaggeration, melodrama, over-expressiveness, or colloquialism. Distinguishing between intentional stylistic choices and genuine errors can be challenging for evaluators.

The following table shows some of the common evaluation techniques used to evaluate LLM:

Evaluation techniques	Description
AI2 Reasoning Challenge (ARC)	It consists of questions that require reasoning, use of commonsense knowledge, and are hard to answer with simple baselines. For example, "A train traveling at 100 mph brakes to a stop in 10 seconds. At what speed (in mph) is the train traveling one second before coming to a complete stop?"
HellaSwag	It aims to assess the ability of language models to understand and apply commonsense reasoning in natural language understanding tasks. For example: "If someone says 'I broke a leg,' the most likely response is...?" (Answer: "Oh no, that sounds painful!"—Empathy over amusement)
Machine Reading Comprehension	It involves providing models with textual passages paired with multiple-choice or open-ended questions, testing their comprehension, reasoning skills, and ability to infer correct answers from text alone. Passage: "Alice traveled to Paris last summer to visit the Louvre Museum. During her visit, she admired the Mona Lisa, one of Leonardo da Vinci's most famous paintings. Afterward, she explored the charming cafes along the Seine River." Question: "Which famous artwork did Alice see during her visit to Paris?" Choices: A) Starry Night by Vincent van Gogh B) The Persistence of Memory by Salvador Dalí C) The Mona Lisa by Leonardo da Vinci D) Girl with a Pearl Earring by Johannes Vermeer Correct Answer: C) The Mona Lisa by Leonardo da Vinci
TruthfulQA	It is a set of questions designed to check if a model can give truthful and accurate answers while avoiding misinformation or biased responses. It includes both straightforward and tricky questions to test the model's reliability. For example, Simple question: What is the capital of France? (correct answer: Paris) Tricky question: What is the capital of Australia, including all historical capitals? (There is no single correct answer because Australia has had several capitals historically)

The following table shows special purpose techniques to evaluate LLM:

Evaluation techniques	Description
Recall-Oriented Understudy for Gisting Evaluation (ROUGE)	It is a set of metrics used to evaluate automatic summarization of texts
Bilingual Evaluation Understudy (BLEU)	It is a metric used to evaluate the quality of text that has been machine-translated from one natural language to another

Evaluation techniques	Description
BERTScore	It uses pretrained contextual embeddings from models like BERT to evaluate the quality of text-generation tasks by computing the cosine similarity between the embeddings of words in the candidate and reference texts

In some cases, for more deterministic outputs, the metrics derived from the confusion matrix can also be used:

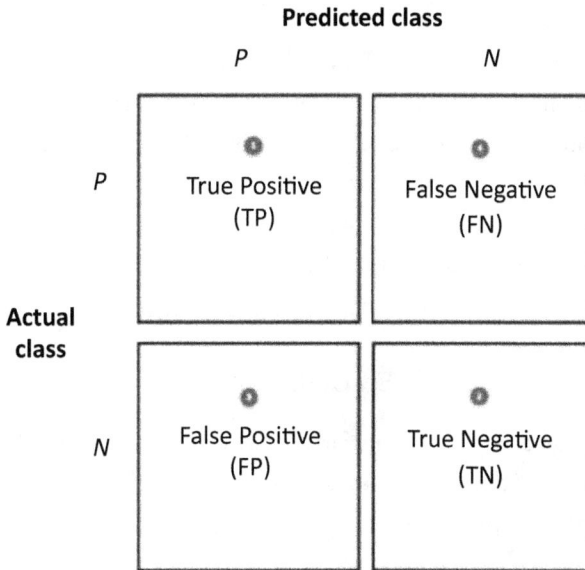

Predicted class

	P	N
P	True Positive (TP)	False Negative (FN)
N	False Positive (FP)	True Negative (TN)

Actual class

Figure 14.1 *Confusion matrix*

Metrics	Description
Accuracy	Proportion of correct predictions overall. (TP + TN) / (TP + TN + FP + FN)
Precision	Proportion of true positives out of all predicted positives. TP / (TP + FP)
Recall	Recall (Sensitivity): Proportion of true positives out of all actual positives. TP / (TP + FN)
Specificity	Proportion of true negatives out of all actual negatives. TN / (TN + FP)
F1	Harmonic mean of precision and recall, balancing both to evaluate model performance. 2 × (Precision × Recall) / (Precision + Recall)

Red Teaming

Red teaming is an essential method for identifying and addressing risks associated with genAI. Each genAI model presents unique vulnerabilities and deployment environments with stochastic outputs, making it crucial for red teams to tailor their approach accordingly. They can be either internal or external, with the intensity of their analysis varying based on the risk level of each system. They launch a deliberate attack on the model to test its security and robustness. The attacks could be of the following types:

1. Injecting code: This involves providing computer code or prompts resembling code to the model to provoke it into generating harmful outputs.
2. Content flooding: Overwhelming the model with large amounts of information to induce undesirable behavior.
3. Hypothetical scenarios: Prompting the model to generate output based on hypothetical instructions that may bypass content controls.
4. Debate on pros and cons: Asking the model to discuss the advantages and disadvantages of controversial topics to elicit harmful responses.
5. Role-playing: Instructing the model to embody a persona associated with negative or controversial statements and encouraging it to produce harmful content.

Example of Training and Evaluating a Model

GenAI model consists of a transformer-based architecture, which is based on neural networks. Figure 14.2 shows the simple form of a neural network known as perceptron.

It consists of an input node x, output node y, activation function f(z), weight w, and bias b. The activation function can be user-defined. The commonly used ones are rectified linear unit, sigmoid function, and tanh.

Output $y = f(z)$, where $z = x.w + b$

Input x is multiplied by weight w, and bias b is added.

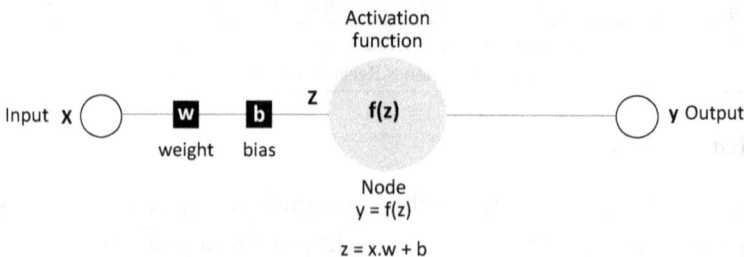

Figure 14.2 Perceptron

Evaluation involves measuring the loss function, which is the delta between actual output and desired output. Training involves minimizing the loss function, continuously adjusting the values of w and b to get the desired output y.

Consider an example of recruiting a candidate, where the candidate is evaluated on the work experience denoted by the variable x. HR gives a rating of 1 to 9 to the candidate. The output y should be either selected or rejected. To enable this, we use a step function that gives the output 1 or 0. When the output is 1, a candidate is selected, and when 0, a candidate is rejected. HR makes a policy to select the candidates with a rating of 5 and above and reject the ones below 5. So, we define a step function with a threshold at $z = 5$. So, when the value of z becomes 5 or more, the step function jumps to 1, which corresponds to selection.

Let us set the weight w to 0.5, and for simplicity, we assume bias $b = 0$.

Imagine you have a candidate with a work experience rating of 8, which is the input value.

$$z = 8 \times (0.5) + 0 = 4$$

When you pass it through the step function, the output will be 0 since $4 < 5$. Even when you have a candidate with the highest rating of 9, the value of z will be 4.5 and he or she will still fail. There is a flaw in the neural network design; it is rejecting candidates even with the highest rating.

One way to remove the flaw is to fine-tune this model by setting the value of b as 2.5. Now this network will select all the candidates with HR rating of 5 and above as shown in the table in Figure 14.3.

Democratize

The output from LLM can be offered as standalone data, dataset, or data product. The business can decide who should have access to data based on policies. This process is known as *data democratization*. For example, a marketing firm utilizing LLM-generated content may choose to offer the resulting data as a subscription service to other companies seeking

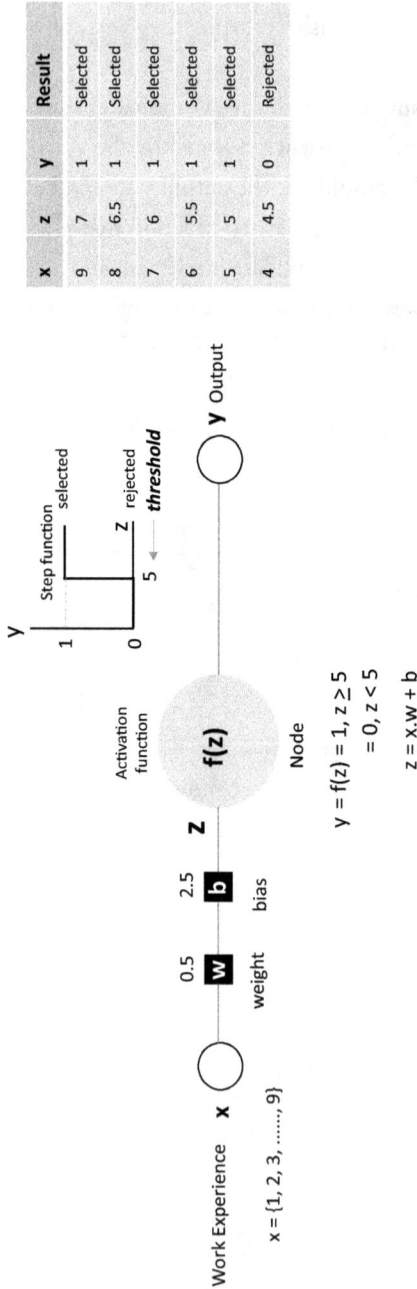

x	z	y	Result
9	7	1	Selected
8	6.5	1	Selected
7	6	1	Selected
6	5.5	1	Selected
5	5	1	Selected
4	4.5	0	Rejected

Work Experience **x**

$x = \{1, 2, 3, \ldots, 9\}$

0.5 **w** weight

2.5 **b** bias

z

Activation function

f(z)

Node

$y = f(z) = 1, z \geq 5$

$= 0, z < 5$

$z = x.w + b$

Step function

selected

rejected

threshold

y Output

Figure 14.3 Fine-tuned HR recruiting system

valuable insights into consumer trends and preferences. By granting access to this data based on carefully crafted policies, the firm ensures that clients adhere to ethical standards and regulatory requirements.

Data democratization can also be applied while preparing the data as an input to LLM. It can be made accessible to the right people, who can work on it and prepare a comprehensive dataset as an input to the LLM. For example, in a recruitment platform leveraging genAI for candidate screening, HR professionals can provide insights on the desired qualifications and skills, while hiring managers can offer feedback based on their experience with successful candidates. Input from industry experts and diversity advocates can further ensure that the dataset reflects diverse backgrounds and perspectives, promoting fairness and effectiveness in identifying top talent.

It is important to implement robust data governance measures to maintain the integrity and confidentiality of the data throughout its lifecycle.

Summary

- There are three stages of training: pretraining, fine-tuning, and custom tuning.
- The process of converting the text into numbers is called vectorization.
- *Embeddings* are a special type of vectors that capture semantic relationships between words and are stored in a vector database.
- The three options for training a model:
  1. Retrain all the parameters
  2. Transfer learning
  3. PEFT
- Training and evaluating the model happen simultaneously and iteratively.
- Red teaming launches a deliberate attack on the model to test its security and robustness.
- The business can decide who should have access to the data based on policies. This process is known as data democratization.

SUMMARY OF PART 5

Readiness Area

Data

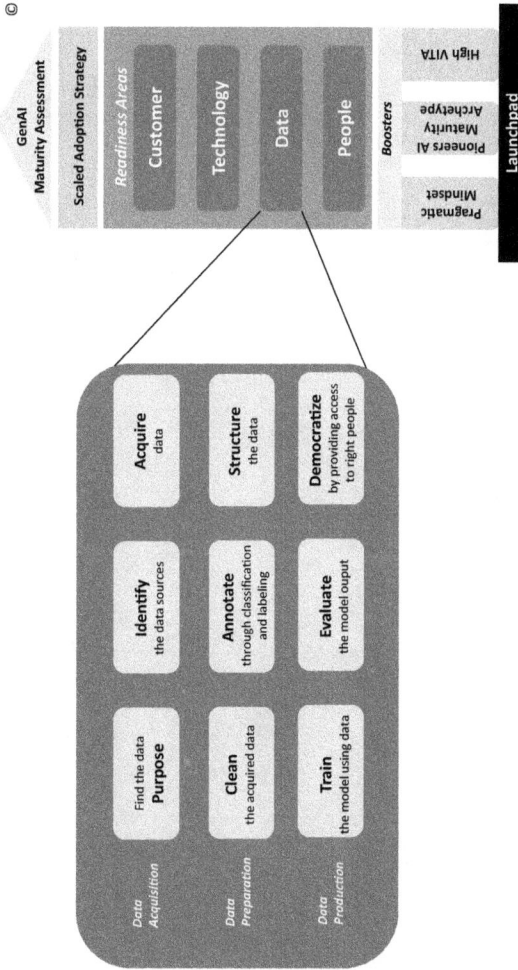

PART 6

Readiness Area

People

CHAPTER 15

Frameworks:

Center of Excellence, Legal, Responsible AI

During the discovery phase of genAI, in the first quarter of 2023, the two rival telecommunication companies, let us call them omega and theta, laid down the foundation of a center of excellence (CoE) to develop the genAI capabilities. Their organizations comprise group functions; three business units: network products, network services, and emerging digital technologies; and three markets: Americas, EMEA, and Asia Pacific.

Omega implemented centralized CoE, and theta implemented federated CoE. The CoEs at both companies were run as cost centers, comprising a central team in the group function and its counterparts in business units and markets. For centralized CoE, the decision-making power lies more with the team in the group than in the business units and markets, whereas for federated CoE, it lies more with the teams in the business units and markets than in the group.

The executive leadership at omega decided to merge the CoEs for AI/genAI, data, cloud, and automation, whereas the respective CoEs at theta decided to remain standalone. The head of group CoE at omega was reporting to the CEO, and the CoE heads in the business units and markets were reporting to the respective heads, with dotted line reporting to the head of group CoE. The head of group CoE for AI/genAI at theta was reporting to the chief data officer (CDO), whereas the heads of CoE for AI/genAI for business units were reporting to the respective marketing heads. The head of CoE for AI/genAI Americas was reporting to the head of market, the head of CoE for AI/genAI EMEA was reporting to the head of marketing, and the head of CoE for AI/genAI Asia Pacific was reporting to the Head of Data.

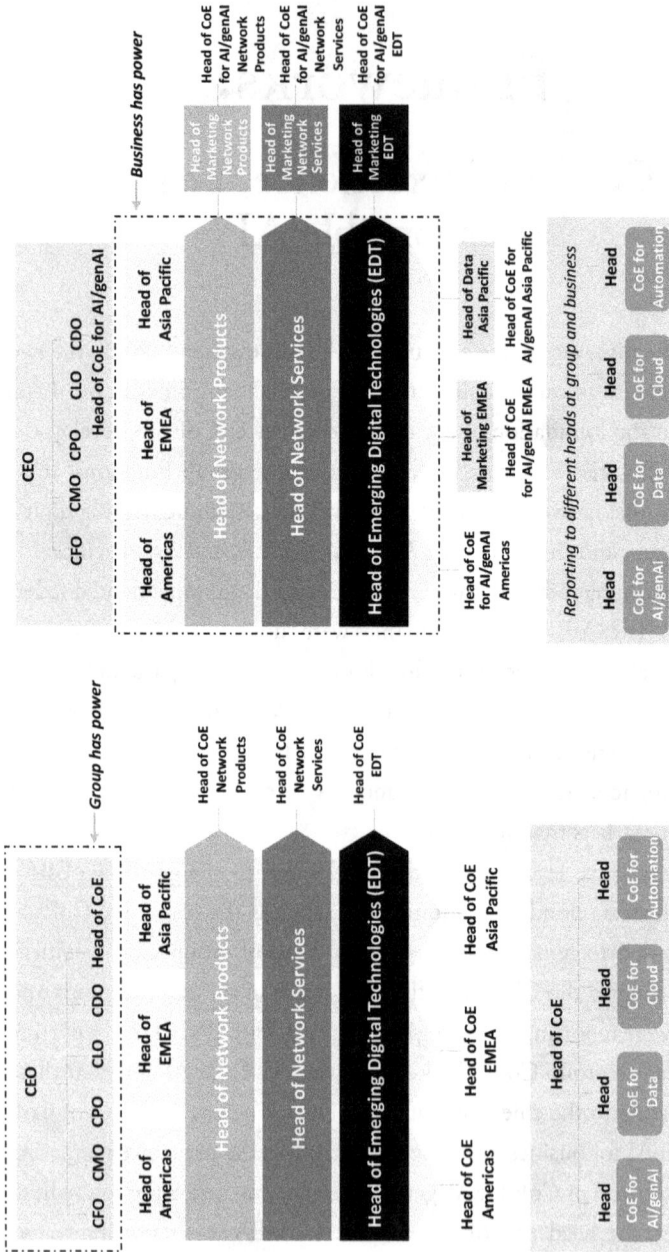

Figure 15.1 *Centralized versus federated and merged versus standalone CoEs*

So, if you want to set up a CoE for your company:

1. Should you adopt centralized or federated structure?
2. Should the head of the CoE report directly to the CEO, his or her leadership team, or a level below the leadership team?
3. Should the AI/genAI CoE be standalone with a sole focus on AI/genAI, or should it be merged with CoEs for data, AI, cloud, and other technologies like automation and analytics?

Before we answer the above questions, let us take a step back and answer the fundamental question: why is it important to establish frameworks for people in your organization?

Establishing frameworks like a CoE, legal, and responsible AI (RAI) is essential for ethical and compliant AI use within your organization, enhancing decision-making transparency and accountability, fostering trust, and mitigating risks.

Center of Excellence

The following are some of the most common objectives of CoEs across different organizations, mostly large-sized, across the globe:

- Creating a genAI vision in the company: understanding where the company is currently on the genAI maturity, where it wants to be in the next three years, and what key strategic priorities would help it reach its objectives.
- Developing an AI portfolio: creating AI and genAI offerings, use cases, capabilities, and applications that can add value to the enterprises and their customers.
- Establishing governance: managing the development of AI programs and initiatives centrally.
- Evaluating business models: deciding whether to continue with the existing business model or adopt a new one.

- Vendor selection: developing evaluation and selection criteria.
- AI upskilling and reskilling program: building the AI and genAI competence among the current employees.
- Hiring and selection: recruiting the right talents to drive AI-enabled transformation.
- Managing external communities: facilitating collaboration with universities, vendors, startups, and other sources of expertise, enabling the development of an AI ecosystem and potential investments in value-adding firms.
- Internal communications team: sharing early success stories and prioritized use cases to foster enthusiasm for driving AI adoption.
- Maintaining a network of AI evangelists and champions: engaging senior executives, key decision-makers, or influencers to take up this additional responsibility.

So, the answer to the first question is that the adoption of centralized or federated CoE depends upon the business requirements. Both come with pros and cons. The advantage of centralized CoE is that it can streamline the AI/genAI developments within an organization. The disadvantage is that it can slow down the processes and decision-making related to managing customer requirements in the markets. The advantage of federated CoE is that it can develop AI/genAI initiatives based on the customer requirements with speed and efficiency. The disadvantage is that it can fail to communicate with CoEs from other markets and reuse learnings and best practices from them.

The answer to the second question is that a clear accountability, ownership, and communication are established if the head of group CoE reports directly to the CEO and the heads of CoE in the business units and markets report to the respective heads with dotted line reporting to the head of group CoE. It sends a positive message to the whole organization that AI/genAI is highly prioritized and business is getting ready for its scaled adoption. It is very confusing if the CoEs are placed under different units in different markets. Once at one of the global telecommunications companies, it was decided by the leadership team of Operations Support Systems/Business Support Systems (OSS/BSS) unit to set up a competence readiness function to develop the internal global competence across all functions such as sales, service delivery, product management, product development, and presales. However, it was placed under sales team, which communicated a wrong message to the rest of the organization that it was a sales initiative only. It failed to manage synergies with other functions, who ran their own competence readiness programs in complete misalignment with the competence readiness function. For successful results, it should have been created as a standalone function with its head reporting to the head of OSS/BSS and a member of the OSS/BSS leadership team.

The answer to the third question is that it is very important to run the AI/genAI CoE in a merged mode combining the CoEs of other technologies too. As seen earlier, for large-scale adoption of genAI, it is important to develop the maturity of the adjacent technologies, alongside genAI, which is effectively achieved in merged mode as opposed to standalone. A study by project Excalibur shows that the chances of scaled adoption of genAI are 45 percent more when the CoEs operate in merged mode than standalone. For example, in a large global organization, the role of CDO was removed and a new role, head of CoE was created, reporting to CEO. All the CoEs were merged under one central CoE. Same structure was replicated in business units and markets. The organization was able to achieve 35 percent more efficiency.

Once the CoE is established, it is important to run regular governance meetings to monitor the progress of initiatives or projects related to AI/genAI. The governance structure is as follows:

- Core committee comprising the CEO; all the heads of CoE of group, business units, and markets; and heads of business units and markets.
- Steering committee comprising the heads of all CoEs and their direct reports or leadership team.
- Operational committee comprising the transformation drivers, program managers, project managers, and solution architects belonging to different CoEs.
- Technology tribes comprising the heads of specific technology CoEs.

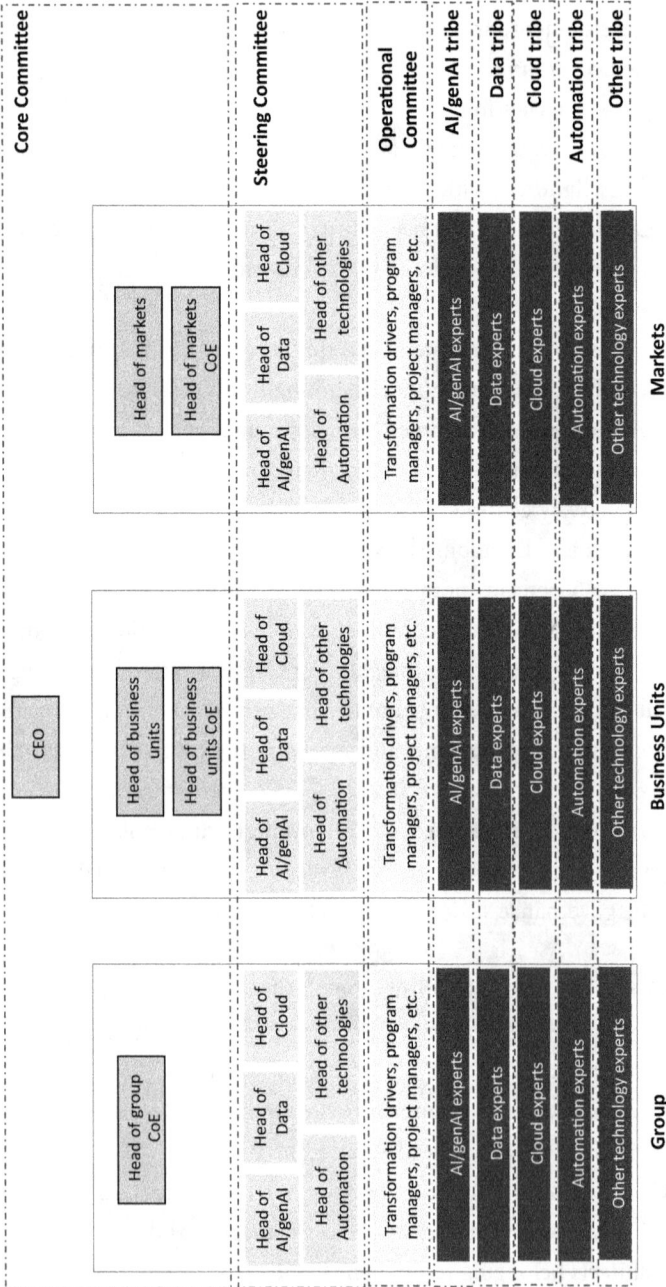

Figure 15.2 CoE governance

The frequency of governance meetings for review is as follows:

- Core committee should meet quarterly.
- Steering committee should meet monthly.
- Operational committee should meet either weekly or biweekly.
- Technology tribes should meet either weekly or biweekly.
- Besides, there should be one all-employee meeting headed by the CEO once in six months.

Legal Framework

The legal team will play a crucial role as business partners in the deployment of genAI right from sales to service delivery. In a sales deal, the legal team is typically involved late in the process, after the content has been drafted, to review and finalize the legal aspects. For genAI sales, the sales, presales, and legal teams need to work very closely, right from the leads to the opportunity phase to ensure compliance with the RAI framework of the organization and regulatory frameworks such as European Union (EU) AI Act. Currently, there are some gray areas where there are no definitive laws yet governing the use of genAI. Hence, the legal team should be consulted before making critical business decisions.

The legal framework of genAI comprises:

- Intellectual property
- Data protection and compliance ownership
- Transparency and explainability
- Confidentiality
- Individual rights

Intellectual Property

AI can process large volumes of data and generate outputs with minimal human intervention. However, there is an ongoing debate about the treatment of intellectual property and confidentiality rights related to the data used to train the AI models. Depending on the jurisdiction, the data used

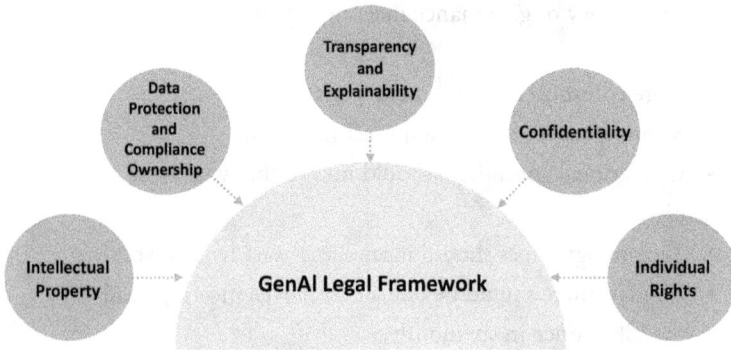

Figure 15.3 Legal framework of genAI

for training could be subject to copyright protection, potentially leading to copyright infringement if reproduced without authorization. Various jurisdictions have different exceptions to copyright laws, such as "fair use" in the United States and exceptions for transient copying and text and data mining (TDM) in the EU, making it challenging to determine which materials can be used for AI training without infringing IP rights. In the context of outputs generated by genAI, it is questionable whether these outputs can be attributed to an author since they are created by an AI system rather than a human mind. Lawmakers in each jurisdiction will need to decide whether granting copyright to the user aligns with the intent of copyright laws, especially considering that the user may not have made any original creative decisions that significantly contribute to the output.

Data Protection and Compliance Ownership

From the EU perspective, an initial step in assessing data protection concerning the use of genAI involves examining the roles of the parties involved to determine the data protection and compliance ownership. We consider three scenarios. In scenario 1, the genAI system provider—it could be an LLM provider, or genAI platform or genAI service provider, has the primary ownership to ensure that data protection and compliance are taken care of while training and testing the first layers of data. When the system providers sell or license their products to the customers, we enter scenario 2, where the customers now have the primary ownership for data protection and compliance while training and testing the model with additional layers of data. We can also have scenario 3 in some cases, where there could be a joint ownership between the genAI system providers and customers. The scenarios mentioned above have not yet been adjudicated by any court or regulatory body. Following are some of the data protection principles that can be applied in all of the above three scenarios:

Explicitness: Organizations should explain clearly in their privacy policies why and how they use data. They should explicitly state all the risks involved.

Data minimization: Organizations using genAI should adopt the minimal data usage policy, ensuring they do not use data more than required. They should consider the option of using synthetic data in place of real personal data.

Public domain data: Even if the data is available in the public domain, one must ensure that it does not violate the owner's copyrights and terms of use.

Transparency and Explainability

Transparency refers to the ability of a specific model to be understood. Explainability concentrates on providing clear and coherent explanations for specific model outputs. The EU AI Act has different rules for different risk levels: minimal risks, high risks, and unacceptable risks.

Minimal risk: This category encompasses AI systems with minimal risk to safety and fundamental rights, typically subject to minimal or no specific legal obligations.

High risk: AI applications in this category have the potential to cause significant harm or adverse effects, especially in critical sectors like infrastructure, education, law enforcement, and justice administration. These high-risk systems must comply with stringent regulatory obligations before deployment to ensure safety and protect fundamental rights.

Unacceptable risk: AI systems categorized as unacceptable risk pose significant threats to safety, livelihoods, and fundamental rights, leading to their outright ban. This includes systems that manipulate human behavior, exploit vulnerabilities, or cause physical or psychological harm to individuals or groups.

However, for AI systems bearing all levels of risk, the following transparency requirements are applicable:

- In situations where AI systems engage with individuals, those individuals should be informed that they are interacting with an AI system.
- Individuals subjected to emotion recognition or biometric categorization systems must be informed and asked for their consent before their biometric data is processed.
- For deepfake-generating systems, it must be disclosed that the content has been artificially generated or manipulated in a clearly visible manner.

The EU AI Act mandates that high-risk AI systems must provide clear and comprehensible information about their capabilities and limitations, and that their decision-making process should be transparent and traceable. Companies deploying AI solutions such as customer service chatbots and product recommendations fall under the minimal risk category. Though such companies are obligated to ensure transparency, there are no stringent regulations for explainability. However, explainable AI enables these organizations to comprehend how their AI systems make decisions and recommendations. This can help them to refine their AI systems to align with business goals, meet customer expectations, and adhere to regulatory standards.

It is not that easy to make the AI systems transparent and explainable due to their "black box" structure and design. The core characteristics that differentiate AI from prior technologies are *invisibility* and *inscrutability*. AI operates invisibly in the background of various technologies and platforms, often without users' awareness. Additionally, even developers may struggle to understand how AI models reach outcomes or identify all the data points they utilize, making AI inscrutable. These characteristics grant AI broad capabilities, allowing it to work behind the scenes and uncover patterns beyond human comprehension. Currently, there is no way to peer into the inner workings of an AI tool and guarantee that the system is producing accurate or fair output.

Confidentiality

Violation of confidentiality, whether by legal requirement or agreement, poses a risk to the rights and privacy of individuals and organizations. It's crucial to maintain data confidentiality throughout the entire life cycle of AI. GenAI models may unintentionally learn and reproduce sensitive data from the training set, potentially leading to the generation of outputs containing confidential information. If a business use case requires confidential information that has been shared by customers, suppliers, or other third parties, the business will need to first consider any duties of confidentiality and other contract terms under which the information was shared and whether they are permitted to use that data within a genAI system.

Individual Rights

These rights could involve accessing and getting a copy of personal data held by an organization, correcting any wrong information, asking for human involvement in important AI decisions, choosing not to have personal data used for certain purposes, and deleting data permanently. However, because of how genAI works, it might be difficult to set up systems that follow these rules.

A New Legal

Maria Varsellona, as the chief legal officer and company secretary at Unilever, has spearheaded a significant transformation in the delivery of legal services within the organization, focusing on efficiency, simplification, and digital enablement. Under her leadership, Unilever's legal team is undergoing a transformation aligned with the company's recent restructuring into five business groups, covering sectors from beauty and well-being to ice cream. Central to this transformation is the establishment of three global legal powerhouses located in cities like Bengaluru, Mexico City, and Barcelona, equipped with genAI tools and staffed by lawyers handling diverse legal tasks. These powerhouses offer ongoing global support to business units, enabling young lawyers to gain valuable skills and experience while enhancing efficiency and streamlining workflows. By leveraging genAI tools for research, drafting, and contract review, the legal teams optimize their time and focus on strategic legal endeavors, thereby strengthening their partnership with business colleagues and contributing to product excellence through intellectual property protection and product claim substantiation.[1] It is an example of the creation of a new *way of working* for legal.

It should be the responsibility of the CoE to ensure the legal implications of AI and genAI are addressed. A new position of *chief legal officer* should be created in the CoE, reporting to its group head of CoE. Similar positions should be replicated in the business units and markets. By doing so, the legal team can work very closely with the business. It is an example of the creation of a new *structure*.

Sales, presales, LLM experts, commercial, and legal teams should work together to ensure the best efforts in making AI transparent and explainable. It is an example of a new *collaboration*.

Sales and presales teams should reskill in the legal domain, and legal experts should have knowledge and understanding of genAI sales. It is likely that enterprises might create a new position in the future combining the sales and legal job descriptions. It is an example of the creation of a new *role*.

Responsible AI

Responsible AI (RAI) is the practice of designing, developing, and deploying AI with good intention to empower employees and enterprises and fairly impact customers and society—allowing companies to engender trust and scale AI with confidence.[2] There is no standard industrialized framework for RAI. Each business has its own framework. However, the following framework has been designed by incorporating the best RAI practices. It is built on three foundational pillars:

1. Legal
2. Ethics
3. Governance

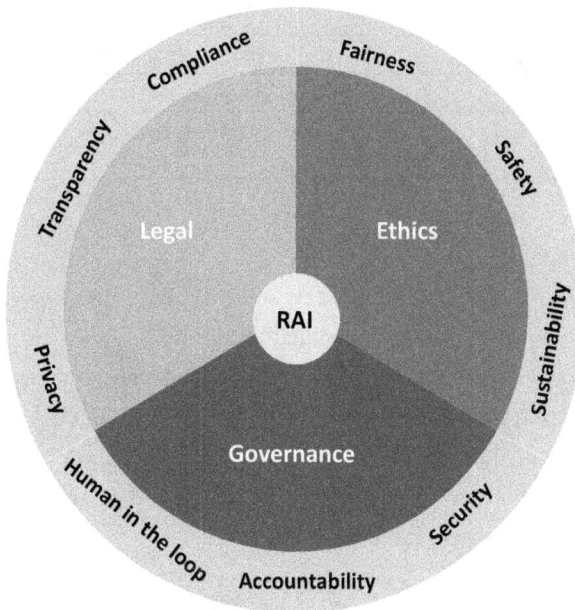

Figure 15.4 Three pillars of RAI

1. Legal
    It comprises
        Privacy: AI systems should respect individual privacy.
        Transparency: AI decisions and reasoning should be comprehensible and explicable to humans.
        Compliance: AI systems should be compliant with the regulations and policies.

Nonlegal teams in the business, such as sales, presales, service delivery, and so on, should not give any legal advice or make any commitments to the clients regarding the RAI. All the legal discussions and engagements should be driven strictly by the legal team.

Note that there is no difference between the legal framework discussed earlier and the legal pillar of RAI. It is the responsibility of the RAI team to drive the legal framework. The following table shows the mapping between them:

Legal pillar of RAI	Legal framework
Privacy	Intellectual property, Confidentiality
Transparency	Transparency and explainability
Compliance	Data protection and compliance ownership, Individual rights

2. Ethics

It comprises

Fairness: AI systems must strive to eliminate bias and guarantee fair treatment for every individual and group.

Safety: AI systems should be developed and managed to reduce risks and harms, including physical, emotional, and economic consequences.

Sustainability: AI should be created and applied in a manner that contributes positively to the society and the environment and enhances the overall welfare of humanity.

3. Governance

It comprises

Human in the loop: Human oversight should be maintained over AI systems and the decision-making procedures associated with them.

Accountability: Individuals and organizations developing and deploying AI should be held responsible for its consequences and impacts.

Security: AI systems need to be resilient to adversarial attacks and malicious exploitation.

New RAI Team

New RAI teams should be created in the group, business units, and markets, with their heads reporting to the respective CoE heads. Three new roles can be created reporting to the head of RAI:

- RAI legal lead
- RAI ethical lead
- RAI governance lead

The RAI legal lead should collaborate with the chief legal officer on the legal pillar, the RAI ethical lead should work with the business team on the ethical pillar, and the RAI governance lead should join the operational committee to oversee the governance pillar of RAI.

Who Is Responsible for AI?

It is the joint responsibility of the leaders and employees to ensure that the principles of RAI are upheld. It requires a collaborative effort where leaders set the vision and direction, while employees implement and adhere to the ethical guidelines in their day-to-day work. This joint responsibility ensures that AI technologies are developed and used in a manner that aligns with ethical standards and societal values.

Summary

- The CoEs can be centralized or federated.
- In the centralized CoE, the group has more power than business units and markets.
- In the federated CoE, the business units and markets have more power than the group.
- Merged CoEs are more efficient than the standalone ones.

- The legal framework of genAI comprises:
  - o Intellectual property
  - o Data protection and compliance ownership
  - o Transparency and explainability
  - o Confidentiality
  - o Individual rights
- Legal, ethics, and governance are the three pillars of RAI.
- Legal comprises privacy, transparency, and compliance.
- Ethics comprises fairness, safety, and sustainability.
- Governance comprises human in the loop, accountability, and security.
- It is the joint responsibility of the leaders and employees to ensure that the principles of RAI are upheld.

CHAPTER 16

Reskilling:

Motivating People, Matching Roles, Personalizing Learning

In one of the Nordic-based global companies, there was an upskilling and reskilling program introduced by HR, for around 1,000 software developers in the EU market, before the pandemic. Out of around 1,000 software developers, 40 percent were front-end developers, 50 percent were back-end developers, and the remaining 10 percent were full-stack developers. A front-end software developer specializes in designing and implementing the user interface and user experience of web applications, focusing on client-side programming languages such as HTML, CSS, and JavaScript. A back-end software developer specializes in developing the server-side logic and database interactions of web applications, using languages such as Python, Java, Ruby, or PHP. A full-stack software developer is proficient in both front-end and back-end development, capable of working on all aspects of web application development from the user interface to the server-side logic. The upskilling program gave all the software developers an opportunity to develop the lacking skillsets. For example, a front-end software developer can learn the back-end development programming languages and make a progression toward becoming a full-stack developer and vice versa. The reskilling program focused on developing data science competence, which gave all the software developers an opportunity to develop skills outside their areas of expertise and become data scientists. The enrollment in the reskilling program was optional. In the first six months of the program launch, only 10 percent of the developers enrolled, out of which 97 percent enrolled in upskilling and only 3 percent enrolled in reskilling. During the pandemic times, when the company decided to do job cuts, the percentage of enrollment

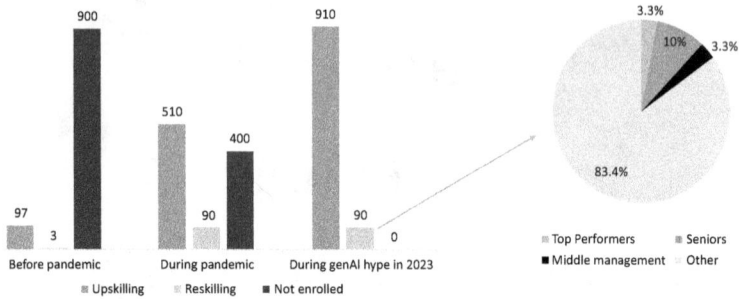

Figure 16.1 Survey of 1,000 software developers

increased to 60 percent, out of which around 85 percent enrolled in upskilling, while 15 percent enrolled in reskilling. In 2023, in the midst of genAI hype, the company made the upskilling and reskilling program mandatory for all the developers. The final enrollment count was 91 percent in the upskilling and only 9 percent in the reskilling, which means out of 1,000 developers, 910 stayed in their areas of domain expertise, whereas 90 decided to pivot their careers into the new domain of data science. Furthermore, out of the 90, only 3 (3.3 percent) were top performers and had won the annual software developer excellence awards more than once, only 9 (10 percent) were senior developers with experience close to 15 years, and only 3 (3.3 percent) were in the middle management: two solution architects and one project manager.

The survey reveals some interesting facts about an employee's approach toward learning. It shows that most of the employees are extrinsically motivated to learn, driven by external factors such as fear of job loss due to pandemic or mandate by the organization. Few are intrinsically motivated to learn. Among those who are motivated either extrinsically or intrinsically, only a few explore new areas outside their domain of expertise or reskill. Most people prefer to stay within their skilled domains. The motivation to reskill in a new area is much less if you are a top performer or at a higher management in your domain. This is proven by the survey results shown in Figure 16.2, which shows that 3 out of 42 top performers, 9 out of 109 seniors, and 3 out of 330 middle management enrolled in reskilling.

In the age of AI, it is very crucial to reskill toward AI, cloud, and data. Every employee is at least expected to know the basics of these

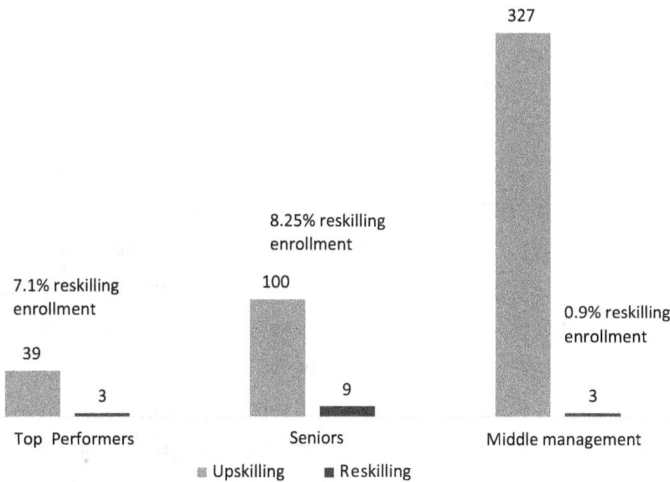

Figure 16.2 Enrollments in reskilling

technologies. In the context of genAI, every professional must know some foundational concepts of genAI, such as what it is, how it works, and what are its short-term and long-term implications on business and society. The average half-life of skills is now less than five years, and in some tech fields, it's as low as two and a half years. *Half-life* refers to the time it takes for skills or knowledge in a particular field to become obsolete or outdated by half. For millions of workers, upskilling alone won't be enough. Some companies now consider reskilling a core part of their employee value proposition and a strategic means of balancing workforce supply and demand. For example, Infosys has reskilled more than 2,000 cybersecurity experts with various adjacent competencies and capability levels. Amazon, through its machine learning university, has enabled thousands of employees who initially had little experience in machine learning to become experts in the field. ICICI Bank, headquartered in Mumbai, employing more than 130,000 people, every year reskills 2,500 to 4,000 employees, mostly graduates from diverse backgrounds for frontline managerial jobs, through an intense academy-like reskilling program.[1]

To ensure successful reskilling, the organizations must:

1. Motivate people toward reskilling.
2. Match individual roles to new roles.
3. Devise a personalized learning plan or pathway for individuals.

Motivating People

Reskilling initiatives are frequently met with apprehension by leaders due to concerns about organizational upheaval and potential job displacement or reassignment. Consequently, they often refrain from openly discussing the purpose and benefits of such programs. Employees are more likely to participate if they comprehend the rationale behind the programs and have been involved in their development. As indicated by a recent report by BCG, just 24 percent of surveyed companies establish a direct link between their corporate strategy and reskilling initiatives.[2] Investing in reskilling requires HR leaders to be fully committed. However, if the broader organization doesn't recognize its importance, gaining commitment for the effort required to make these initiatives successful becomes challenging. Generally, the middle managers who work under strict deadlines and pressures are resistant to the idea of reskilling. They are concerned about the following:

- Their team members won't manage their usual tasks while getting reskilled.
- It could be costly and logistically challenging to take their team members away from their daily jobs to participate in training.
- After being reskilled, their team members might leave for other parts of the company or even outside the company.
- The reskilled employees won't bring in the same level of competence and work efficiency as compared to the traditionally skilled employee.

This can cause *talent hoarding*, where managers try to keep their favorite team members by not letting them take part in reskilling.

Thus, it is important to motivate people about reskilling, which can be done as follows:

- Creating AI reskilling awareness
- Cultivating growth mindset
- Managing middle managers
- Continuous coaching and mentoring

Creating AI Reskilling Awareness

The right awareness should be created in the organization for employees at all levels to address the apprehension toward the impact of AI by addressing the following questions:

- Why is AI reskilling important for every employee?
- How does AI reskilling contribute toward the corporate strategy?
- How would an employee and organization benefit from reskilling?
- Why is it important to also reskill in adjacent technologies such as cloud, data, and automation?

While not all knowledge workers will face job loss in the future, many may find that AI and other emerging technologies have changed their tasks so much that they are essentially working in entirely new areas. It is not that AI will replace human jobs. But those who work with AI will replace those who don't work.

Cultivating Growth Mindset

As per the research by Carol Dweck, there are two mindsets, fixed and growth, that determine our attitude toward learning and eventually our career success. People with fixed mindsets believe that skills are born, whereas people with growth mindsets feel that skills are built. People with a fixed mindset focus on the outcome or results. They are more concerned or worried about how they would look or feel if they fail to learn a new skill. People with a growth mindset focus on the process of learning, without worrying much about the outcomes. They focus on how to get better and better every single day. Usually, the top performers or the seniors in the team have fixed mindsets. They are so comfortable in the bubble of success or seniority that they don't want to try something new outside their area of expertise. To enable reskilling, it is important to change their mindsets from fixed to growth by making them aware of the importance of AI or genAI for the future of the business and their personal careers. In my book *Digital Leadership Framework,* I have explained how to cultivate a growth mindset.

Managing Middle Managers

To avoid talent hoarding by middle managers, it is important to make talent management and development a managerial responsibility, besides solely an HR responsibility. For example, companies such as Wipro assess managers based on their teams' involvement in training opportunities, while Amazon advances leaders through a performance evaluation that considers their contributions to their team's development. One of the best ways to secure commitment and support from the middle managers is to involve them in the reskilling programs.

Continuous Coaching and Mentoring

Reskilling programs require time investment and a strong commitment from the employees. Most of the employees are reluctant to participate as they find it difficult to take time from their busy work and personal life schedules. Another reason is that some employees may find some concepts too technical and difficult to grasp due to their nontechnical backgrounds. This can be overcome by offering them continuous coaching and mentoring through their learning journeys, even before they enroll in a reskilling program. An IT company has introduced the concept of genAI office hours, where the employees who have enrolled in the reskilling programs or would like to enroll in one, can book 15-to-30-minute slots to interact with the experts. This has helped them stay motivated and focused on the program.

Matching Roles

Employees should be aligned with suitable new positions. When their destination roles are clearly outlined beforehand and if the program is centered around the needs and benefits of employees more than the needs and benefits of an organization, they show greater interest in reskilling. For example, Amazon's career choice program enables employees to pursue various educational opportunities, ranging from bachelor's degrees to certificates, with all expenses covered upfront. This approach has played a significant role in expanding the program, which has seen over 130,000 participants already.[3] The matching of roles involves the following three steps:

1. Creating attractive roles
2. Assessing skills gap
3. Presenting new role options

1. Creating attractive roles
Organizations can either create attractive roles for the employees by creating completely new roles that require AI skillsets or by adding AI skillsets in the existing ones.

Some of the proposed roles are shown in the tables below:

Specialized technical roles	Description
AI/genAI developer	To develop AI or genAI applications or agents using the latest coding languages
LLM fine-tuner	To pretrain, fine-tune, and custom-tune an LLM using best tuning practices
LLM evaluator	To evaluate the LLM outputs and provide fine-tuning and guardrail development recommendations
LLM designer	To design an LLM or Small Language Model (SLM) architecture
Prompt engineer	To design best-in-class prompts to generate relevant output
LLMOps specialist	To manage the deployment, maintenance, and optimization of LLM to ensure their reliable and efficient operation within an organization's infrastructure
MLOps specialist	To oversee the deployment, monitoring, and optimization of machine learning models to ensure their scalability, reliability, and efficiency in production environments
AI tester	To develop test cases and ensure quality assurance of AI/genAI applications
AI solution architect	To design and implement AI/genAI solutions as per specific business requirements

Specialized technical roles	Description
Data scientist	To manage the overall process of acquiring, preparing, and processing data for LLM
Data engineer	To clean and prepare data for LLM
Data analyst	To analyze the input and output LLM data to develop insights
Cloud architect	To design and implement a cloud infrastructure to host data and AI/genAI applications
Cloud developer	To develop cloud applications and platforms using latest coding languages
Automation expert	To manage end-to-end processes for AI/genAI, cloud, and data using methodologies such as continuous integration and continuous deployment (CI/CD)

Generic technical roles	Description
DAC solution architect	To design and implement an overall DAC solution
DAC migration expert	To manage migrations of data and IT applications cloud
DAC engineer	To develop, test, and deploy DAC solutions
DAC industry SME	To develop and deploy DAC solutions to a specific industry
DAC infrastructure expert	To manage infrastructure for DAC solutions
System integration expert	To integrate and configure DAC solutions into the existing IT environment
Platform engineer	To develop a platform to host DAC applications and solutions

Note that DAC stands for data, AI, and cloud.

Specialized managerial roles	Description
AI/genAI strategy manager	To develop AI/genAI strategy for a business unit or entire organization
AI consultant	To develop AI/genAI business case, value propositions, and operational roadmap
Data strategy manager	To develop data strategy for a business unit or entire organization
Data consultant	To develop data business case, value propositions, and operational roadmap

Specialized managerial roles	Description
Cloud strategy manager	To develop cloud strategy for a business unit or entire organization
Cloud consultant	To develop cloud business case, value propositions, and operational roadmap
Automation strategy manager	To develop automation strategy for a business unit or entire organization
Automation consultant	To develop automation business case, value propositions and operational roadmap
DAC sales manager	To sell DAC solutions to clients
DAC legal advisor	To offer legal expertise in selling DAC solutions to clients
DAC LLM presales manager	To offer technical LLM expertise in selling DAC solutions to clients
DAC commercial manager	To offer commercial expertise in selling DAC solutions to clients

Generic managerial roles	Description
DAC program manager	To execute an organizationwide DAC transformation program
DAC project manager	To drive a specific DAC project, a part of the overall transformation program
DAC transformation expert	To strategize and execute an organizationwide DAC transformation program
DAC industry transformation expert	To strategize and execute an industry-specific DAC transformation program
Responsible AI Lead	To ensure execution and governance of the RAI framework in an organization
DAC sales expert	To ensure coordination between sales, presales, legal, and commercial during DAC sales

Note that the organizations can customize the above roles or create new ones as per their business requirements.

2. Assessing skills gap

Every company should create a skill list, known as *skill taxonomy*. It's a structured way to identify and measure the abilities of a business. Companies can develop their own skill taxonomies or source them from external providers. For instance, HSBC has incorporated the skill list developed by the World Economic Forum with some adjustments to include skills relevant to its various departments. Likewise,

SAP, previously managing its own skill list of 7,000 items, has partnered with Lightcast, a platform that continuously maintains an
updated database of skills.[4]

Figure 16.3 shows the sample skills taxonomy for genAI. Organizations can customize them or create new ones based on their business
requirements.

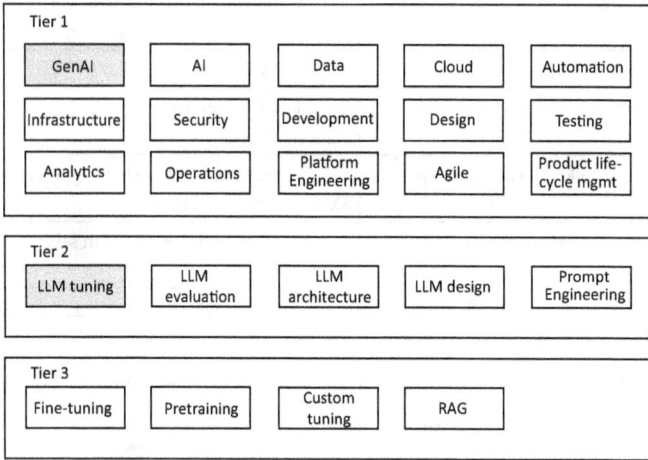

Figure 16.3 Skills taxonomy

For every skill, there are four levels: not started, beginner, intermedi-
ate, and advanced. Upskilling involves moving upwards to higher levels
for a specific skill. Reskilling involves moving horizontally or diagonally
downwards from one skill to another as shown in Figure 16.4. One
always starts from the beginner level while reskilling, which means one

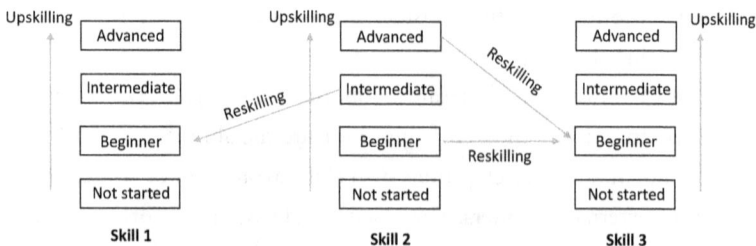

Figure 16.4 Upskilling and reskilling

can move only diagonally down from higher levels and horizontally from the beginner level of other skills. It is not possible to move horizontally: intermediate-to-intermediate or advanced-to-advanced or diagonally up, from one skill to another.

The skills gap analysis can be done using the following:

- For every individual, use the skills matrix below to fill in the current and future technical and nontechnical skills.

	Technical skills	Nontechnical skills
Current	- Skill 1 - Skill 2 - Skill... n	- Skill 1 - Skill 2 - Skill... n
Future	- Skill 1 - Skill 2 - Skill... n	- Skill 1 - Skill 2 - Skill... n

- For every technical and nontechnical skill, do the gap analysis using the sheet below:

Current skill	Gap analysis	Future skill
Skill description	• Identify the gaps between the skills. • Write down the steps to be taken to bridge the gap.	Skill description

3. Presenting new role options

Employees show strong motivation to reskill if they are provided with the visibility on new roles. It is important to analyze the skills gap between the current role and the future new role.

Use the sheet below:

Current role	Gap analysis	Future role
Skill 1 description	• Identify the gaps between the roles. • Write down the steps to be taken to bridge the gap.	Skill 1 description
Skill 2 description		Skill 2 description
...Skill n description		...Skill n description

Personalized Learning

Once the new role is identified for an employee, it is important to have a personalized learning plan. It enhances engagement and motivation of employees by aligning training with their specific interests and career goals, leading to higher productivity and job satisfaction. This tailored approach fosters a culture of learning and development, ultimately driving organizational success.

Key elements of a personalized learning plan include:

1. Individual courses: Tailored courses that address specific skill gaps or areas of interest for the employee.
2. Learning pathways: Curated sequences of courses or training modules designed to support career progression or skill development goals.
3. Certifications: Opportunities for employees to earn recognized certifications in relevant areas, validating their expertise and enhancing their credentials.
4. Job rotations: Structured opportunities for employees to gain experience in different roles or departments within the organization, broadening their skillset and perspective.
5. On-the-job training (OJT): Hands-on experiences, projects, or assignments that allow employees to apply newly acquired knowledge and skills in real-world scenarios, facilitating deeper learning and mastery.
6. Coaching and mentorship programs: Pairing employees with experienced coaches and mentors who can provide guidance, advice, and support as they navigate their career paths and personal development goals.

Group Activity

With the key stakeholders in your organization, based on the guidelines provided in this chapter:

1. Discuss the right strategy to motivate people using the following guiding questions:
   a. Have you launched a reskilling program before? What was the experience?
   b. Are people aware of the importance of reskilling?

c. Is there a high willingness to learn and grow among the people?

d. Are managers supportive? Do they encourage reskilling?

e. Do you provide coaching and mentoring?

2. Develop new matching roles for employees based on their skills and interests, using the following guiding questions:

a. Are the roles attractive? How do you measure the attractiveness?

b. Do you have tools to assess the skills gap on a large scale?

c. Do you have a skills taxonomy?

d. Are you providing enough career progression options for people?

3. Create a personalized learning plan for all the individuals, using the following guiding questions:

a. Does the personalized learning plan include all the elements?

b. Are people motivated to learn?

c. Do we collect continuous feedback from people?

Summary

- Motivating people about reskilling can be done by creating AI reskilling awareness, cultivating growth mindset, managing middle managers, and continuous coaching and mentoring.

- The matching of roles involves the following three steps:

  1. Creating attractive roles

  2. Assessing skills gap

  3. Presenting new role options

- Upskilling involves moving upwards to higher levels for a specific skill.

- Reskilling involves moving horizontally or diagonally downwards from one skill to another.

- The key elements of personalized learning include individual courses, learning pathways, certifications, job rotations, OJT, and coaching and mentorship programs.

CHAPTER 17

Leadership:

Right Balancing, Cultivating Competencies, Championing GenAI

Imagine you are the CEO of a leading European-based tech firm; let us call it VisionTech. The financial health of your firm is not looking good. It has faced losses for three consecutive quarters. Your job is at risk. You desperately want to turn around the business and make it profitable. Recently, your firm has developed an AI-driven sophisticated facial recognition product designed for law enforcement agencies in several EU states. The product promises unprecedented accuracy in identifying suspects, aiding in crime prevention and public safety. You have signed deals worth millions of euros with a distributor, who would resell the product to law enforcement agencies. It is a great opportunity not only for your company to turn around its business but also for you as CEO to build your brand and reputation as a global business leader in AI.

However, as the launch date approaches, you receive troubling reports from your team about potential biases in the algorithm, particularly in its recognition of individuals from minority communities. The only way to address this problem is to delay the product launch by a quarter and invest significant resources in implementing guardrails to address these biases. The installation of these guardrails would incur substantial costs, both financial and temporal, requiring extensive retraining of the algorithm and rigorous testing to ensure fairness and accuracy across all demographic groups. Additionally, the company would need to navigate intricate legal and regulatory frameworks governing the use of facial recognition technology, further adding to the complexity and expense of the endeavor.

Your legal team has advised you not to move ahead with the launch without addressing the bias issues, as they fall under the *high-risk* category as per the EU AI Act. The fines would be huge for failing to conduct adequate risk assessments. You discuss with your executive team. All of them advise you to delay the launch and invest in ethical guardrails, because it could position the company as a leader in RAI development, earning the trust and loyalty of both customers and stakeholders. Finally, you turn to your board members. One of them asks you to check with the distributor if they are fine with the delay in launch by a quarter. At the meeting, the distributor warns you that if the launch is delayed, your company might lose the contract and it might go to your competitors. Disappointed, you bring this matter before the board. You have a very difficult discussion with them. If this deal is lost, there would be another two quarters of losses, resulting in heavy downsizing. You might also lose your job as the CEO. Your board advises you to roll out the product with biases at the announced launch date and fix these issues later during the product maintenance and upgrades. They tell you to be discreet about this matter and brush it under the carpet. To make it easier for you, they even offer you alluring monetary incentives in the form of equity.

You weigh all the options. You find yourself conflicted between the ambitious you and the ethical you. The ethical you tells you not to move ahead. There could be public backlash, legal challenges, and damage to the company's reputation and your reputation as the CEO. The ambitious you tells you that it is a great opportunity to outsmart your competitors, turn around your business, grow your equity value, and shine as a global AI business leader.

What decision will you make? Will you go ahead with the launch? What will you select: profits or ethics?

Right Balancing

Right balancing involves choosing the right balance between AI profits and AI ethics. As a leader, you bear the ultimate responsibility for ensuring both profitability and ethical conduct. This requires navigating complex decisions where short-term gains must be weighed against long-term ethical implications, all while upholding the values and integrity of your organization. The decisions that are profitable and ethical in the near and long term are easy choices for leaders. But choices become difficult when leaders must decide between what is ethical but not profitable, and what is profitable but not ethical. In choosing ethics over profits, leaders must assess a term called *acceptable loss*. It indicates the amount of loss you are willing to absorb. If the choice exceeds the acceptable loss limits, then it is a no-go. In choosing profits over ethics, leaders must do an *ethical risk assessment*. It indicates the degree of ethical risk. If the ethical risk is minimal or limited, then it is a go. But if it is a high or unacceptable risk, it is a no-go. The choices become even more difficult when choosing between ethical and non-ethical and short-term loss but long-term gain or short-term gain but long-term loss.

There are four profit–ethics possibilities as shown in the matrix:

1. Short-term loss but long-term gain, non-ethical: acceptable loss and ethical risk assessments
2. Short-term gain but long-term loss, non-ethical: acceptable loss and ethical risk assessments
3. Short-term loss but long-term gain, ethical: acceptable loss assessment
4. Short-term gain but long-term loss, ethical: acceptable loss assessment

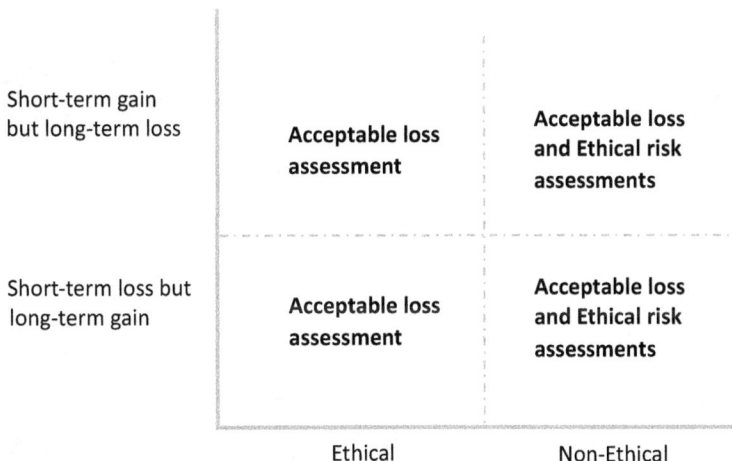

Figure 17.1 Profit–ethics matrix

The leaders should seek guidance from the RAI ethics team within the CoE in preparing an ethical risk assessment.

Cultivating Competencies

In a survey by project Excalibur, the case described at the beginning of this chapter was presented to 150 business leaders across the globe: Americas, EMEA, and Asia Pacific. Their responses were collected anonymously. It contained a question: Would you go ahead with the launch?

Out of 150 participants, 62 percent said *no*, whereas 38 percent said *yes*. Among those who said no, 47 were from EMEA, 25 were from Asia Pacific, and 21 were from Americas. Among those who said yes, 26 were from Americas, 22 were from Asia Pacific, and 9 were from EMEA.

Those who said yes were asked further the reason for doing so. To which most of them replied that since the product was to be used by law enforcement agencies and not by the enterprises, they saw fewer implications of bias or harm. They were further asked if they would have proceeded with the launch had the product been intended for commercial use. The number of 'yes' dropped from 38 to 15 percent.

Further studies revealed that the 62 percent who said no to the first question scored relatively higher on the competency rating for the following four key competencies of a digital leader: growth mindset, empathy, informed decision-making, and fast execution, as stated in my book, *Digital Leadership Framework*. The 15 percent who still maintained their 'yes' scored the lowest on the competency rating, especially on empathy.

These competencies are important for an AI leader to cultivate as they drive key behaviors that can enable scaled adoption of genAI. Growth

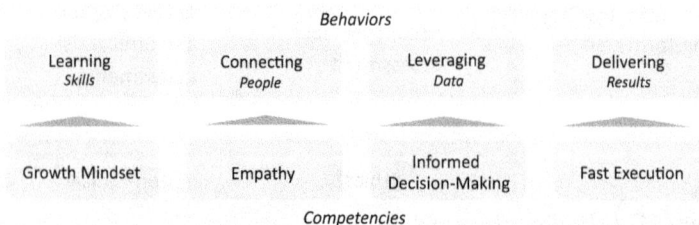

Figure 17.2 Relationship between competencies and behaviors

mindset enables learning, empathy enables people connections, informed decision-making enables leveraging data, and fast execution enables delivering results.

Please refer to my book, *Digital Leadership Framework*, to understand more on how to cultivate these competencies.

Championing GenAI

Business leaders play a crucial role in driving the scaled adoption and integration of genAI within the organization. Without support from the top management, the chances of its success are very low. By championing genAI, leaders can foster a culture of innovation, efficiency, and competitive advantage while ensuring alignment with strategic objectives. Following are some of the best practices:

1. Set a clear vision: articulate a clear vision for genAI adoption aligned with business objectives.
2. Drive cultural change: foster a culture of innovation and data-driven decision-making to embrace genAI initiatives.
3. Invest in talent: invest in AI/genAI talent recruitment, training, and development to build internal expertise.
4. Provide resources: allocate sufficient resources, including budget and technology infrastructure, to support AI projects.
5. Promote collaboration: facilitate collaboration between different teams and departments to leverage genAI capabilities across the organization.
6. Ensure ethical use: establish guidelines and processes for the ethical development and deployment of genAI technologies.
7. Measure impact: define key performance indicators to measure the impact of genAI initiatives on business outcomes.
8. Communicate value: communicate the value of genAI initiatives to stakeholders, including employees, customers, and investors.
9. Adapt to change: remain agile and adaptive to changes in technology and market dynamics to capitalize on new genAI opportunities.
10. Lead by example: lead by example by embracing genAI technologies yourself and demonstrating their value in driving business success.

The Rule of 3

Normally, it is observed that the power in any organization follows the rule of 3—it is concentrated in the hands of three people. They are the ones who carry maximum weight and can influence the outcome of any decision. It is a common phenomenon in any group or team meeting. The top three people, or *heavyweights*, normally drive and influence the outcome of the meeting. We have seen in Chapter 3 that the weights increase as we move up the corporate hierarchy. And at the top, it is again three who have maximum weights than most others. One of them is the CEO, and the other two are his/her trusted advisors: the right hand and the left hand. And in most cases, these three individuals are allies of each other.

How AI will phase out in the future? Will it benefit humanity or do more harm? It depends on the decisions made by the top three heavyweights. If they choose the wrong balance between profits and ethics, it will cause harm. If they get the right balance, it will benefit individuals, businesses, societies, and the environment. However, right balancing is not easy. In fact, it is going to be the toughest challenge faced by a leader in the near future. Thus,

Leadership is the launchpad of genAI.

Summary

- Right balancing involves choosing the right balance between AI profits and AI ethics.
- In choosing ethics over profits, leaders must assess a term called acceptable loss.
- In choosing profits over ethics, leaders must do an ethical risk assessment.
- The leaders should seek guidance from the RAI ethics team within the CoE in preparing an ethical risk assessment.
- Growth mindset, empathy, informed decision-making, and fast execution are the important competencies for an AI leader to cultivate as they drive key behaviors that can enable scaled adoption of genAI.

- By championing genAI, leaders can foster a culture of innovation, efficiency, and competitive advantage while ensuring alignment with strategic objectives.
- *Leadership is the launchpad of genAI.*

SUMMARY OF PART 6

Readiness Area

People

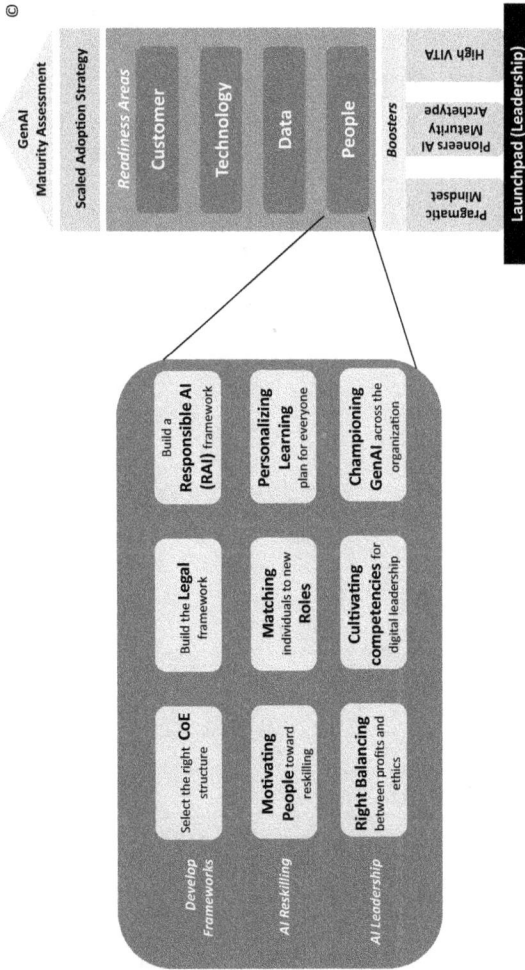

GenAI Maturity Assessment

Scaled Adoption Strategy

Readiness Areas
- Customer
- Technology
- Data
- People

Boosters

High VITA

Pioneers AI Maturity Archetype

Pragmatic Mindset

Launchpad (Leadership)

Readiness Rocket

Develop Frameworks
- Select the right **CoE** structure
- Build the **Legal** framework
- Build a **Responsible AI (RAI)** framework

AI Reskilling
- **Motivating People** toward reskilling
- **Matching** individuals to new **Roles**
- **Personalizing Learning** plan for everyone

AI Leadership
- **Right Balancing** between profits and ethics
- **Cultivating competencies** for digital leadership
- **Championing GenAI** across the organization

## PART 7

Practical Application of Operational Readiness Framework

CHAPTER 18

Talent XYZ:

A Fictitious Case Study

It was the third week of April 2023. People were back in the office from the Easter holidays. Achintya, the CEO of Talent XYZ, a Stockholm-based human resource management (HRM) software company, was leading the first executive leadership meeting of the second quarter. The hot topic on the agenda was genAI. Since the launch of ChatGPT in November 2022, Talent XYZ had been in the discovery phase, exploring the technology, and had not taken any action. Achintya, being a doer and a risk-taker, wanted to take some action. Joining him in the meeting room was Vrinda, the AI transformation consultant at Digiculum, a Stockholm-based firm offering digital transformation services such as consulting, learning, and ecosystem orchestration. Digiculum was the digital transformation partner of Talent XYZ.

Earlier, during the pandemic, Digiculum had proposed a new structure for Talent XYZ to support digital transformation, retaining the workforce of 2,500 employees located in 12 countries across the globe. The headcount was still the same.

The executives at Talent XYZ were planning to experiment with non-convertible pilots. However, Vrinda quickly dismissed their plan and instead proposed before them a scaled adoption with two tracks: convertible pilot or genAI solution, together with the readiness rocket.

While the executives were deciding which option to choose, Vrinda suggested that they start with operational readiness. A one-day workshop was planned with the L1 and L2 leadership teams, the following week, at an offsite location.

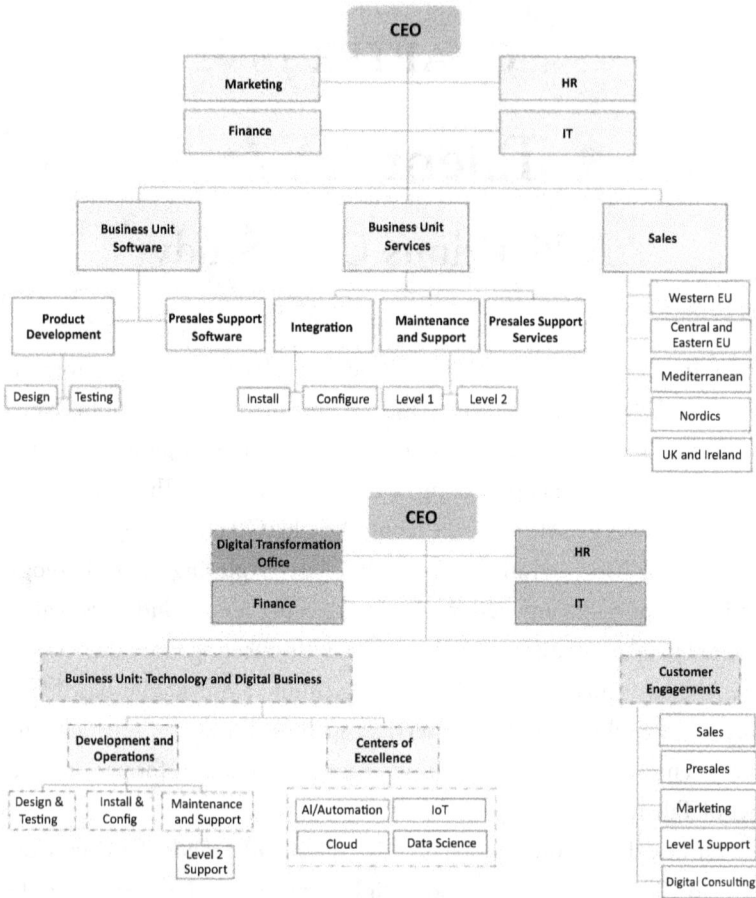

Figure 18.1 Old and new organization chart of Talent XYZ

Note: Boxes in dotted lines show the changes

The L1 leadership comprises:
- Maria, head of digital transformation office
- Dario, head of finance
- Anna, head of HR
- Sandeep, head of IT
- Hardik, head of business unit: technology and digital business
- John, head of customer engagements

The L2 leadership comprises:

- Ricky, head of development and operations
- Farah, head of centers of excellence (CoE)
- Maurice, head of sales
- Angel, head of presales
- Wenhong, head of marketing
- Sanne, head of level 1 support
- Vineet, head of digital consulting

A week before the workshop, Vrinda emailed the links to the online genAI maturity and AI maturity assessments to the key stakeholders, including L1 and L2. She also emailed the link to the AI/GenAI mindset assessment to the entire organization. Both assessments had to be completed and submitted within the next three days.

GenAI Maturity Assessment

The final average genAI maturity of Talent XYZ was at Level 2. Vrinda shared the results with Achintya. The results did not surprise him much. He was eager to see what solution Vrinda had to offer at the workshop. Achintya emailed all L1 and L2 leaders, urging them to prioritize this workshop.

It was Monday, the day of the workshop. After the round of welcomes, Vrinda quickly jumped onto the first item on the agenda, genAI maturity assessment. The final average score was 2.2. It did not surprise the audience either.

It was decided to raise the genAI maturity level to 4 within 24 months.

Scaled Adoption Strategy

Next, Vrinda asked if the team had decided on the track for the scaled adoption strategy—convertible pilot or genAI solution.

"We are yet to decide," replied Achintya.

She started the situation analysis with the participants. Following was the response:

Situation analysis	Questions
Industry	1. What is the level of genAI hype in our industry? >> Very high. 2. What are the popular genAI use cases for our industry? >> Chatbot using RAG. 3. Are there any regulatory or compliance requirements specific to our industry that may impact the implementation of genAI solutions? >> EU AI Act.
Customer	1. What are the main needs and pain points of our customers that could potentially be addressed by genAI? >> New content, new experiences, better efficiency, reduced costs. 2. What percentage of our customers are in the piloting phase? What is their feedback or experience? >> 30 percent. There are challenges with data. 3. What percentage of our customers are in the discovery phase? What is their feedback or experience? >> 70 percent. They have adopted a wait-and-see approach.
Process	1. What specific processes could be impacted by genAI? >> Sales, service delivery, customer support. 2. Are there any potential risks? >> Higher costs of implementation, inaccuracies of genAI output. 3. By how much can the lead times be reduced? >> 70 percent.
Data	1. Are we aware of our critical data? >> No. 2. Where is it located? >> Scattered across multiple locations. 3. Is it easily accessible? >> No.
People	1. What is the current AI, data, and cloud competence? >> Low. 2. Are people eager to develop genAI competence? >> Not many. 3. Are there any reskilling programs in place? >>No.

Situation analysis	Questions
IT tools and infrastructure	1. Do we have adequate IT infrastructure and tools to support genAI initiatives? >> No. 2. Are there any gaps in our existing IT capabilities that need to be addressed? >> Not sure. 3. Are our IT systems scalable to support genAI? >> Not sure.

After discussing with the team, the following strategic priorities were discussed:

Analysis	Preliminary strategic priorities	Final strategic priorities
Industry/Customer	1. AI/genAI-driven products 2. Convertible pilots 3. GenAI solution	2. or 3. (undecided)
Process	4. Automate wherever possible 5. Automate customer support 6. Invest in automation tools	Automate wherever possible
People	7. AI/genAI reskilling 8. Upskilling 9. Invest in learning and development	AI/genAI reskilling
Data	10. Data acquisition and cleaning 11. Data-driven decision-making 12. Data security	Data acquisition and cleaning
IT tools and infrastructure	13. Invest in AI/genAI tools 14. Build AI/genAI capabilities 15. Digitalize core IT	Build AI/genAI capabilities

The participants were unable to decide between the final strategic priority for industry/customer.

"Let us evaluate the pros and cons of convertible pilot v genAI solution," said Vrinda.

"With genAI solution, we would start with MVP and develop it incrementally further. We estimate the scope, budget, timelines, and risks to be much larger than the convertible pilot. Do we even have the right competence?" asked Vineet.

"No, we don't," replied Ricky.

"Do we even know which use case to select if we go for convertible pilot option?" asked Hardik. "Same goes for genAI solution," said Farah.

"Let us park this for the moment," said Vrinda.

Boosters

The following table shows the net mindset scores of Talent XYZ based on the assessment outcome:

Mindset	Score
Net optimistic score	2.13
Net skeptic score	1.97
Net pragmatic score	1.65

The overall mindset of the organization was optimistic. The total executives (L1 and L2) were 14, middle management (L3, L4, L5) was 556, and lower management was 1,930.

The table below shows the mindset split:

Head counts	Executives	Middle management	Lower management	Total
Optimistic	8	166	868	1,042
Skeptic	5	269	552	826
Pragmatic	1	121	510	632

The table below shows the mindset split percentagewise:

Percentage	Executives (%)	Middle management (%)	Lower management (%)
Optimistic	0.76	15.93	83.3
Skeptic	0.6	32.56	66.82
Pragmatic	0.15	19.14	80.69

Out of 2,500, 632 people had pragmatic mindset. The executives and middle management with higher weights comprised only 19.3 percent. This was the reason behind low net pragmatic score of 1.65.

The overall target pragmatic score to be achieved is ≥ 2.2.

Vrinda recommended the instructor-led course Cultivating AI/GenAI Mindset by Digiculum.

Vrinda started with Booster 2: AI maturity. She displayed the following average AI maturity assessment result. The average AI understanding score was 60, and the AI adoption score was 37.

The AI maturity archetype was investigators, with medium AI understanding and low AI adoption.

"Our customers gave us feedback that our product lacks AI capabilities as compared to our competitors. We were not proactive enough," said Angel.

"There was less development budget for AI. We couldn't do much," said Ricky.

"We had to prioritize fund allocations for current business," said Dario.

"We will prioritize AI/genAI going forward," said Achintya.

Vrinda said:

While you develop genAI capabilities, it is also possible to build the ones for the traditional AI. We need to upgrade Talent XYZ to the AI maturity archetype of pioneers from investigators. You lie in the investigators– optimistic (IO) zone in the archetype–mindset map. Our target is to bring you to pioneers–pragmatic (PiP) zone. I have some suggestions. Make sure you create an enterprisewide AI strategy, which should be primarily driven by the executives. You can start building AI capabilities in the customer-facing functions and cultivate AI competence through reskilling programs.

Next, she moved to Booster 3: VITA.

"We have the HRM software, our mainstream product. It has 7 key modules: hiring, onboarding, developing, appraising, compensating, retaining, and exiting We have two services: install and config, and maintenance and support. The product comprises 35 percent of our revenue, whereas the major 65 percent comes from services," said Hardik.

Vrinda started the VITA component calculation activity with the participants. Following was the response:

#	Products/Services	V (%)	I (%)	T (%)	A (%)
1	HRM software	5	20	70	5
2	Install and config	0	20	80	0
3	Maintenance and Support	0	5	40	45
	Average percentages of each VITA	1.67	15	63.33	16.67

"We see that text has a high VITA score, whereas video, image, and audio are the ones with lower scores," said Maria.

"Will improving VITA components such as video, image, and audio enhance the customer experience?" asked Vrinda.

"Yes certainly! It can also help us generate more revenues," said Maurice.

"We can develop videos for troubleshooting, technical descriptions, and user manuals. We can use images to create visual diagrams that could simplify technical explanations. And we could use genAI to create them. I do not see much of an audio component in HRM product," said Farah.

"We should also increase the video and image component in the install and config service," said Wenhong.

"And for maintenance and support, we can increase the video component only," said Sanne.

"I agree with your suggestions. Let us do it," said Wenhong.

Readiness Areas

"Can you please list the names of all your customers?" asked Vrinda.

"Total we have 10 customers. Our biggest customer is Haveth International, one of the largest pharmaceutical companies in Europe. They have been using our product for over a decade. It is an account that fetches us millions of euros per year," said Maurice.

"Next ones are Xylem and Phloem, a life sciences company based in Nordics. X-dent, a company offering dental care services in the Nordics. Winner, a sporting goods company based in Finland. Mobicota, a Swedish telecommunications operator. Triumph, one of the largest insurance providers in Nordics. Bilbil, an auto dealer based in Sweden. Acu, one of the largest consumer goods retailers in Sweden. Freya, one of the largest consumer goods retailers in Oslo. And, TechHarvest Software, one of the largest IT consulting companies in Scandinavia," said Achintya.

"What is your revenue model?" asked Vrinda.

"The customers pay for a perpetual software license based on number of users. There is a one-time deployment fees that include customization, installation, and configuration. We charge annual fees for application development and maintenance (ADM), which includes ongoing development and a 24x7 operational support. Major portion of our revenue comes from the recurrent ADM fees," said Dario.

Following was the response by the team to the high-readiness customer selection matrices:

List of Customers	Matrix 1 Quadrant	Matrix 2 Quadrant	Matrix 3 Quadrant	Revenue Current Year	Profit Current Year
Haveth Int	III	III	III	20	6.1
X&P	II	NA	NA	20	5.8
X-dent	II	NA	NA	19	3.95
Winner	III	II	NA	18.5	2.95
Mobicota	III	III	II	18	2.66
Triumph	I	II	NA	8	1.15
Bilbil	II	NA	NA	8.5	1.12
Acu	I	II	NA	8	1.1
Freya	IV	I	III	10	1.1
TechHarvest	III	IV	IV	10	1.09

(in million EUR)

"We have Haveth International, Freya, and TechHarvest as the high-readiness customers. I suggest you finalize only one," said Vrinda.

"But why do we need to finalize one? Can't we start with all the top 3 simultaneously?" asked Sandeep.

"I would suggest you start with one customer. Instead of doing non-convertible pilots with several customers, it is a much better strategy to do a scaled adoption with one. Pick the best one," replied Vrinda.

"I agree," said Achintya.

"We shall continue with the remainder of this readiness area after you finalize the customer. Let us move to the next readiness area: technology. We need to wait for inputs from the customer before we cover the LLM, ecosystems, and vendor selection. But as of now, we can cover capabilities, infrastructure assessment, and technical debt management. While exploring this area, I would suggest you all think long-term till 2030," said Vrinda.

Vrinda gave 20 minutes to the participants to discuss among themselves and rank the top capabilities they would like to build. Following was the response:

Capabilities	Rank
Generative	1
Personalization	2
Predictive	3
Pattern recognition	4
Classification	5
Speech to text/text to speech	6
Facial recognition	7

"Can you explain the rationale behind selecting the top three capabilities?" asked Vrinda.

"They would add the most value to our HRM product, and thus the customer experience," replied Ricky.

"With generative we can enable text-to-text, text-to-image, text-to-video, and so on. With personalization, we can offer specific customer experiences. With predictive, we can make predictions such as which employee is likely to perform, or likely to leave based on their observed behaviors and relevant data," replied Farah.

"It can also help us build and sell new genAI standalone products in the future," said Angel.

"How do we plan to build the competence?" asked Maurice.

"We will start with AI reskilling programs for internal employees. But we do not know how to begin," said Anna.

"We will be covering this in detail in the readiness area: people," said Vrinda.

"I estimate at least a couple of million dollars to build each one of them," said Dario.

"We should work on the budget estimation for the capabilities development on priority. We should brand ourselves as a data and AI company. Kindly ensure that we ramp up competence on this as soon as possible and adequately support our development team with all the resources," said Achintya.

"Also, it is important that we have a clear communication plan, both internal and external," added Wenhong.

Next, Vrinda started with the infrastructure assessment with the relevant key stakeholders, such as Achintya, Maria, Sandeep, Hardik, John, Ricky, Farah, and Vineet. Each of them was provided with assessments. The final average score was 2.67, corresponding to low infrastructure readiness.

"The assessment scores tell us that we need to modernize our existing infrastructure at least to the level of medium readiness," said Sandeep.

"How would you improve the infrastructure? Do you have any long-term strategy?" asked Vrinda.

"We have already kicked off the modernization program six months ago. However, due to lesser budget allocation and lack of availability of dedicated resources, we were unable to achieve the desired outcome. Now we will ensure that we allocate more of resources and budget," said Sandeep.

"Our long-term strategy with infrastructure is to cloudify it. We would like to migrate most of the IT applications to the hybrid cloud and ensure that the cloud remains always upgraded and updated on the latest release by the provider. We shall be using a multi-vendor model with all the three hyperscalers such as AWS, Azure, and Google Cloud," said Hardik.

"We are currently experimenting with IaC. We can see the clear value and benefits. Over the next 2 years, we plan to transform 40 percent of our infrastructure using IaC," said Sandeep.

"How do we rate our technical debt on a scale of 1 to 10, 1: lowest and 10: highest?" asked Vrinda.

"I would like to provide a rating of 6. It is at a medium level," replied Sandeep.

"We often encounter some performance issues in our tools and systems due to lack of technical debt management," said Hardik.

"Going forward, we shall ensure that we have clear coding standards, better documentation and version control, CI/CD and automated testing, regular code reviews, and continuous learning and improvement to manage it better," said Sandeep.

Vrinda moved to the next important readiness area: data.

"The fundamental question to answer is, what is your data purpose? Direct monetization, indirect monetization, or non-monetization?" asked Vrinda.

"At this stage, with data we are looking at reduced costs, increased customer satisfaction, and increased employee satisfaction. It means indirect monetization and non-monetization," said John.

"Can you elaborate more on how do you plan to reduce costs?" asked Vrinda.

Angel replied:

If we are able to access and acquire the right data, we can automate our internal processes. It can improve the lead times up to 70 percent. We can expect to reduce costs in the range of 30 to 45 percent. We need to collaborate with a partner who can guide us through the end-to-end process and help us with preparing datasets for training AI/genAI models.

"How do you plan to increase the customer satisfaction?" asked Vrinda.

Maurice replied:

The current overall customer satisfaction score is 5 out of 10. The score dropped due to some of the major IT escalations we had last year. We want to improve it to 7 and above. We plan to reduce the delivery lead times for the customers. Also, we plan on providing them a better experience by adding AI capabilities and reducing product and service complexity. We are exploring how we can simplify explanations using genAI through text, image, and video. Another way of increasing the customer satisfaction is by improving our support services.

"You can also explore some of the popular industry-agnostic use cases such as implementing an AI-enabled chatbot either using RAG and developing knowledge base from the daily customer interactions. This new data created will be your very useful asset, with which you can train the future genAI models," said Vrinda.

"How do you plan to increase the employee satisfaction through data?" asked Vrinda.

"If employees get access to the right data, it can help them reduce their workloads and help them achieve speed and efficiency. It can provide them meaningful and real-time insights that can add value to their business, enabling them to make data-driven decisions. Better access and control over data can help us drive AI/ genAI upskilling and reskilling programs effectively," said Anna.

Vrinda gave them the sheets to capture the data flows at customer touchpoints, between functions, and within functions.

"We shall acquire data from these sources and store them temporarily in the data lakes," said John.

Next, the participants started with the data cleaning.

"Look at all the three types of data flows. Do you notice any biases?" asked Vrinda.

"There could be a few biases in estimating the deal size at the customer opportunity touchpoint. Also, in HR activities such as hiring, onboarding, training, employee motivations, appraisals, compensation, employee retention, and exiting," said Achintya.

"Make sure that you benchmark the deal size with industry standards or with your competitors. For example, you might categorize a deal worth 1 million U.S. dollars as large. But as per industry standards, the same deal might be classified as medium," said Vrinda.

"I would suggest the hiring managers from different teams be more involved in HR activities. It would help in reducing biases," said Anna.

Vrinda asked the participants to add the seven main classifiers, stated in Chapter 13, to all data flows according to the old organizational structure, as the processes and workflows for the new one were still under development.

Following was the response:

Customer touchpoints	Data flowing IN	Data flowing OUT
Lead	High-level description of lead, point of contact at customer (ext, c, ns, nr, ar, ni, nm)	Company info, product/service description, point of contacts at Talent XYZ (ext, c, ns, nr, ar, ni, nm)
Opportunity	Customer requirements, deal size, business value to customer, timelines (ext, c, ns, nr, ar, ni, m)	Business case, scope of work, technical solution, delivery timelines, team competence (ext, c, ns, nr, ar, ni, nm)
Contract	Signed copy of contract (ext, c, s, nr, ar, ni, m)	Signed copy of contract (ext, c, s, nr, ar, ni, m)
Order	PO (ext, c, s, nr, ar, ni, m)	Quotation (ext, c, s, nr, ar, ni, m)
Delivery	Customer feedback, signoffs, phase approvals (ext, c, ns, nr, ar, ins, nm)	Agreed deliverables (ext, c, s, nr, ar, ni, m)

Customer touchpoints	Data flowing IN	Data flowing OUT
Acceptance	Acceptance certificate (ext, nc, ns, nr, ar, ni, nm)	Acceptance certificate request (ext, nc, ns, nr, ar, ni, nm)
Invoice	Invoice acknowledgment (ext, nc, ns, nr, ar, ni, nm)	Invoice (ext, c, s, nr, ar, ni, m)
Payment	Payment transfer notification (ext, nc, ns, nr, ar, ni, nm)	Payment reminders (ext, nc, ns, nr, ar, ni, nm)

All the data in the data flows at customer touchpoints were given the following three labels as per Figure 13.3:

Label: Industry: Software/Platforms

Label: Function: Sales

Label: Category: Consumer transaction

Functions/ units	Data flow
Sales	Leads, new opportunities, orders booked, net sales booked, work in progress, customer information, contracts, P&L, sales reviews, OPEX (int, c, s, nr, ar, ins, m)
Business unit software	Product releases, product development plans, technical documentation, sales reviews (int, nc, ns, nr, ar, ni, nm) P&L, OPEX (int, c, s, nr, ar, ins, m)
Business unit services	Project delivery, issues and escalations, service level agreement (SLA) reviews, sales reviews (int, nc, ns, nr, ar, ni, nm) P&L, OPEX (int, c, s, nr, ar, ins, m)
Finance	Payroll, accounts, taxation, compliance, P&L reviews, budget reviews, procurements (int, c, s, nr, ar, ins, m) annual reports (ext, nc, ns, nr, ar, ins, nm)
Marketing	Leads, product campaigns, market research and development (int, nc, ns, nr, ar, ins, nm) budget (int, c, s, nr, ar, ni, m)
HR	Hiring, onboarding, training, employee motivations, employee retention, exiting (int, nc, ns, nr, ar, ni, nm) appraisals, compensation (int, c, s, nr, ar, ins, m)
IT	IT tools development and maintenance, updates, upgrades, performance (int, nc, ns, r, im, ni, nm) budget (int, c, s, nr, ar, ins, m)

Only two labels: Function and Category, were used to label the above data flow as per respective data types.

For the data flowing between the functions, the sub-labels from Figure 13.3 were used as shown in the table below:

Data flowing between units / functions	Business unit software	Business unit services	Finance	Marketing	HR	IT
Sales	Sales: Sales & commerce	Sales: Sales & commerce	Sales: Sales & commerce	Sales: Sales & commerce	HR: People	IT: Process
Business unit software		Product development: Product info	Finance: Company news and financials	Marketing: Sales & commerce	HR: People	IT: Process
Business unit services	X		Finance: Company news and financials	Marketing: Sales & commerce	HR: People	IT: Process
Finance	X	X		Finance: Company news and financials	HR: People	IT: Process
Marketing	X	X	X		HR: People	IT: Process
HR	X	X	X	X		HR: People IT: Process

"Now that your data is annotated, how would you structure it?" asked Vrinda.

"We shall go with data warehouse, datasets, and data products. We want to keep our data clean and simple. Hence, we will not go for knowledge graphs for now," said Hardik.

Hardik then drew the following structures on the whiteboard:

Data Warehouse

Data 1	Classifier 1	Label 1
Data 2	Classifier 2	Label 2
...Data n	...Classifier n	...Label n

Datasets

PO	Invoice	Points of contact	Orders booked	Net sales
Contracts	Work in progress	P&L	OPEX	Product releases
Technical documentation	Product development plans	Project delivery	Issues and escalations	Payroll
Accounts	Taxation	Compliance	Budget	Procurement
UX	Campaigns	Leads	HR processes	IT updates
Annual reports	Market research	...	...	...

Data Products

Sales product	PO	Invoice	Points of contact	Orders booked	Net sales	Contracts	Work in progress	P&L
	OPEX	Budget	Leads	UX				
Finance product	PO	Invoice	Budget	OPEX	Payroll	Taxation	Accounts	Compliance
Marketing product	Leads	Campaigns	Market research					
HR product	HR processes	Budget						
Delivery product	Project delivery	Contracts	Work in progress	Procurement	Budget	OPEX	P&L	

"Nice job, Hardik! So, HR data product contains datasets such as HR processes and budget; Marketing data product contains datasets such as leads, campaigns, and market research, and so on. Let us try to extract value from them," remarked Maurice.

All the participants worked out the following data democratization policy:

- By default, no one has access to data. Users need to make a basic request to obtain one.
- Users with basic requests will have access to non-confidential and/or non-sensitive data only related to their respective functions and/or markets.
- Users must request in advance to acquire access to confidential and/or sensitive data within their respective functions and/or markets. It would require approvals from the respective data owners.

- Users must request in advance to acquire access to confidential and/or sensitive data outside their respective functions and/ or markets. It would require approvals from the respective data owners, business controller, and compliance officer.

"We shall cover the remainder of readiness area: data later. Now let us move to readiness area: people," said Vrinda.

Vrinda began by discussing the pros and cons of centralized and federated CoE with the participants. She asked, "I see that you have an established CoE. Can you tell me more about how it operates?"

Farah explained, "We have the CoE within the business unit for technology and digital business," Vineet added, "We have 4 markets: Nordics, UK and Ireland, Rest of EU (RoEU), and non-EU. There are 3 CoEs: one in Nordics, one for UK and Ireland, and one combined for RoEU and non-EU, driven by digital consulting in the markets."

After evaluating, Achintya stated, "I believe a centralized CoE structure is best for us. Farah, the head of group CoE, will report to me and join my leadership team. The 3 market CoE heads will report to John, the head of customer engagements, with dotted line reporting to Farah. Our governance will include a core committee, steering committee, operational committee, and technology tribes."

Vrinda noted, "I see you don't have an internal legal team."

Achintya replied, "Yes, we have outsourced our legal function to a partner."

"The roles and responsibilities of legal in the context of genAI have changed. You may continue working with your external partner, but ensure that they report to the head of group CoE and work very close to the business," said Vrinda.

Next, Vrinda moved to another important framework: RAI. She explained the details of the framework and gave options to Talent XYZ to adopt as-is or with some customizations as per business requirements.

"For now, we shall adopt the framework as-is. We will create new roles: RAI Leads, reporting to the respective heads of CoE in group and markets," said Achintya.

Next on the agenda was AI/genAI reskilling.

"Do you have an ongoing AI/genAI reskilling program?" asked Vrinda.

"No. But we ran a reskilling program on cloud earlier. The participation was low in the beginning. But as cloud got matured, we saw more enrollments," said Anna.

"Is there a high willingness to learn and grow among people?" asked Vrinda

"People want to learn. But time is a constraint for them. Constant motivation and frequent communications explaining them the benefits can increase their willingness," replied Anna.

"Are managers supportive with reskilling?" asked Vrinda.

"Some of them are but some are not," replied Anna.

"Do you have a strategy going forward to motivate people to reskill on AI/genAI?" asked Vrinda.

Anna replied:

We first need to bring their mindsets to pragmatic. I have observed either a lot of optimism or skepticism regarding genAI. We need to constantly communicate and motivate them about enrolling them in these programs. I am planning a coaching session with managers on how to manage the employee expectations. We need to assess skills gap and match new roles for employees. We can add AI in their current roles or completely create a new role for them.

Vrinda then presented the list of new roles to the team, including the data, AI, and cloud (DAC) ones. She asked which existing roles they would modify immediately with an AI/genAI component and which new roles should be created immediately, within the next six months, within one year, and within the next two to three years. Following was the response:

Modify immediately	Create immediately	Within next 6 months	Within 1 year	Within next 2 to 3 years
Cloud architect	AI/genAI developer	Automation strategy manager	LLMOps specialist	LLM fine-tuner
Cloud developer	AI tester	Automation consultant	DAC solution architect	LLM evaluator

(Continued)

Modify immediately	Create immediately	Within next 6 months	Within 1 year	Within next 2 to 3 years
Data scientist	AI solution architect	Data strategy manager	DAC migration expert	LLM architect
Data engineer	AI consultant	Data consultant	DAC engineer	LLM designer
Data analyst	AI/genAI strategy manager	Cloud strategy manager	DAC industry SME	DAC transformation expert
Automation expert	RAI lead	Cloud consultant	DAC infrastructure expert	DAC industry transformation expert
Platform engineer	DAC legal advisor	Prompt engineer	DAC sales manager	DAC LLM presales manager
System integration expert			DAC commercial manager	DAC program manager
			DAC sales expert	DAC project manager

Vrinda then asked the participants to list the current and future technical and nontechnical skills. Following was the response:

	Technical skills	Nontechnical skills
Current	• Software development • Software testing • System engineering • Database management • Storage management • Network engineering • IT administration • Datacenter management • Process modeling • Agile • Product life cycle management	• Project management • Program management • Strategy • Consulting • Sales • Accounting • Marketing
Future	• AI/genAI • Data • Cloud • Automation • Infrastructure • Security • Development • Design • Testing • Analytics • Operations • Platform engineering	• Digital leadership • Digital strategy • Legal AI

Then, the team did the gap analysis, matching current skills to the future ones and eventually mapping them to the new roles. The following table shows an example of gap analysis and matching roles for AI/genAI skills:

Skill type	Current skill	Gap analysis/gap mitigation	Future skill	Matching roles
Technical	• Software development • Software testing • System engineering • Database management • Storage management • Network engineering • IT administration • Datacenter management • Process modeling • Agile • Product life cycle management	Programming languages such as Python, R. Hyperscaler AI platforms such as Google Cloud AI, AWS SageMaker, Azure AI, AI data pipelines	AI	• AI developer • AI tester • AI solution architect • AI consultant
		All above plus API programming, LLM parameter optimization, evaluation, frameworks, Azure OpenAI studio	GenAI	• LLM fine-tuner • LLM evaluator • LLM architect • LLM designer
Nontechnical	• Project management • Program management • Strategy • Consulting • Sales • Accounting • Marketing	AI/genAI fundamentals, RAI, use cases, case studies, courses, events and seminars, learning from experts, legal counsel	AI	• AI strategy manager
			GenAI	• GenAI strategy manager • RAI lead • DAC sales manager • DAC commercial manager • DAC program manager • DAC project manager • DAC transformation expert

Following were the personalized genAI learning plans for technical and nontechnical roles:

Component	Technical role	Nontechnical role
Individual courses	ChatGPT API, LangChain for LLM application development, vector databases, building RAG applications, LLMOps, red teaming, RAI principles	GenAI fundamentals, reinforcement learning through human feedback (RLHF), red teaming, prompt engineering techniques, RAI principles
Learning pathways	For developers, for solution architects	For project managers, for leaders
Certifications	GenAI reskilled developer, GenAI reskilled solution architect	GenAI reskilled project manager, GenAI reskilled leader
Job rotations	CoE, product development, digital consulting	CoE, markets
On-the-job training (OJT)	On different client projects	On different client projects
Coaching and mentoring	With Ricky and his development team	With Farah and her CoE team

Next, Vrinda started with the AI leadership module. She presented the VisionTech case study from Chapter 17 to read and asked the leaders to vote anonymously using the Menti app if they would go ahead with the launch, yes or no? Out of 14 executive leaders of Talent XYZ, 10 said no and 4 said yes.

"What are the standard guidelines for right balancing between profits and ethics?" asked Vrinda.

Achintya said:

It is very important to draw the line between profits and ethics. It is perhaps the most challenging task for a leader as the line is very thin. Also, it is very hard to pinpoint where to draw the line. But let us make a guideline that whenever Talent XYZ would confront a situation where it has to make a hard choice between profits and ethics, it will make a decision through consensus. First, L1 leadership will try to reach a consensus. If unable then L2 will be involved. If we are still unable to reach, we can seek for external guidance. At every step of the decision-making, we will involve legal and RAI leads.

Vrinda said:

It is a great approach. Next, it is important for leaders to cultivate the four key competencies of a digital leader. I shall recommend you the book, Digital Leadership Framework: Cultivating the four key competencies. Remember, it is the responsibility of every leader to be the champion of genAI. The executive leadership at Talent XYZ is the launchpad of genAI.

"We like the 10 best practices outlined by you and we shall do our best to adhere to them," said Achintya.

Thus, the workshop was concluded.

A team led by John began engaging with the top three best customers: Haveth International, Freya, and TechHarvest.

Among the high-readiness customers shown in the table on the next page, TechHarvest placed in quadrant IV of matrix 3 was the most preferred. Haveth International was the second most preferred as it showed high revenue and profitability. Freya was the third most preferred.

(in million EUR)

List of Customers	Matrix 1 Quadrant	Matrix 2 Quadrant	Matrix 3 Quadrant	Revenue Current Year	Profit Current Year
Haveth Int	III	III	III	20	6.1
Freya	IV	I	III	10	1.1
TechHarvest	III	IV	IV	10	1.09

A team led by John began scheduling introductory meetings with them. Among all the CTOs met, the CTO of Freya showed the most interest. It was due to a healthy and informal business relationship and a high trust level between Talent XYZ and Freya.

Thus, Freya, one of the largest consumer goods retailers in Oslo, was shortlisted as the final customer. Freya wanted Talent XYZ to enhance their HRM product with AI and genAI capabilities. It was important first to understand their needs. The sales team headed by Maurice started engaging with them using the SPIN methodology.

Following was the outcome:

SPIN categories	Questions
Situation	• What is your current approach to genAI? Are you leveraging the AI technology? >> We see genAI as the game-changer, a technology that can cause disruption and provide better experiences to customers. We had begun AI transformation before the pandemic. We would be leveraging AI for the genAI deployment. • What specific AI tools or platforms are you currently using, if any? >> AWS SageMaker, Jasper, Grammarly. • How do you currently handle tasks that could benefit from genAI capabilities? >> We handle it manually, which is sometimes tedious and time-consuming. • How do you currently measure the success or effectiveness of your AI initiatives? >> We use the following metrics: reduction in time, costs saved, and increase in revenue. • What is the size and composition of your AI development team? >> We have a CoE in Oslo, comprising a team of 11: 1 CoE head, 5 AI experts, 3 data scientists, and 2 cloud experts.

(Continued)

SPIN categories	Questions
Problem	• What challenges do you encounter when implementing AI solutions? >> Data quality, data availability, data accessibility, lack of skilled resources, complexity, scalability, interpretability, integration with existing workflows, high risks, and uncertain costs. • Can you identify inefficiencies in your current AI workflows? >> Data collection and preparation, model development and training, model deployment and monitoring, integration with legacy systems, feedback loops, and iterative improvement. • What are the data challenges? >> Quality, availability, accessibility. • What limitations do you encounter with your current AI tools or platforms? >> Scalability, flexibility, customization, security, and integration with existing systems. • Have you noticed any recurring issues about the performance of your AI models? >> Scalability and integration with existing systems.
Implication	• What impact do these challenges have on your business operations or outcomes? >> Operational efficiency, competitive disadvantage, stifled innovation, poor customer experience. • How do these AI-related issues affect your team's productivity? >> Low morale, high risks of error and rework, innovation stagnation. • Are there any potential risks in not addressing these challenges? >> It can reduce the team's trust in using these tools. • How do the challenges impact your organization's ability to innovate? >> It does not motivate people to step out of their comfort zones to try and experiment with new things. • What are the potential consequences if these AI-related issues worsen over time? >> We are likely to see attrition, reduced growth and profitability.

SPIN categories	Questions
Need-payoff	• What are the benefits of implementing genAI capabilities? >> Reduced costs, new customer experiences, new employee experiences. • How do you foresee genAI enhancing creativity and innovation? >> Through content differentiation, productivity gains • What specific efficiency gains or cost savings do you expect to achieve? >> We want to increase overall productivity gain by 60%. Cost savings of a minimum of one million U.S. dollars annually. • What are the new revenue streams? >> We have not monetized yet. But we have ambitions to monetize soon, either directly or indirectly. • How would genAI assist in personalizing customer experiences or loyalty? >> Offering dynamic pricing and discounts and personalized recommendations to customers through sentiment analysis, predictive analysis, and pattern recognition.

The sales team in Nordics had a workshop with Freya's marketing team where they developed the customer journey maps as shown in Figure 18.2.

The following week, the Talent XYZ leadership team met again with Vrinda.

"It is great that you have finalized Freya as your customer. Do you have any reflections from the SPIN engagement and customer journey maps?" asked Vrinda.

"We categorize Freya as AI archetype pioneers. From the interactions we had so far, we can describe their mindset as pragmatic," said Maria.

"They have deployed considerable amounts of AI in their operations. However, they are facing lots of issues and are unable to offer better experiences to their customers," said Vineet.

"Their chatbot has a low rating and is able to troubleshoot only 20 percent of the time," said Angel.

Customer Journey Map for online shopping at Freya

Need	Website visit	Browsing	Checkout	Post-Visit
New customers discover Freya through online search, referrals, or advertisements	Type the url	Search the products in the search engine	Online Shopping cart	Reflecting on the shopping experience. In store pick-up or home delivery. Consuming the purchased products
Existing customers visit website to get exclusive online deals on specific products	Greeted on home page. View latest promotional offers	Access using the catalog	Payment using existing cards, new cards, or installments	

"My friend recommended me Freya."

"Good website design."

"Chatbot was unable to help."

"I do not like to store my card details."

"On-time home delivery."

"Slow page loading time during peak hours."

"Sometimes it is difficult to find the right products."

"Card declined."

"Card details are stored by default."

"It is not the same product I ordered."

Customer Journey Map for in store shopping at Freya

Visiting decision	The Visit	Shopping	Checkout	Post-Visit
New customers discover Freya through online search, referrals, or advertisements	Parking vehicles in the lot	New customers explore all the aisles	Customers have 3 options: 1) Checkout at normal counter 2) Express checkout with 10 items or less 3) Self-checkout	Reflecting on the shopping experience, consuming the purchased products
Existing customers do weekly grocery shopping, redeem vouchers, get discounts or promotional offers on certain products	Greeted by a welcome sign and top promotional offers	Existing customers know where to find their products. They fill their carts with the essentials first and then explore new products in remaining time		
	Access to shopping carts			

"My friend recommended me Freya."

"It is difficult to find parking on busy hours and weekends."

"Good ambience."

"Wide range of consumer products available."

"Attendant was available to help."

"Slow checkout."

"Self-checkout often need attendant support."

"Long queue for express checkout."

"I received discount coupons on future purchase."

"Quality groceries. Fresh and cheaper fruits and vegetables."

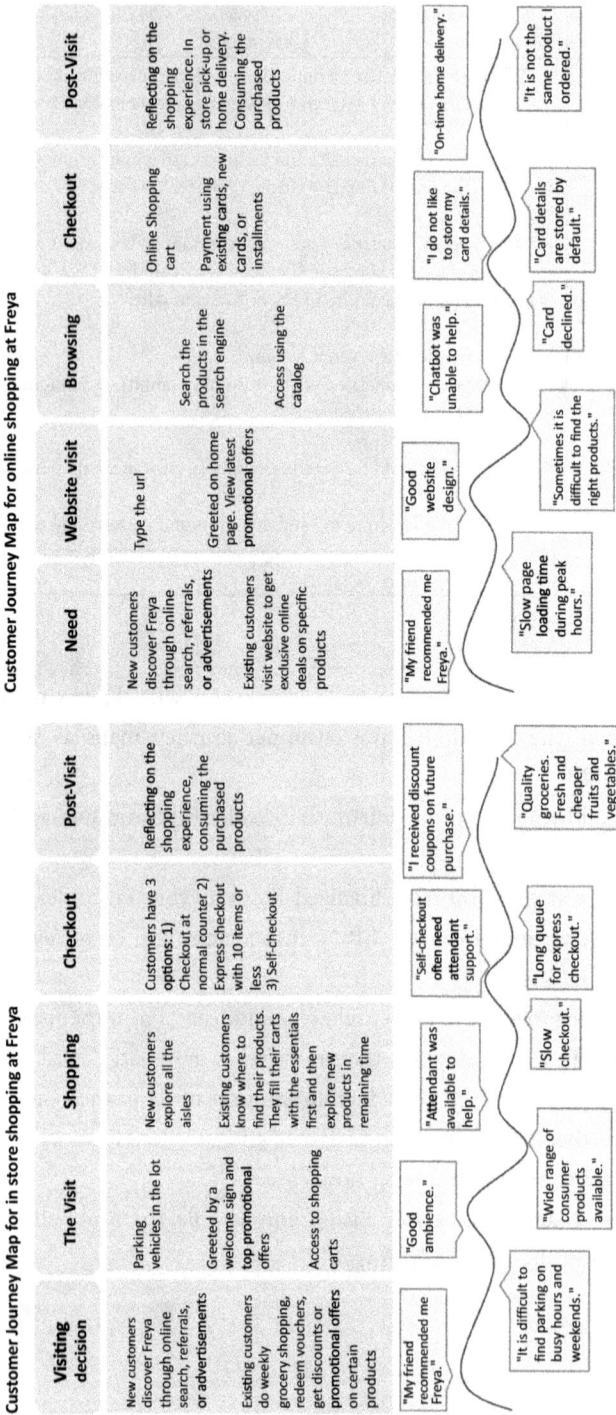

Figure 18.2 Customer journey maps

Customer Journey Map for online Customer support by chatbot

Need for Info/Support	Open chatbot	Q&A	Conclusion	Post-Call
Follow-up on a refund on a returned product	Interacting with the bot	Responding to all bot queries	End of bot session	Reflecting on the experience

"Refund overdue by 5 days."

"Bot asked me my name and email."

"Bot asked too many questions."

"Asked to call the Freya customer support."

"It was annoying to provide details."

"Questions were vague."

"Waste of time chatting with a bot."

Customer Journey Map for Customer support over phone

Need for Info/Support	The Call	Call Escalation	Conclusion	Post-Call
Decision to call Freya was to follow-up on refund on a returned product	Dialing the Freya helpline. Interacting with the IVR	Speaking with a customer support representative	Ending the call with the representative	Reflecting on the call experience

"Refund overdue by 5 days."

"IVR was complicated."

"Wait time of 15 minutes."

"Asked to call back in next 3 days, if not received."

"IVR is annoying."

"I was told that my refund is in process."

"Not a good experience."

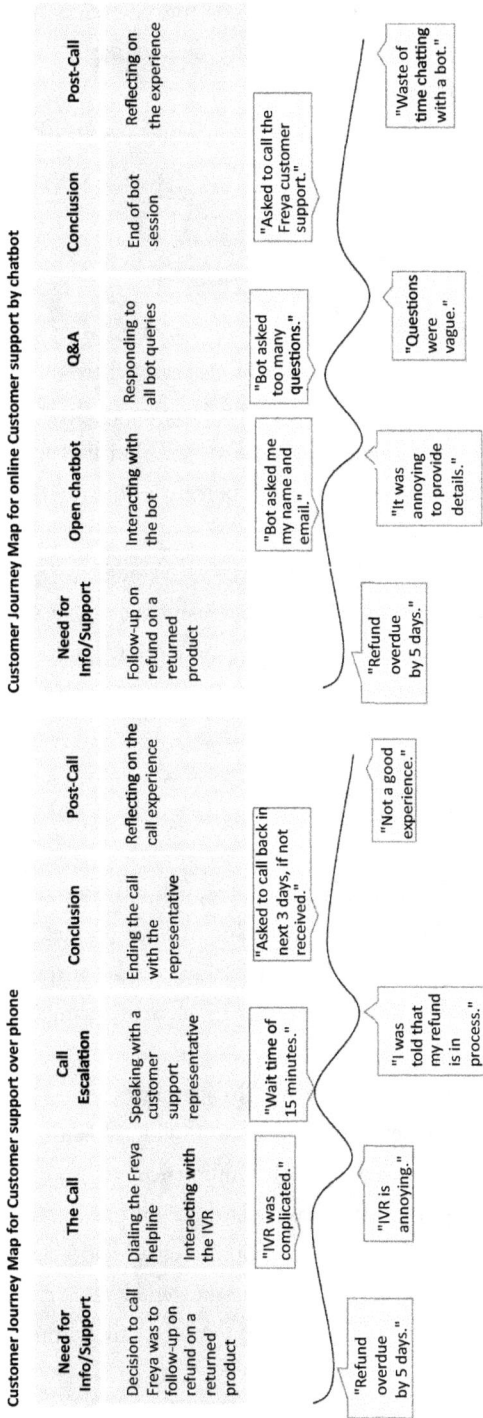

Figure 18.2 (Continued)

"I am not sure how Freya's customer journey maps are relevant to us. We provide them our HRM software that manages their workforce of 3,000 across Europe," said Anna.

"Yes, you are right. The journey maps may not be directly relevant to your product. But it can provide you a better understanding of their pain points and challenges," said Vrinda.

Vrinda started the discussion on the use case.

"We would like to go for infusion use case where we want to add the AI/genAI capabilities into our product," suggested Ricky.

Maurice pitched this proposal to the CTO at Freya. It was accepted. In fact, Freya decided to sponsor 50 percent of the development costs. It was a big win for Talent XYZ.

The following week the team met with Vrinda.

"Congratulations on the win! Now you have a clear strategic priority. It's a genAI solution. And not a convertible pilot," said Vrinda.

She began with the next exercise, product.

"In which quadrant do you categorize this genAI product?" asked Vrinda.

"It is a multimodal current product. It will produce both text and image as output. We can use a licensing business model," said Hardik.

"Next, it is important that you position yourself correctly in the genAI value chain. It can give you clarity on LLM, ecosystem, and vendor selection, which we will begin shortly," said Vrinda.

"Since we are infusing the genAI capabilities into our existing product, we position ourselves as AI copilot providers," said Achintya.

"Since we do not have genAI competence, we need to partner with vendors. It is important that we select the right ones," said Maria.

"So, let us do the vendor selection exercise," said Vrinda.

She projected the slide containing the genAI value chain.

"Can you list the key players in the value chain whom you would like to partner with?"

"LLM providers, system integrators, tuning specialists, cloud hyper-scalers, inference evaluators, and guardrail providers," said Ricky.

"Why are we not considering genAI service or platform providers?" asked Hardik.

"Because we are building copilots that are specific to our product. These platform or service providers provide a generic platform where one can build various AI and genAI apps," replied Ricky.

"We should think long term here. We don't want to restrict ourselves as copilot providers. We will have an edge over our competitors if we offer new products and solutions. These platform providers already have partnership with LLM providers. Some providers offer LLM curation too. It will improve our time to market," counterargued Hardik.

"This means we cannot control the LLMs, we won't be able to fine-tune them, nor we can improve inference," said Ricky.

He continued, "It would be better if we fine-tune our own LLM."

"But it will be expensive. Also, we don't know if we can find a skilled vendor to do so," said Hardik.

"We should develop internal competence," said Ricky.

"We started ramping up our AI competence before the pandemic and we are not even halfway," said Hardik.

"That's because we always faced budget crunch. Now, since we have a sponsorship from Freya, we should ensure that we capitalize on every single penny," replied Ricky.

Vrinda saw the argument heating up, so she interjected:

"Talent XYZ can reposition itself in the value chain later. But as of now, you position yourself as AI copilot providers. So, I would like you to discuss among yourself and come up with a draft list of these vendors,"

The following was the first draft of the list of vendors:

LLM providers	System integrators	Tuning specialists	Cloud hyperscalers	Inference evaluators	Guardrail providers
OpenAI+ Azure (GPT-4)	Accenture	Hugging Face	AWS	Arthur	OpenAI Moderation API
Google (Gemini)					
Meta (Llama-2)	Tata Consultancy Services	Entry Point AI			
AI21 Labs (Jamba 1.5)			Azure		Perspective API
Mistral AI (Mistral)	Infosys				
Anthropic (Claude)		Cohere		Arize	
Cohere (Aya)	Wipro				Hugging Face
EleutherAI (GPT-NeoX)		SambaNova	Google Cloud		
DeepSeek (DeepSeek-R1)	Other				

All the vendors stated in the table above are multi-value vendors.

Based on the vendor selection guidelines, the final shortlisted vendors, except the LLM providers, were:

System integrators: local third party

Tuning specialists: Entry Point AI

Inference evaluators: Arize

Guardrail providers: Perspective API

Vrinda started the next exercise, ecosystem selection.

"Do you have in mind any ecosystems that you would like to be part of or start on your own?" asked Vrinda.

"We have heard about the promise of the ecosystems but never explored anything like that before in our business. Can you suggest some ecosystems which would be suitable for us?" asked Maria.

"The ecosystem that you can pioneer could be the one with your existing customers who use your product. Let them connect and share the best practices and experiences with one another. Talent XYZ could be the main orchestrator of the ecosystem, managing the information and interactions,"

replied Vrinda.

"But we have different pricing for our different customers. We have sold them the customized products as per their requirements. What if the customers learn this vital piece of information from one another?" asked Sandeep.

"That's a good question. We don't share the sensitive and confidential data and information on the ecosystem. But we can share the product experiences, implementation, and operational best practices, which can be valuable for one another," replied Vrinda.

I can recommend some ecosystems where you can be a good follower, and seek and share value. We at Digiculum orchestrate ecosystems with software and IT consulting companies in the Nordics, an AI ecosystem for companies in Nordics, and human resource management teams from different companies. It would be beneficial for you to join them where you can understand the challenges and pain points of other players in the ecosystem and modify your products and services accordingly.

"Seems to be a good idea! So, we have four ecosystems to evaluate. Let's begin the exercise," said Achintya. After an hour of evaluation, the following was the exercise outcome:

Based on the outcome, it was decided that Talent XYZ would pioneer the Talent XYZ product ecosystem with support from Digiculum and follow the Nordic AI ecosystem.

Ecosystems	Objective	Differentiation	Trust	Governance	Flexibility	Score
Talent XYZ product	4	2	5	4	3	18
Nordics software and IT	3	2	2	3	3	13
Nordic AI	5	4	4	4	3	20
HR ecosystem	4	4	3	3	3	17

Next, Vrinda started a very important exercise, selecting LLM. She first started with the business requirements. Following was the response:

Business requirements	Questions
Primary goal	- What specific problem are you addressing with the LLM? >> Provide customers fast and easy access to information, provide new business insights, ability to summarize content, generate new content, and increase their productivity gains. - Are you aiming to improve customer engagement, internal operations, or corporate culture? >> Customer engagement. If we successfully deliver the genAI solution at Freya, we would like to scale the solution with other customers.
Expected tasks	- What kinds of tasks do you intend for the LLM to perform: text generation, sentiment analysis, summarization, translation, question answering, or something else? >> All of the above. We also want it to generate images. - Do you require a model that can handle multiple tasks simultaneously (multitask learning)? >> Yes. - Would your tasks include any one or more of the VITA: video, image, text, and audio? >> Text and image. - Is there any specific industry or domain you would like to develop your model for? >> No. It will be industry or domain agnostic.

Business requirements	Questions
Expected scale	-What is the expected volume of data and traffic that the application will handle? >> 100 employees in the first three months, 500 within six months, 1,500 within a year, 3,000 within two years. - Are you deploying the model for a small-scale project, a medium-sized business application, or an enterprise-level deployment? >> Enterprise-level deployment. - Will the application need to scale dynamically to accommodate fluctuations in demand? >> Yes.
Computational resources	-What are the computational resources available for model training, inference, and deployment? >> None. -Do you have access to high-performance computing resources such as GPUs or TPUs? >> No. -Are there limitations on memory, storage, or processing power that may influence your choice of model? >> Yes. -Are the resources energy efficient? >> No.
Data availability and quality	-What is the availability and quality of data for pretraining and fine-tuning the LLM? >> Need to prepare. -Do you have access to labeled datasets relevant to your use case, or will you need to collect and annotate data? >> Need to collect and annotate data. -Are there concerns about data privacy, bias, or representativeness that need to be addressed? >> It should be compliant with the regulations. Need to check if the data needs to stay in Norway or can be stored across the border in Sweden too.

Based on the business requirements, the following two LLMs were shortlisted: Mistral and Jamba 1.5. They were further subjected to evaluations for core model characteristics. Following was the response:

Core model characteristics	Questions
Transformer architecture	-Which transformer architecture do you consider: encoder–decoder, decoder only, or encoder only? >> Not sure.
Model size	- How many parameters does the model comprise? >> Mistral has 7 billion parameters. Jamba 1.5 large has 94 billion, whereas Jamba 1.5 mini has 12 billion parameters.
Model interpretability and explainability	-How important is it for the model's predictions and decisions to be interpretable and explainable? >> It is a requirement as per the EU AI Act. -Do you need tools or techniques to provide insights into how the model arrives at its conclusions? >> Yes.
Robustness, privacy, and security	-How robust and generic does the model need to be across different domains, languages, or data distributions? >> The model needs to be specialized around providing HR-related information. -Are there specific edge cases or challenging scenarios that the model must handle effectively? >> Not sure. -Is the model compliant with privacy and security standards such as General Data Protection Regulation (GDPR), EU AI Act, and Health Insurance Portability and Accountability Act (HIPAA)? >> Yes, both are compliant.
Fine-tuning and customizability	-Can we fine-tune or tailor the model to specific needs? >> Yes. -How feasible is transfer learning? Is it possible to transfer data from one domain to another when it is limited? >> Both excel at transfer learning.
Integration with existing systems and workflows	-How seamlessly can the LLM be integrated with your existing systems, applications, and workflows? >> Not sure. But from the demo, both seem compatible. -Are there APIs or interfaces available for integrating the model with other software components? >> Yes. - Will there be a need for custom development or modifications to existing systems to support the LLM? >> Yes.

Core model characteristics	Questions
Cost and licensing considerations	-What are the upfront and ongoing costs associated with acquiring, deploying, and maintaining the LLM? >> LLMs will be managed by the providers. -Are there licensing agreements or usage fees that need to be considered? >> Yes.
Knowledge cutoff	-Is the knowledge cutoff date recent? >> No. -How often is the cutoff date updated? >> Annually.
Open source	-Are the models open source? >> Both are open source.
Modality	-Do you require a single modal or multimodal model/LLM? >> Multimodal. -In case of multimodal requirements, which specific modes are you looking at: video, image, text, or audio? >> Text and image.

Following was the response for model performance evaluation:

Performance	Questions
Accuracy	-What is the accuracy level of output desired? >> High accuracy, greater than 90%. -What is the model's tolerance to noise, misspellings, grammatical errors, or incomplete sentences? >> Both models show good tolerance.
Performance versus resource trade-off	-How do you find the desired level of balance between accuracy and resource efficiency? >> It needs to be accurate.
Latency and throughput	-What is the desired model latency? >> Low latency.
Consistency	-How consistently is the model able to produce desired output? >> High consistency.
Deployment	-Where would the model be hosted, on-premises or cloud? >> On provider's cloud.
Real-time adaptation or continuous learning	-Is the model able to learn and improve on an ongoing basis, either through fine-tuning on new data or other adaptation techniques? >> Yes.

(Continued)

Performance	Questions
Multilingual capabilities	-Is the model able to support multiple languages, which can be beneficial for diverse applications? >> Yes.
Support and maintenance	-What are the support and maintenance SLAs? Is there community support available? >> Yes. -What is the frequency of updates and upgrades? >> There will be weekly minor updates. Major upgrade every six months. It will be managed by the provider. -How good is the documentation? >> It is user-friendly.

Ethical Considerations

The table below shows some of model's ethical considerations:

Ethical considerations	Questions
Bias assessment and mitigation	Do you have a good procedure to assess the biases in the model? >> No. Do you have an effective bias mitigation strategy in place? >> No. How frequently do you reassess and update your bias mitigation procedures? >> It is continuous, based on reported hallucinations.
Ethical guidelines	Does the model adhere to established ethical principles for AI development such as fairness, transparency, and accountability? >> Yes. Have you conducted comprehensive audits to ensure that the model's decision-making processes align with ethical standards and legal regulations? >> Yes.

Considering the green AI aspects such as carbon emissions during training and energy consumption during inference, and based on the flowchart in Figure 9.4, it was decided to go for fine-tune based SLM, as not very large amounts of datasets were expected to fine-tune the model. RAG and LLM curation options were not considered.

Based on the evaluation assessment, risk diversification analysis, and final vendor interviews, both Mistral and Jamba 1.5 mini were selected as the LLMs.

There were a few meetings between the product development team led by Ricky, and HR from Freya, who were the product owners of the software to discuss the design of genAI solution. It was decided to create a new prompt-like interface for the HRM software where the users can type a prompt and the tools should be able to display the output provided by the LLM. The output should be unique and interesting for the user, providing some added value.

For example, suppose a user gives a prompt: tell me the number of annual vacations left for me. Besides the correct answer, the LLM would also provide information on the top vacation destinations or some important business or self-help books to read while on vacation.

Following were the business requirements for the different modules of HRM:

Modules	Requirements Model should:
Hiring	1. Write creative job descriptions. 2. Provide workforce planning recommendations. 3. Generate tailored interview questions. 4. Create a knowledge base of interview transcripts and provide insights. 5. Craft personalized offer letters.
Onboarding	1. Help HR design a creative onboarding program. 2. Provide a personalized onboarding experience for the new joiners. 3. Suggest a list of internal speakers along with reasoning. 4. Suggest a list of external speakers along with reasoning. 5. Provide assistance in building a community of new joiners.
Developing	1. Provide personalized training. 2. Suggest a list of coaches or mentors for employees. 3. Nurture the high-potential employees. 4. Create innovative development programs for top performers. 5. Recommend new job rotations or OJT positions.
Appraising	1. Generate good constructive feedback for employees. 2. Provide appraisal recommendations to line managers. 3. Detect bias in appraisals. 4. Recommend personalized appraisal goals for the employees. 5. Suggest self-appraisals and peer appraisals to employees.

Modules	Requirements Model should:
Compen- sating	1. Suggest competitive compensation packages. 2. Suggest the right bonuses and rewards. 3. Suggest personalized benefits for employees. 4. Provide recommendations on investment opportunities. 5. Provide personalized recommendations to employees on payroll, such as possible destinations to visit and books to read, based on remaining vacation days.
Retaining	1. Estimate the likelihood of an employee leaving the company. 2. Suggest personalized retention solutions for individual employees. 3. Analyze employee sentiments. 4. Provide work-life balance suggestions. 5. Provide emotional and wellness support.
Exiting	1. Design personalized farewells for exiting employees. 2. Create tailored exit interviews. 3. Provide a summary of employee contribution to the company. 4. Provide career development recommendations. 5. Provide outplacement and rejoining suggestions.

It was decided to develop a collaborative genAI solution in three phases, comprising technologies such as AI, data, cloud, and automation. Following is the outline of the development plan for a total budget for U.S. $17 million for 24 months:

Phases	Modules	Budget (USD in millions)	Timeline (months)
MVP 1.0	Hiring	3	6
MVP 2.0	Onboarding, Developing	5	9
Full product	Appraising, Compensating Retaining, Exiting	9	9

The following were the estimated productivity gains for the following activities:

Activities	Estimated productivity gains (%)
Writing job descriptions	60
Workforce planning	30
Generating tailored hiring interview questions	95
Crafting personalized offer letters	15
Overall onboarding program design	120
Creating development programs	155
Overall appraisal for employees	98

Activities	Estimated productivity gains (%)
Designing compensation packages	35
Generating tailored exit interview questions	95

Following is the estimated business case for Talent XYZ:

(all numbers in USD)	Year 1	Year 2	Year 3	Year 4	Year 5
GenAI solution development cost	6,333,000	10,666,000	0	2,000,000	0
GenAI solution operational cost	1,200,000	2,200,000	2,000,000	2,000,000	3,000,000
Income	−7,533,000	−12,866,000	3,000,000	1,000,000	12,000,000
Value (revenues from licensing genAI solution)	0	0	5,000,000	5,000,000	15,000,000

Explanation/assumptions:

- Annual license cost estimated for full product is U.S. $5 million to be charged at the start of year 3.
- Operational costs are high and variable in Year 1 and Year 2 due to non-standardized operations. From Year 3 onward, costs stabilize at around U.S. $2 million as processes become standardized.
- In Year 4, solution is custom developed for Haveth International and TechHarvest with a budget of one million USD each.
- Licenses are sold to them at the beginning of year 5.
- Additional operational cost per client is U.S. $500k annual.

Following were the key metrics designed:

#	Name	Target
1	Number of active users	#Active users ≥ 50 percent
2	Frequency of usage	Average usage per week per user ≥ 2
3	Session duration	Average time per session ≤ 5 minutes
4	Customer satisfaction	Score ≥ 7 (1: lowest, 10: highest)
5	Ease of use	Score ≥ 7 (1: lowest, 10: highest)
6	Output accuracy	Accuracy ≥ 90%
7	Performance	Rating ≥ 6 (1: lowest, 10: highest)
8	Integration	Score ≥ 6 (1: lowest, 10: highest)

After weeks of resource planning and preparation with Freya, the kickoff date of genAI solution development arrived. It was the coming Monday. Talent XYZ leadership team met with Vrinda the previous Friday.

Achintya said:

It is going to be the most uncertain project in my 30-year career. We are placing a big strategic bet along with our esteemed customer Freya. I would like to highlight the top three risks. First, the accuracy of the business case estimates. Second, acquisition of high-quality training data for the model. Third, development of genAI competence.

Vrinda concluded:

As Talent XYZ develops genAI solution, operational readiness should also be the key focus. Both should be developed parallelly and learn from each other. We should start preparing the business case for operational readiness focusing on gap mitigation and strengthening the four readiness areas: customer, technology, data, and people. If things go as per plan, the full genAI solution will be ready in around two years and Talent XYZ will be operationally ready.

Conclusion

Start operational readiness now if you haven't done so. It is the foundation of scaled adoption, combined with either of the two tracks: convertible pilot or genAI solution. It might be very difficult for enterprises to decide which track to follow. But while you decide, start applying the readiness rocket in your business.

If you finalize one of the above tracks, you should develop it in parallel with operational readiness. You can take learnings from one another.

Do not repeat the mistake of most enterprises by opting for non-convertible pilots. There will be learnings from it. No doubt. But why spend time, money, and resources in developing something that is not going to scale? Instead, develop a convertible pilot or genAI solution with higher chances of scaling and derive learnings from it at every stage of its deployment.

AI/genAI is going to scale and jobs that use AI will replace those that don't. The same goes for enterprises. Enterprises with scaled adoption of AI/genAI will replace those that don't.

So, start your scaled adoption journey now!

If you need advice and support, you can visit www.scalinggenai.com and book a consultation.

If you have any questions or feedback about the book, connect with me through LinkedIn through the link: www.linkedin.com/in/amit-prabhu26

or QR code:

Or through my website: www.amitprabhu.net

Hope you have enjoyed reading the book, as much as I have enjoyed writing it. Remember, this book is not just about information ... It's all about transformation!

Notes

Introduction

1. Bant, et al., "5 Forces That Will Drive the Adoption of GenAI."
2. Chui, et al., McKinsey.
3. Luther, "What GenAI's Top Performers Do Differently."
4. Ibid.
5. Bakshi, "90% of Generative AI Pilot Projects May Not Make It to Production in 2024."

Chapter 1

1. Web article, *Statista.* https://www.statista.com/outlook/tmo/artificial-intelligence/generative-ai/worldwide   last accessed March 15th 2025.
2. Davenport and Mittal, *Harvard Business Review Press*, 165–168.
3. Kaniora and Lucini, "A Radical Solution to Scale AI Technology."

Chapter 3

1. Youngdahl and Ramaswamy, "The Digital Transformation of CX at Albright Cancer Centers: The Generative AI Journey."
2. Bharti, "AI and Cost Cutting Biggest Reasons Why Tech Layoffs Have Surged by 136 Percent in 2024, Reveals Study.

Chapter 4

1. Tan, "How DBS Is Industrializing AI Across Its Business."
2. Olavsrud, "Unilever Leverages GPT API to Deliver Business Value."
3. Toyota newsroom, "Toyota Research Institute Unveils New Generative AI Technique for Vehicle Design."
4. Ramlochan, Prompt Engineering and AI Institute.

Chapter 5

1. Gartner webinar, "How Generative AI Will Impact Business Leaders Plans in 2024."

Chapter 6

1. Youngdahl and Ramaswamy, "The Digital Transformation of CX at Albright Cancer Centers: The Generative AI Journey."

Chapter 7

1. Google Cloud, "AI21 Labs: Rewriting the Rules on Natural Language Processing With Google Cloud."
2. Klubnikin, ITRex group.

Chapter 8

1. Nielsen, Nielsen Norman Group.

Chapter 9

1. Amazon Web Services. "Amazon Bedrock."
2. Accenture newsroom, "Accenture Launches Specialized Services to Help Companies Customize and Manager Foundation Models."

Chapter 10

1. Davenport and Mittal, *Harvard Business Review Press*

Chapter 11

1. Catlin, et al., McKinsey & Company.
2. Pidun, Reeves, and Schüssler, BCG.

Chapter 12

1. Databricks,"Data Lakehouse."
2. Barbara H. Wixom, Cynthia M. Beath, Leslie Owens, "Creating Value from Data: A Monetization Framework."

Chapter 13

1. Rosling, et al., *Factfulness: Ten Reasons We're Wrong About the World–and Why Things Are Better Than You Think.*
2. Nexla, "LLM Hallucination–Types, Causes, and Solution."
3. OpenAI, "Aligning Language Models to Follow Instructions."
4. Reuters YouTube video, "Google AI Chatbot Vard Flubs an Answer in ad."
5. Coulter, and Bensinger, "Alphabet Shares Dive After Google AI Chatbot Bard Flubs Answer in ad."
6. Oremus, The Washington Post.
7. Dhillon, "India Confronts Google Over Gemini AI Tool's Fascist Modi' Responses."
8. Rosling, et al., *Factfulness: Ten Reasons We're Wrong About the World–and Why Things Are Better Than You Think.*

Chapter 15

1. "Legal Leadership: Harnessing GenAI to Revolutionise Our Legal Teams," Unilever news.
2. Accenture,"Responsible AI: Scale AI With Confidence."

Chapter 16

1. Jorge Tamayo, Leila Doumi, Sagar Goel, Orsolya Kovacs-Ondrejkovic, Raffaella Sadun, "Reskilling in the Age of AI."
2. Ibid.
3. Ibid.
4. Ibid.

References

"Legal Leadership: Harnessing GenAI to Revolutionise Our Legal Teams." February 23, 2024. *Unilever.*

Accenture newsroom. November 30, 2023. "Accenture Launches Specialized Services to Help Companies Customize and Manager Foundation Models." https://newsroom.accenture.com/news/2023/accenture-launches-specialized-services-to-help-companies-customize-and-manage-foundation-models.

Accenture. n.d. "Responsible AI: Scale AI With Confidence." www.accenture.com/sk-sk/services/applied-intelligence/ai-ethics-governance.

Amazon Web Services. "Amazon Bedrock." https://aws.amazon.com/bedrock/.

Bakshi, S.R. December 29, 2023. "90% of Generative AI Pilot Projects May Not Make It to Production in 2024." www.financialexpress.com/business/digital-transformation-90-of-generative-ai-pilot-projects-may-not-make-it-to-production-in-2024-3350304/.

Bant, A., H. Poitevin, N. Green, and E. Brethenoux. December 14, 2023. "5 Forces That Will Drive the Adoption of GenAI." *HBR.*

Barbara H. Wixom, Cynthia M. Beath, Leslie Owens. "Creating Value from Data: A Monetization Framework." *Harvard Business Review.*

Bharti, D. February 9, 2024. "AI and Cost Cutting Biggest Reasons Why Tech Layoffs Have Surged by 136 Percent in 2024, Reveals Study." *India Today.* www.indiatoday.in/technology/news/story/ai-and-cost-cutting-biggest-reasons-why-tech-lays-offs-have-surged-by-136-per-cent-in-2024-reveals-study-2499830-2024-02-09.

Catlin, T., U. Deetjen, J-T. Lorenz, J. Nandan, S. Sharma. n.d. "Ecosystems and Platforms: How Insurers Can Turn Vision Into Reality." Accessed April 24, 2024. www.mckinsey.com/industries/financial-services/our-insights/ecosystems-and-platforms-how-insurers-can-turn-vision-into-reality.

Chui, M., L. Yee, B. Hall, A. Singla, A. Sukharevsky, and QuantumBlack AI. August 1, 2023. McKinsey. "The State of AI in 2023: Generative AI's Breakout Year." www.mckinsey.com/capabilities/quantumblack/our-insights/the-state-of-ai-in-2023-generative-ais-breakout-year.

Coulter, M. and G. Bensinger. February 9, 2023. "Alphabet Shares Dive After Google AI Chatbot Bard Flubs Answer in ad." Reuters. www.reuters.com/technology/google-ai-chatbot-bard-offers-inaccurate-information-company-ad-2023-02-08/.

Databricks. n.d. "Data Lakehouse." www.databricks.com/glossary/data-lakehouse.

Davenport, T.H. and N. Mittal. "All in on AI: How Smart Companies Win Big With Artificial Intelligence." *Harvard Business Review Press.*

Dhillon, A. February 26, 2024. "India Confronts Google Over Gemini AI Tool's Fascist Modi' Responses." *The Guardian.* www.theguardian.com/world/2024/feb/26/india-confronts-google-over-gemini-ai-tools-fascist-modi-responses.

Gartner Webinar. "How Generative AI Will Impact Business Leaders Plans in 2024."

Google Cloud. "AI21 Labs: Rewriting the Rules on Natural Language Processing With Google Cloud." https://cloud.google.com/customers/ai21; https://bloggingwizard.com/generative-ai-statistics/.

Jorge Tamayo, Leila Doumi, Sagar Goel, Orsolya Kovacs-Ondrejkovic, Raffaella Sadun. "Reskilling in the Age of AI." *Harvard Business Review.*

Kaniora, A. and F. Lucini. April 13, 2020. "A Radical Solution to Scale AI Technology." *Harvard Business Review.*

Klubnikin, A. February 28, 2024. ITRex Group. "Generative AI in Business: Top 5 Use Cases Every Company Should Consider." https://itrexgroup.com/blog/generative-ai-use-cases-in-business/.

Luther, A., R. de Laubier, N. de Bellefonds, T. Charanya, S. Shah, K. Ifiora, and P. Forth. February 9, 2024. "What GenAI's Top Performers Do Differently." BCG. www.bcg.com/publications/2024/what-gen-ais-top-performers-do-differently.

Nexla. n.d. "LLM Hallucination–Types, Causes, and Solution." https://nexla .com/ai-infrastructure/llm-hallucination/.

Nielsen, J. July 16, 2023. "AI Improves Employee Productivity by 66%." *Nielsen Norman Group.* www.nngroup.com/articles/ai-tools-productivity-gains/.

Olavsrud, T. March 10, 2023. "Unilever Leverages GPT API to Deliver Business Value." *CIO.* www.cio.com/article/464190/unilever-leverages-chatgpt-to-deliver-business-value.html.

OpenAI. January 27, 2022. "Aligning Language Models to Follow Instructions." https://openai.com/index/instruction-following.

Oremus, W. December 15, 2023. The Washington Post. "AI Chatbot Got Election Info Wrong 30 Percent of Time, European Study Finds." www .washingtonpost.com/technology/2023/12/15/microsoft-copilot-bing-ai-hallucinations-elections/.

Pidun, U., M. Reeves, and M. Schüssler. September 27, 2019. "Do You Need a Business Ecosystem?" *BCG.* Accessed April 24, 2023. www.bcg.com/publications/2019/do-you-need-business-ecosystem.

Ramlochan, S. September 21, 2023. Prompt Engineering and AI Institute. "The Yin and Yang of AI: How Traditional and Generative Models Differ and Complement Each Other." https://promptengineering.org/the-yin-and-yang-of-ai-how-traditional-and-generative-models-differ-and-complement-each-other/.

Reuters YouTube video. February 8, 2023. "Google AI Chatbot Vard Flubs an Answer in ad." www.youtube.com/watch?v=oGPEL9EVOyA.

Rosling, H., O. Rosling, A.R. Ronnlund. April 3, 2018. *Factfulness: Ten Reasons We're Wrong About the World–and Why Things Are Better Than You Think.* Publisher Flatiron Books.

Tan, A. February 14, 2024. "How DBS Is Industrializing AI Across Its Business." *ComputerWeekly.com.* www.computerweekly.com/news/366569993/How-DBS-is-industrialising-AI-across-its-business.

Toyota Newsroom. June 20, 2023. "Toyota Research Institute Unveils New Generative AI Technique for Vehicle Design." https://pressroom.toyota.com/toyota-research-institute-unveils-new-generative-ai-technique-for-vehicle-design/.

Web article. *Statista.* Accessed March 15, 2025. https://www.statista.com/outlook/tmo/artificialintelligence/generative-ai/worldwide.

Wildwood, L. April 29, 2024. "25 Top Generative AI Statistics For 2024." *Bloggingwizard.* www.statista.com/outlook/tmo/artificial-intelligence/generative-ai/worldwide.

Youngdahl, W. E and K. Ramaswamy. 2023. "The Digital Transformation of CX at Albright Cancer Centers: The Generative AI Journey." Thunderbird Global School of Management. Reprinted with Permission.

About the Author

Amit Prabhu is an AI consultant, author, speaker, business trainer, policy-maker, and entrepreneur. He has consulted various corporate clients and trained 1000+ people on AI, Data, and Cloud. Besides being an author of two business books, *Digital Strategy Framework* and *Digital Leadership Framework*, he is a regular speaker on Generative AI at global conferences and events. As an Independent Consultant to the European Commission AI Office, he is actively involved in drafting the EU's first General-Purpose AI Code of Practice. He is the mastermind behind entrepreneurial ventures such as Digiculum and Scaling GenAI. *Explorer* and *Teacher* are the two words that describe him vividly. He holds a master's degree in telecommunications and networking from the University of Pennsylvania and lives in Stockholm, Sweden, with his wife and a son.

Index

www.ingramcontent.com/pod-product-compliance
Lightning Source LLC
Chambersburg PA
CBHW061136220326
41599CB00025B/4249